DIMENSIONS OF SOCIAL EXCLUSION

DIMENSIONS OF SOCIAL EXCLUSION

Edited by
Dr. A.Mani
M.A., M.Sc. (Psy), M.Phil, Ph.D.
Assistant Professor cum Assistant Director
Centre for Study of Social Exclusion & Inclusive Policy (CSSEIP)
Gandhigram Rural University
Gandhigram - 624 302 (Tamil Nadu)
(India)

&

Dr. M. Ponniah
M.Com., M.phil, PGDCA, PGHRM, Ph.D.
Associate Professor cum Deputy Director
Centre for Study of Social Exclusion & Inclusive Policy (CSSEIP)
Gandhigram Rural University
Gandhigram (Tamil Nadu)
(India)

DPH

DISCOVERY PUBLISHING HOUSE PVT. LTD.
NEW DELHI-110 002

Published by:
Tilak Wasan
DISCOVERY PUBLISHING HOUSE PVT. LTD.
4383/4B, Ansari Road, Darya Ganj
New Delhi-110 002 (India)
Phone : +91-11-23279245, 43596064-65
Fax : +91-11-23253475
E-mail : discoverypublishinghouse@gmail.com
sales@discoverypublishinggroup.com
parul.wasan@gmail.com
web : www.discoverypublishinggroup.com

First Edition: **2013**

ISBN: 978-93-5056-250-5

Dimensions of Social Exclusion

Printed at:
Aditi Fine Art Press
Delhi

Preface

Social exclusion refers to the complex processes that deny certain groups full participation in society. Social exclusion is the process through which individuals or groups are wholly or partially excluded from the society in which they live. The phrase "Social Exclusion" to refer the processes by which entire marginal groups like Dalits, Adivasis, and Subalterns etc. are systematically denied rights, opportunities and resources that are ensured for all citizens to accomplish their full participation in society. Social exclusion is multi-dimensional since exclusion processes are caused by various factors and manifest in different forms and types. Due to its multi-dimensionality, the nature, forms and dimensions of social exclusion varies from one society to another or one country to another across the world. Though, the term social exclusion is of recent origin, the prevalence of exclusive practices occurred since the time immemorial. Various terms/nomenclatures were used to describe these exclusive practices in society. Slavery, apartheid, untouchability, racism, sexism, male chauvinism, anti-Semitisms are cruel dimensions of exclusion in the world. Also the magnitude and rigidity in the nature, forms and types of exclusion vary across the world.

Whether an open society like western countries where mobility or change from one status/ position to another is possible, or a closed society like India where mobility or change from one status/position is impossible, the process of exclusion occurs at various forms and dimensions with relative variation in the magnitude and extremity of exclusion. In India, social exclusion is multi-dimensional. In India, people are hierarchically divided and accorded caste status as higher, backward and lower whatever called due to their birth which established entrenched inequality in Indian sub-continent groups in different compartments from there they cannot. Caste and untouchability are cruel manifestations of social exclusion under which people are degraded due to their birth rather than their intellectual trait/ qualities.

Under caste system, untouchables, now assertively call themselves as Dalits and other lower castes were treated as subhuman and meted out cruel atrocities on them. Untouchability is an institutional form of discrimination and exclusion under which untouchables/Dalits are precluded from elementary rights such as right to entry of temples, public places, public roads, wells, tanks etc. Over the centuries, various socio-economic, political educational, cultural, and religious disabilities were imposed on them. Traditionally, they were debased socially, ritually, economically, politically and culturally. It was forcefully imposed on these people with the support of the ideologies of caste, varnashrama order and doctrine of karma and dharma etc.

Over the centuries, tribals, the indigenous people of India, conquered and subs equated by later immigrant people like Dravidians, Aryans, Muslim rulers, British, now Multi-National Corporations. They are the most vulnerable group and have undergone various forms the exclusion like land encroachments, land displacements due to developmental activities. They are worst in receiving end and the scum of the soil. Due to their continued exclusion, they were pushed into extremist path for survival through armed struggle.

Women – Mao said 'women hold up half of the sky'. Women are another larger excluded group. Traditionally under the Hindu patriarchical setup they were excluded in various dimensions. Over the centuries they were denied access to resources, wealth, rights, power etc. Sati is the most extreme dimension. Purdah (seclusion), forced widowhood etc. are other dimensions of exclusive practices for Indian women.

India is a multi-religious plural society where all the religions of the world professed/followed. Minorities' are other excluded groups who are excluded and discriminated due to their numerical insignificance, conversion activities particularly under the era of politization of religion in India. They are passive victims and experience hidden exclusion in everyday life which created a feeling of insecurity in India. Some minorities, particularly Muslims are equated with terrorists. Ghettoisation (communal living), communal riots, attacks on minorities are manifestation of exclusion of minorities in India.

More recently, Population ageing, differently-abled, people with HIV/AIDS, transgender is considered on as socially excluded references to be concerned with more inclusive strategies. State and civil societies are important agents of social change. Indeed, it is the role of State to frame a policy to integrate the excluded marginal groups into the mainstream. In India, plethora policies and welfare programmes were launched towards establishing more inclusive and just society. But rather most of these state's endeavours were not successful and did not produce result at expected level. It is due to lack of understanding of the dimensions of social exclusion which is multi-dimensional in nature in India to frame a suitable, appropriate policy for more inclusive society. In this context, formulation of various multi-dimensional strategies is very imperative and urgent need to fill the void in the unmet needs of policies to include these excluded groups into mainstream.

Editors

Acknowledgments

We fall short of words to express our gratitude for constant encouragements and guidance from our Vice-Chancellor Dr. SM. Ramasamy and Dr. N. Narayanasamy, Registrar, Gandhigram Rural University, Gandhigram.

We acknowledge with a deep sense of gratitude Dr. T. Rajendran, Dean, Faculty of Rural Social Sciences, and Dr. P. Anandharajakumar, Associate Professor, Dept. of Rural Development, Dr. Nehuru, Dr.B.Tamilmani, Gandhigram Rural University, Gandhigram for their concern.

We express our heartfelt thanks to Dr. C. Ramanaujam, Coordinator, CSSEIP, Mr. Sam Velladhurai and Dr. Anjuli Chandra, Assistant professors, CSSEIP, Gandhigram Rural University, Gandhigram.

We thank to all the authors for their support and contribution of their knowledge through their research papers, articles and paper presenters of the National seminar held in Gandhigram Rural University, Gandhigram.

We also thankful the supporting staffs Dr. V. Thirukkani, Dr. P.S. Swathi, Research Associates, Mr. Sudhikumar and Mrs. Rajalakshmi for their constant support at facilitated every moment of this task.

We greatly thankful to our family members Mrs.M.Subthramani, A. Chellammal, Mrs. D. Anitha Ponniah, M.P. Diviyan for their constant support at every moments of life.

We also thankful to Discovery Publishing House Pvt. Ltd., New Delhi for their support in publishing this book with professional zeal and perfection in short span of time.

Dr. A. MANI

Dr. M. PONNIAH

Contents

SECTION-V : EXCLUSION OF TRANSGENDER

SECTION–I

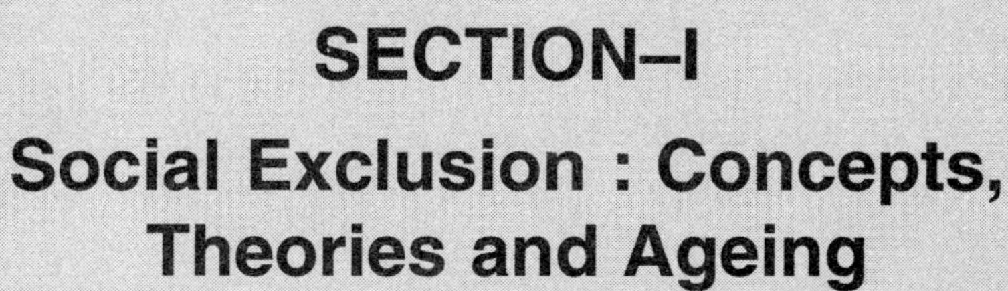

Social Exclusion : Concepts, Theories and Ageing

1
CHAPTER

Social Exclusion
Concept, Forms and Perspective

Dr. A. Mani
Asst. Professor cum Asst. Director, CSSEIP, GRI, Gandhigram

The concept of "Social exclusion" in social science literature is of recent origin. Social exclusion is a complex and multidimensional concept having social, cultural, political and economic ramifications. These dimensions are interwoven. The relations of social exclusion can be differentiated in several ways. One can talk of systemic or constitutive exclusion which is inbuilt in hierarchical social system. It excludes certain communities from interaction and access to social resources through social arrangements, normative value systems and customs. The exclusion based on caste is one example. Patriarchy is another example.

Social exclusion not only generates tension, violence and disruption but also perpetuates inequality and deprivation in Society. Overcoming 'exclusion' constitutes the most elementary pre-requisite for the building of a democratic society.

This concern is the centre of our Constitution. Indian Constitution provides equality to all citizens irrespective of caste, creed, region and gender. It also directs the State to take various measures to remove the different forms of discrimination, inequality and thereby help to eradicate social exclusion.

People are excluded when they are not part of the networks which support most people in ordinary life-networks of family, friends, community and employment. Among many others, poor people, ex-prisoners, homeless people, people with AIDS, people with learning disabilities or psychiatric patients might all be said to be at risk of exclusion. This is a very broad concept: it includes not only deprivation, but problems of social relationships, including stigma, social isolation and failures in social protection.

In practice, the idea of exclusion is mainly used in three contexts. The first is financial: exclusion is identified with poverty, and its effect on a person's ability to participate in normal activities. The second is exclusion from the labour market: exclusion is strongly identified with long-term unemployment (though there is some research evidence to question whether long-term unemployed people are really excluded). Third, there is exclusion in its social sense, which identifies exclusion partly with alienation from social networks, and partly with the circumstances of stigmatised groups.

The idea of social exclusion comes from France, where it was the basis for a policy of 'insertion' or social inclusion, combining benefits with plans and agreements to integrate people into society. This policy has been widely imitated, and the idea of exclusion has become one of the main concepts in the European Union.

What is Social Exclusion?

Social exclusion describes a process by which certain groups are systematically disadvantaged because they are discriminated against on the basis of their ethnicity, race, religion, sexual orientation, caste, descent, gender, age, disability, HIV status, migrant status or where they live (Gareth Thomas MP, Parliamentary Under-Secretary of State for International Development, UK; DFID Policy Document).

Social exclusion relates to the alienation or disenfranchisement of certain people within a society. It is often connected to a person's social class, educational status and living standards and how these might affect their access to various opportunities. It also applies to some degree to the disabled, to racial minorities, women and to the elderly. Anyone who deviates in any perceived way from the norm of a population can become subject to coarse or subtle forms of social exclusion.

"Social exclusion is about the inability of our society to keep all groups and individuals within reach of what we expect as a society...[or] to realise their full potential."

Social exclusion is the unique interplay of a number of factors, whose consequence is the denial of access, to an individual or group, to the opportunity to participate in the social and political life of the community, resulting not only in diminished material and non-material quality of life, but also in tempered life chances, choices and reduced citizenship"(*Kenyon, S., Lyons, G. and Rafferty, J.: 'Transport and Social Exclusion: Investigating the Possibility of Promoting Inclusion Through Virtual Mobility. 'Journal of Transport Geography 10:3)*

People who are excluded are not 'just like' the rest of the poor. They are also disadvantaged by *who they are or where they live*, and as a result are locked out of the benefits of development.

Social exclusion has been defined by the Department of International Development (DFID) as "a process by which certain groups are systematically disadvantaged because they are discriminated against on the basis of their ethnicity, race, religion, sexual orientation, caste, descent, gender, age, disability, HIV status, migrant status or where they live. Discrimination occurs in public institutions, such as the legal system or education and health services, as well as social institutions like the household" (DFID, 2005, Reducing Poverty by Tackling Social Exclusion: A DFID Policy Paper).

Social exclusion refers to the loss of social cohesion resulting from growing inequalities and the return of mass social and economic vulnerability for an increasing part of the population.

Social exclusion is related not only to a lack of material wealth but also to symbolic exclusion, social deprivation and incomplete participation in the main social institution (Silver, 1995).

Social Exclusion refers to the impossibility of an individual or a social group to participate actively in the economic, cultural, political or institutional spheres of society.

It is both an objective and a subjective condition that can change over time and space as it is shaped by specific historical and social processes.

"Social exclusion is a broader concept than poverty, encompassing not only low material means but the inability to participate effectively in economic, social, political and cultural life and in some characterisations alienation and distance from mainstream society" (Duffy, 1995). Social exclusion is multidimensional—it encompasses social, political, cultural and economic dimensions, and operates at different social levels. It is also dynamic, in that it impacts people in various ways and to differing degrees over time. And it is relational—it is the product of social interactions which are characterised by unequal power relations, and it can produce ruptures in relationships between people and society which result in a lack of social participation, social protection, social integration and power. However, since there is rarely a complete lack of access, there is some arbitrariness in where the social exclusion lines are drawn, and therefore who is perceived to be excluded.

The concept of social exclusion is particularly useful because of its focus on process and relations. Thus it complements the concept of inequality which focusses more on disparities between different categories of people. 'Social inequality', for example is conceptualised as constraints on opportunity, in accessing education or healthcare for example, which are based on class and other status ascriptions such as gender, age or ethnicity. However, such a focus on structures and constraints can ignore the actors who are continuously building and transforming these structures. Thus many believe that the utility of social exclusion is in that it offers an actor-oriented approach which points to who is doing what, and in relation to whom. It also allows us to identify and tackle issues of power.

As a result, in development practice, the term 'exclusion' has become popular with non-economic social scientists because it focuses on societal institutions, actors, relationships and processes, of which measured disparity in income or lack of access to social services may be both an indicator and outcome.

Social Exclusion as a Process

Social exclusion is a process. It can involve the systematic denial of entitlements to resources and services, and the denial of the right to participate on equal terms in social relationships in economic, social, cultural or political arenas. Exclusionary processes can occur at various levels – within and between households, villages, cities, states, and globally. This is an actor-oriented approach which is useful because it points to who is doing what and in relationship with whom. It also provides information for international development agencies to identify those dynamic processes already extant which they could aim to strengthen or minimise. In a situation where there is a disparity in social power relationships, the question of who has the prerogative to define, who is the definer and who is the defined, becomes a site of conflict.

People are excluded by institutions and behaviour that reflect, enforce and reproduce prevailing social attitudes and values, particularly those of powerful groups in society.

Exclusion is frequently more subtle and unintentional: when disabled people are excluded from services, markets and political participation through a lack of awareness of their needs or by social attitudes, or when minority groups are excluded by language barriers.

The excluded people are not 'just like' the rest of the poor. They are also disadvantaged by who they are or where they live, and as a result they are locked out of the benefits of development. People living in remote and isolated areas are not taken into consideration on important matters; people from wrong part of the town find it difficult to find jobs or partners. They are more likely to be denied access to income, assets and services. They often end up being excluded from society, the economy and political participation.

Social exclusion is a multidimensional concept, people may be excluded from livelihoods, employment, earnings, property, housing, minimum consumption, education, the welfare state, citizenship, personal contacts or respect etc. but the concept focuses on the multidimensionality of deprivation, on the fact that people are often deprived of different things at the same time. It refers to exclusion (deprivation) in the economic, social and political sphere.

The Links between Exclusion and Inequality

The concepts of social exclusion and inequality are closely linked. Unequal societies in which certain groups are discriminated against can lead to exclusion. Likewise, social exclusion involves inequality. Unlike vertical inequalities, which focus on individuals, horizontal inequalities concern inequalities between groups, as does social exclusion. Both horizontal inequalities and social exclusion are multidimensional, encompassing social, economic and political forms of exclusion. However, horizontal inequalities are not always severe enough to lead to a situation defined as social exclusion.

Policies and initiatives to reduce horizontal inequalities and social exclusion can be quite similar; both take a multidimensional approach and generally target groups rather than individuals. Both are also concerned with the responsibility of richer groups in bringing about social exclusion/horizontal inequality, and are conscious of the need to address policies towards richer as well as poorer people to reduce social exclusion/horizontal inequality.

Social exclusion refers to lack of participation in society and emphasizes the multi-dimensional, multi-layered, and dynamic nature of the problem. Definitions of the concept emanate from diverse ideological perspectives, but most share the following features:

1. ***Lack of participation:*** Protagonists differ over which aspects of society are important and where responsibility for non-participation resides. Most agree that exclusion is a matter of degree, since individuals may be participating to a greater or lesser extent, and that it is relative to the society in question.
2. ***Multi-dimensional:*** Social exclusion embraces income-poverty but is broader: other kinds of disadvantage which may or may not be connected to low income, such as unemployment and poor self-esteem, fall within its compass.
3. ***Dynamic:*** The advent of dynamic analysis and a demand from policy makers to investigate cause as well as effect has generated an interest in the processes which lead to exclusion and routes back into mainstream society.

4. ***Multi-layered:*** Although it is individuals who suffer exclusion, the causes are recognized as operating at many levels: individual, household, community, and institutional.

The Conceptual Links between Exclusion and Poverty

People who are socially excluded are generally also poor, particularly if poverty is defined in a multidimensional way. Some differences, however, are: (*i*) that the majority of people in a society may be poor, (i.e. suffer from adverse incorporation) but it does not make sense to say that the majority are excluded; (*ii*) in most cases social exclusion implies inequality or relative deprivation, whereas poverty need not; (*iii*) social exclusion implies that there are processes of exclusion and institutional processes and actors responsible for excluding, whereas poverty does not.

Forms of Social Exclusion

In the Indian context, socially excluded groups can be identified at two levels:

(*a*) *Social groups:* Dalits or untouchables, Adivasis or Tribals, religious and linguistic minorities, the most backward castes, especially women and children among these social groups.

(*b*) *Sectoral groups:* Agricultural labourers, marginalized farmers, child labourers, domestic workers, informal workers/unorganized sector workers, contract workers, plantation workers, fisher communities, manual scavengers, rural and forest based communities, vernacular social groups, people living with disability etc.

The excluded also includes those excluded form:

- a livelihood; secure, permanent employment; earnings; property,
- credit, or land; housing; minimal or prevailing consumption levels;
- education, skills, and cultural capital;
- the welfare state; citizenship and legal equality; democratic participation; public goods;
- the nation or the dominant race; family and sociability; humanity, respect, fulfillment and understanding (Silver, 1995).

Gender

Discrimination against women is widespread and systemic, and they are subject to exclusion in various spheres. Women continue to face barriers to their political participation, and are vastly under-represented in local and national governing bodies worldwide. There are also gender differences in terms of inclusion in the labour market. Most women are concentrated in the informal economy, which is characterised by job insecurity, poor working conditions and low pay. The persistence and reproduction of women's exclusion is also supported by social norms and religious values. In many communities, traditional barriers still prevent women from going out of their homes to work. For some women, having primary or sole responsibility for household duties, including childcare, also prevents them from working outside their homes or areas of residence.

Social exclusion has some powerful advantages for gender analysis: it is dynamic and process-oriented; it enables a focus on the excluded and included as well as the excluders and includers, and it allows for the kind of multilayered analysis that is needed for a better understanding of gender and other complex social relations.

Old Age

As with youth, the intersection of old age with gender, ethnicity and disability, for example, can result in discrimination against, and the marginalisation of, older women and men. They can face multi-dimensional disadvantages including lack of assets, isolation and physical infirmity. These are closely related to the processes and institutional arrangements that exclude them from full participation in the economic, social and political life of their communities. These include the discriminatory laws and practices of governments as well as the negative attitudes and discriminatory practices of family members, healthcare providers, employers, etc. Age-based prejudice isolates older people from consultation and decision-making processes at family, community and national levels, and can lead to the denial of services and support on the grounds of age.

Disability

Disabled people often have limited access to education, employment, and public services. Some of the barriers to their inclusion are physical, such as inaccessible buildings and transport; institutional, such as discriminatory legislation; and attitudinal, for example stigma.

HIV/AIDS

Social exclusion can increase the risk factors leading to HIV infection, making the disease much harder to prevent. The stigma associated with the infection also means that in many countries people living with HIV and AIDS are likely to be socially excluded. Some groups will find their exclusion compounded by contracting the virus and being blamed for their condition, for example gay men, young women and widows. This can make HIV and AIDS more difficult to treat.

Dimensions of Social Exclusion

Exclusionary processes can have various dimensions:

Political exclusion can include the denial of citizenship rights such as political participation and the right to organise, and also of personal security, the rule of law, freedom of expression and equality of opportunity. Bhalla and Lapeyre (1997: 420) argue that political exclusion also involves the notion that the state, which grants basic rights and civil liberties, is not a neutral agency but a vehicle of a society's dominant classes, and may thus discriminate between social groups.

Economic exclusion includes lack of access to labour markets, credit and other forms of 'capital assets'.

Social exclusion may take the form of discrimination along a number of dimensions, for example gender, ethnicity, age – which effectively reduces the opportunity for such groups to gain access to social services and limits their participation in the labour market.

Cultural exclusion relates to the extent to which diverse values, norms and ways of living are accepted and respected. At one extreme, diversity is accepted in all its richness and at the other there can be situations of stigma and discrimination.

These relationships are all interconnected and overlapping, and given the complexity of influences on individuals, it is impossible to identify a single specific cause in the context of social exclusion. People may be excluded because of deliberate action on the part of others (e.g. discrimination by employers); as a result of processes in society which do not involve deliberate action; or even by choice. However, more generally, the causes of social exclusion that lead to poverty, suffering and sometimes death, can be attributed to the operations of unequal power relations.

Perspectives on Social Exclusion

In the Aristotelian perspective, an impoverished life is one without the freedom to undertake important activities that a person has reason to choose.

Adam Smith too felt impelled to define "necessaries" in terms of their effects on the freedom to live non-impoverished lives (such as "the ability to appear in public without shame").

According to an Amartya Sen: Poverty results in capability failure: "the idea of social exclusion has conceptual connections with well-established notions in the literature on poverty and capability deprivation.

Impoverishment of our lives results frequently from the inadequacy of income and thus low income is an important cause of poor living. But poor living cannot be seen just as lowness of income. Income may be the most prominent means for a good life without deprivation, but it is not the only influence on the lives we can lead. If our paramount interest is in the lives that people can lead—the freedom they have to lead minimally decent lives—then it cannot but be a mistake to concentrate exclusively only on one or other of the means to such freedom." We must look at impoverished lives, and not just at depleted wallets".

Thus, Amartya Sen views poverty as capability deprivation (that is, poverty to be seen as the lack of the capability to live a minimally decent life).

Effects of Social Exclusion

To describe persons as "socially excluded" (rather than to describe them as "poor") is to suggest that they are socially isolated in some sense, that they "have" or experience weak social relatedness. The socially excluded may lack social ties to the family, local community, voluntary associations, trade unions or even the nation. They also may be disadvantaged in terms of the extent of their legal rights or in their ability to effectively realize them.

It hurts them materially – making them poor in terms of income, health or education by causing them to be denied access to resources, markets and public services. It can also hurt them emotionally, by shutting them out of the life of their community.

Socially excluded people are often denied of choices and opportunities available to others to increase their income and escape from poverty by their own efforts. Simply because of *who they are,* certain groups cannot fulfill their potential, nor can they participate equally in society. An estimated 891 million people in the world experience discrimination on the basis of their ethnic, linguistic or religious identities alone (DFID).

It makes them voiceless to claim their rights. Even though the country's economy may grow and general income levels may rise, excluded people are likely to be left behind, and make up an increasing proportion of those who remain in poverty.

The sense of powerlessness among the excluded can rob people of their self-confidence and aspirations and their ability to challenge exclusion.

Social exclusion causes the poverty of particular people, leading to higher rates of poverty among the affected groups by denying them access to resources, markets and public services.

It reduces the productive capacity – and the rate of poverty reduction – as a whole. Social exclusion is often a cause not only of poverty, but also of conflict, violence and insecurity.

Tackling Social Exclusion

Poverty reduction policies often fail to reach the excluded unless they are specifically designed to do so. If we are to tackle it effectively, we need to recognize where it is a problem, understand it better and, find different ways of working with partner governments, the international community and civil society organizations to overcome it.

Ways of governments, civil society and donors tackling Social Exclusion:

- Creating legal, regulatory and policy frameworks that promote social inclusion;
- Ensuring that socially excluded groups benefit from public expenditure as much as other groups;
- Improving economic opportunities and access to services for excluded groups;
- Promoting their political participation in society, and their capacity to organise and mobilize themselves;
- Increasing accountability to protect citizens' basic human rights;
- Tackling prejudice and changing behaviour.

DFID Policy Paper Recommendations

- Analyze the impact of exclusion on poverty reduction in all our country programmes, in order to decide priorities for work by region, country and sector;
- Promote exchanges of best practice between national and regional organizations;
- Work with other government departments and development partners to include analysis of exclusion as a cause of conflict and insecurity in our approaches and responses to conflict prevention and reduction;
- Identify opportunities to address social exclusion in fragile states;
- Strengthen the collection and analysis of statistics on excluded groups;
- Work with the World Bank and regional development banks, United Nations agencies, the European Community and other donors to make development work better for excluded groups.

The Spaces of Social Exclusion

Social exclusion can occur in different sites and spaces. These include state institutions, access to services and markets. Exclusion can also occur in the market place (e.g. social norms can exclude women in traditional societies from participating in the physical space where buying and selling takes place);

through community norms; and within the family. A person can be denied access completely or given only unequal access – both can constitute exclusion.

Exclusion can result from the power relations that shape these spaces. John Gaventa argues that in this sense, the idea of the boundaries is important: "Power relations help to shape the boundaries of participatory spaces, what is possible within them, and who may enter, with which identities, discourses and interests" (2006: 26). Therefore, power needs to be understood in relation to how spaces of engagement are created, the levels of power within, and the different forms of power across them.

The social exclusion discourse in Latin America, for example, emerged partly as a result of widespread recognition of the high levels of inequality throughout the region. In sub-Saharan Africa, debates on poverty reduction are increasingly focused on inequality, providing entry points for social exclusion to be addressed.

Social Exclusion as a Consequence of Conflict

There are close links between social exclusion and conflict and insecurity, both in terms of causes and consequences. There are now convincing arguments that some forms of social exclusion generate the conditions in which conflict can arise. This can range from civil unrest to violent armed conflict and terrorist activity. Severely disadvantaged groups with shared characteristics (such as ethnicity or religion) may resort to violent conflict in order to claim their rights and redress inequalities. Group differences are not enough in themselves to cause conflict, but social exclusion and horizontal inequalities provide fertile ground for violent mobilisation. Hence, the concept of social exclusion can help in conflict resolution because it identifies some of the causes of conflict. However, here it is more helpful to focus on horizontal inequality because it is unequal relative position which underlies much conflict, including relative riches as well as relative poverty. Moreover, analysing why some societies with sharp horizontal inequalities suffer conflict and others do not, it has become evident that conflict is particularly likely when there are both socio-economic and political horizontal inequalities or exclusion. Becoming aware of exclusion and inequality, therefore, can be an essential first step for international development practitioners in contributing to conflict prevention and resolution in fragile states.

As well as being a common cause of conflict, social exclusion can also occur as a result of conflict. Pervasive conflict can marginalise whole societies, and is a major cause of refugees who then become excluded in the place or country to which they move.

Identifying and Measuring Social Exclusion

The measurement of social exclusion is tied to the definition of social exclusion. Different approaches have been adopted to defining social exclusion in developing countries, including: according to whether people do not benefit from modern opportunities (e.g. those not employed in the formal sector or those not receiving state social protection); those who fall a certain distance below average achievements (e.g. less than two thirds average incomes); according to some prior conception of groups who are excluded (e.g. people living in remote areas; tribal groups); and by asking people about who they perceive to be excluded. These approaches all tend to identify different people as excluded, as the 'states' of exclusion are highly diverse and of differing salience globally. As a result, there can be no single set of indicators that would be equally relevant to all contexts.

Social anthropologists argue that exclusion is a process and that identifying and measuring it risks essentialising statistical categories into groups. On the other hand, economists argue that gathering and analysing statistical information relating to social exclusion can help to identify which groups are excluded, identify the forms and levels of exclusion they face, and quantify the impact of exclusion. Disaggregated data allows progress to be monitored and change relating to specific groups to be tracked over time. Statistical information can also draw attention to exclusion, strengthening influencing strategies and creating leverage. Raising the profile and visibility of excluded groups can also be a powerful act in itself.

In addition, the collection of multidimensional data – including not only economic and social, but also political dimensions - by group is essential if policies are to be designed and monitored, and aimed at reducing group inequalities and increasing social inclusion. Without such data it is impossible to know what sort of action is needed, and if action has been taken, whether it is being effective. However, an important problem remains the availability of disaggregated data across countries and regions.

REFERENCES

Burchardt T., Le Grand J., and Piachaud D., 2002, 'Introduction', in Hills, J., Le Grand, J. and Piachaud, D., *Understanding Social Exclusion*, Oxford University Press, Oxford.

Louis Prakash, "Social Exclusion", *Social Action*, Vol. 58, October-December, 2008, pp. 343-345.

NCERT Book on Sociology, Class XI, Chapter 5, Patterns of Social Inequality and Exclusion.

Ramiah, lecture note on the workshop Social exclusion in India.

2
CHAPTER

Social Exclusion and Social Inclusion

A. Joseph Xavier
Assistant Professor, Department of Commerce, Ayya Nadar Janaki Ammal College, Sivakasi
Ramya
Assistant Professor, Department of Management Studies, Avinashilingam University of Women, Coimbatore
R. Selvakumari
Research Scholar, Department of Commerce, Ayya Nadar Janaki Ammal College, Sivakasi

Social exclusion is a multidimensional process of progressive social rupture, detaching groups and individuals from social relations and institutions and preventing them from full participation in the normal, normatively prescribed activities of the society in which they live.

Social exclusion is evident in deprived communities, it is harder for people to engage fully in society. In such communities, weak social networking limits the circulation about information about jobs, political activities, and community events. But many social workers believe that exclusion in the countryside is as great as, if not greater than, that in cities. In rural areas there is less access to goods, services and facilities, making life difficult in many respects.

Causes

Whilst recognising the multi-dimensionality of exclusion, policy work undertaken at European Union level focuses on unemployment as a key cause of, or at least correlating with, social exclusion. This is because in modern societies, paid work is not only the principal source of income with which to buy services, but is also the fount of individuals' identity and feeling of self-worth.

Most people's social networks and sense of embeddedness in society also revolve around their work. Many of the indicators of extreme social exclusion, such as poverty and homelessness, depend on monetary income which is normally derived from work.

Poverty

Just as the conceptual slippage from exclusion to inclusion has happened without much debate, the assumptions which underpin this shift have not been examined. Social inclusion initiatives which attempt to simultaneously fuse the identification of the socially excluded with attempts to incorporate them into the mainstream of society, confuse the identification and tackling of social exclusion with promoting inclusion. In doing so, such initiatives make a series of assumptions about the excluded, the society they are seen to be excluded from, and the solutions that are deemed necessary.

While it seems well evidenced that social exclusion has a negative impact on health and well-being, there is an accompanying widespread assumption that 'inclusion' in mainstream social settings is important for mental health and wellbeing. In other words, people with mental health problems should *want* to be involved and take part, as it is undeniably good. However, it is precisely this 'common sense' idea that is problematic. One of the problems with the move to 'promoting inclusion' is that inclusion in practice implicitly assumes that the quality of mainstream society is not only desirable, but unproblematic and legitimate.

In addition, social inclusion discourse implies that society is comprised of a comfortable and satisfied 'included majority' and a dissatisfied 'excluded minority'. This focuses attention on the excluded minority and fails to take seriously the difficulties, conflicts and inequalities apparent in the wider society which actually generate and sustain exclusion *and* mental health problems. Moreover, this implicitly assumes that the so-called 'normal' population are themselves 'socially included' in a variety of aspects of social and community life. Yet it is well-known that people in full time work spend little time on non-work related activities and full time work negatively affects people's ability to socialise, volunteer or help others. Similarly, research has noted how the inhabitants of middle class suburbs are often socially isolated and rarely mix with others outside their own socio-cultural group. Furthermore, some people actually *choose* their own exclusion as exemplified through the phenomenon of 'gated communities' where the affluent develop enclave-style housing developments where they segregate themselves from the rest of society yet are rarely, if ever, a target of social inclusion initiatives.

1. On the one hand, to make individuals at risk of exclusion more attractive to employers, i.e. more "employable".

2. On the other hand, to encourage (and/or oblige) employers to be more inclusive in their employment policies.

In some circumstances, transport may be a factor in social exclusion—for instance, if lack of access to public transport or a vehicle prevents a person from getting to a job, training course, job centre or doctor's surgery. Some schemes therefore promote accessibility, for instance:

- By ensuring public transport is available, which is particularly relevant for women.
- By subsidising the purchase of a scooter, which is relevant to young people living in rural areas.

Links between Exclusion and Other Issues

The problem of social exclusion is usually tied to that of equal opportunity, as some people are more subject to such exclusion than others. Marginalisation of certain groups is a problem even in many economically more developed countries, including the United Kingdom and the United States, where the majority of the population enjoys considerable economic and social opportunities.

Social Inclusion

Social inclusion, the converse of social exclusion, is affirmative action to change the circumstances and habits that lead to (or have led to) social exclusion.

Social Inclusion is a strategy to combat social exclusion, but without making reparations or amends for past wrongs as in *Affirmative Action*. It is the coordinated response to the very complex system of problems known as social exclusion. The notion of social inclusion can vary, according to the type of strategies organisations adopt.

Social exclusion is a concept used in many parts of the world outside of the United States to characterise contemporary forms of social disadvantage. Dr. Lynn Todman, director of the Institute on Social Exclusion at the Adler School of Professional Psychology, suggests that social exclusion refers to processes in which individuals and entire communities of people are systematically blocked from rights, opportunities and resources (e.g. housing, employment, healthcare, civic engagement, democratic participation and due process) that are normally available to members of American society and which are key to social integration.

These concerns have led some commentators to argue that we need to move away from status based consumerism towards recognising other types of contribution in society, not just those dependent upon money, paid work and status. Yet these are precisely the qualities of mainstream society which people with mental health difficulties are increasingly being encouraged to aspire to, under the promise of social inclusion, primarily through paid work. Although social inclusion initiatives are intended to promote choice in living one's desired life in the community and emphasising involvement in all potential elements of social life, including sports and leisure 2002; the main route to inclusion is usually seen as paid work. For example, it is commonly argued that 'employment *must* become a fundamental part of *every* service user's care plan'. The 'hard outcomes' measured to assess inclusion usually relate primarily to employment, or at least proximity to, and involvement in, the labour market. This often means that other outcomes such as improving self esteem and participation—themselves not without criticism—are merely viewed as 'distance travelled' towards these government defined outcomes, rather than ends in themselves.

Whilst there are many good reasons for considering employment as an important agenda for mental health services, the relationship between work and health is complex. A recent review concluded that the 'evidence is clear that, for working people, the design and management of work can be a major threat to their mental health'. Modern employment is increasingly poorly paid, un-unionised, insecure and characterised by longer working hours, short term contracts, increasing workloads, stress and uncertainty. In addition, focusing on employment as the route to inclusion ignores the necessity, value and gendered nature of unpaid work and also undermines the legitimacy of non-employment'.

Consequences of 'Inclusion'

The ways in which the socially excluded are constructed within policy and practice discourse can result in a number of potential consequences. In particular, it can lead to a focus on changing the individual's choices and aspirations, rather than the social context which constrains their choices. In assuming that the 'mainstream' is ideal and desirable, it is possible that discourses around mental health are increasingly constructed within a deficit model, which constructs the socially excluded as lacking in the skills and dispositions required for paid work and other mainstream activities. In this way, the problem which needs to be addressed is not social inequality, oppression or discrimination, but cultures of low aspiration and fatalism. The moral imperative for service users to engage in a way which is defined as appropriate by government, policy makers and services can lead to those who do not co-operate being viewed as dysfunctional.

This is apparent with modern policy concerns about the issue of 'dependency'. Increasingly, service users are constructed as being 'dependent' on welfare services if they use services in particular ways. The notion of dependency is almost invariably constructed in negative terms and is opposed to the ideal of 'independence'. In this way, service users' reliance on benefit payments, services and/or other people with mental health difficulties becomes a 'moral hazard' which encourages dependency, rather than a social good which prevents destitution or provides support, solidarity and care. It is interesting to note that some elements of the service user/survivor movement also place a lot of emphasis on independence from services as part of their aspiration for greater autonomy and may view 'getting back to work' as a particular individual mark of achievement.

As we have seen, the notion of 'social exclusion' as a dynamic term focusing attention on the power dynamics involved in social practices of exclusion and marginalisation has given way to notions of the 'socially excluded' as a particular set of individuals who require social inclusion. Thus 'exclusion' has been turned from a process into an outcome, a 'condition people are in' which can be measured, monitored and rectified by initiatives to change the behaviour of the excluded by influencing choices made about their lives and welfare services. Indeed, the priority placed on particular 'mainstream' opportunities such as paid work results in the promotion of particular individualised therapeutic and behavioural interventions, as evidenced by the trend of giving people Cognitive Behavioural Therapy for long term depression and anxiety to help them get back to work.

Many proponents of social inclusion are well-intentioned in their aim to liberate mental health services from a primary concern with 'care' and 'treatment'. However, because psychiatry is largely, and it might be argued, unavoidably, an individualistic and interventionist discipline characterised by management and social regulation, social inclusion could become another form of treatment or technique which is imposed on service users 'for their own good'. In this way, mental health services are given the task of social engineering/regulation by imposing and reinforcing particular dominant cultural values and practices. Paradoxically, such policy measures may actually reproduce exclusion by enforcing a moral conformism. For example, the more social inclusion is seen to relate to paid work, the more those *not* in paid work will feel excluded and marginalised. In this way, the inclusion imperative could actually increase the gap between the supposed 'included majority' and the 'excluded minority'.

Moreover, social inclusion has a *conditional* element in which coercion can be used to ensure compliance. Thus, alongside seemingly progressive modernisation strategies which promote greater choice, control and independence for welfare service users, we are also witnessing a growth in the social control of people with mental health difficulties. Recent moves towards compulsory treatment in the community, supervision orders and assertive outreach services have often been viewed as mental health 'anti social behaviour orders' which function to exclude certain undesirable people from the rest of society. Such treatment of the issue bears similarity to the way in which the tenants of social housing are compelled to behave 'properly' or have their tenancies revoked. Mental health service users are being urged to exercise greater choice and control, but only if they make the 'right' decisions. Moreover, reforms of the benefits systems may result in the withdrawal of welfare benefits to people on long term sickness benefits.

Conclusion

Finally, the demand for social inclusion is paradoxical in that it both expresses a genuine desire to tackle the consequences of social inequality and yet at the same time could become co-opted as a modern form of moral and social governance which reproduces and legitimises the prevailing socio-economic order. On the one hand it offers the promise of emancipation through the resolution of social exclusion and yet it simultaneously becomes another way in which the 'mentally ill' are subject to social, moral and economic regulation.

REFERENCES

Angus, J. (2002) *A Review of evaluation in community-based art for health activity in the UK*. London, Health Development Agency, http://www.dur.ac.uk/resources/cahhm/reports/CAHHM%20for%20HDA%20J%20Angus.pdf

Atkinson, A.B. (1998) Social Exclusion, Poverty and Unemployment. In A.B. Atkinson and J. Hills (eds) *Exclusion, Employment and Opportunity*. CASE paper no. 4. London: Centre for Analysis of Social Exclusion, London School of Economics.

http://www.mentalhealthalliance.org.uk/ and www.criticalpsychiatry.co.uk

3
CHAPTER

Ageing - Boon or Curse
A Case Study on Elders in Rural Community

M. Jeyaseelan
Assistant Professor, Department of Sociology, Periyar University, Salem-636 011

Introduction

Aging is natural, inevitable and ubiquitous phenomenon. Everyone should confront this process, if he/she lives. It is Irreversible one. Literally it refers to the effects of age. Commonly speaking, it means the various effects or manifestation of old age. In this sense, it refers to various deterioration in the organisms. Aging has been viewed differently by different persons. To politicians and Industrialists, it means power and wealth whereas to a middle class employee, it amounts to a forced retirement. To biologists and social scientists, it is a field of research on biological cells and problems on individual respectively.

The population ageing is the one of the serious social problem for the entire world especially the developing countries. Ageing population is ever increased due to longevity of life span on an individual. The family, commonly the joint family type, and social networks provided an appropriate environment in which the elderly spent their lives. The advent of modernization, industrialization, urbanization, occupational differentiation, education, and growth of individual philosophy has eroded the traditional values that vested authority with elderly. These have led to defiance and decline of respect for elders among members of younger generation. There is a stereotyped view is being prevailed among the youngsters about the aged people.

In lieu of old age homes, it is advocated that the old aged people in community set up may feel well and good. But the aged people in community setup also experiencing some problems.

Elders in India

India's elderly population (aged 60 and above) is expected to increase from 71 million in 2001 to 179 million in 2031 and further to 301 million in 2051. The proportion is likely to reach 12 per cent in 2031 and 17 per cent in 2051. As of 2001, south India has the highest number of elderly persons above 60 years and maintains its lead in the next 40 years (19 million in 2001 to 70 million in 2051). In fact, one-fourth of India's elderly persons live in south India, indicating the low fertility and high expectation of life at birth in the region (Guilmoto & Irudaya Rajan, 1998; Irudaya Rajan & Zachariah, 1998). The lowest numbers are expected in North-East India. In fact, Central India, with the second highest number of elderly in 2001, is projected to increase its population at the same rate as South India by 2051. East India also follows South and Central India and is expected to reach 67 million in 2051. The number of elderly persons above 70 years of age (old-old) is likely to increase more prominently than those 60 years and above. The old-old are projected to increase five-fold between 2001 to 2051 (from 27 million in 2001 to 132 million in 2051). Their proportion is expected to raise form 2.7 to 7.6. Although we have found excess males in the females. In 2051, south India is expected to lead with the highest number (34 million) of old - old, followed by East and Central India, and the lowest in Central India. South and West India and the lowest in Central India. South and West India are projected to have excess females throughout the study periods; other regions show excess females only in some periods.

The oldest–old group (80+) in India is expected to grow faster than any other age. In absolute numbers, it is likely to increase six-fold from 5.4 million in 2001 to 32.0 million in 2051. As expected, south India will lead with the highest numbers and proportions of oldest-old in the next half of the 21st century. From 2011 onwards, all regions are expected to have excess oldest - old females.

Methodology

The present study was carried out at Sangeethapatty village of Sangeethapatty panchayat, Omalur taluk of Salem district. The village is selected by using random sampling method. It is approximately five kilometre far away from Omalur town and located behind the Periyar University. It is a multi-caste village. This village has both traditional and modern aspects. It is in transition.

Objectives

1. To study the socio-economic status of elders.
2. To find the living arrangement of elders.
3. To find out the problems of elders in community setup.

4. To understand the perception of elders on the present changes and developments.
5. To come out with suggestions.

Sampling: In order to carry out the present study, purposive sampling method is adopted to call out the necessary information from the elders. The sample size is 80. The *descriptive research* design method is used to describe the status of elders. *First hand information* is collected from the field. As a tool, *the interview schedule* is constructed to find out personal details. The simple statistical tool like percentage is used to draw inferences.

Results

1. Most of the elders are women and married. The mean age of the men is 71.54 and mean age of the women is 75.01. The most of the respondents are illiterates and belong to scheduled caste category.
2. The main calling is agricultural coolie and engaged in quarries. Since they are the unskilled workers in their later age financial dependency is obvious.
3. They accept that the decline and change in the role reduce the importance of the elders in the family especially the role of taking important decision in the family.
4. According to the disengagement theory, many of the relationships between a person and other members of society are severed and those remaining are altered in quality. In the study area also, withdrawal of elders from community participation is manifested.
5. On the part of living arrangements, they are stayed along with sons. But there is no separate room for them. No special arrangements are made for them.
6. The verbal abuse is the common problem prevailing the in study area.
7. Old age pension scheme is not reached this village. Most of elders made complaint that they are struggling very hard to get this scheme. In spite of the repeated attempt, their application is one or another way delayed.
8. Most of the elders have an eye problem. They insists the free eye camps and follow ups. According to them, in reality free eye camps were arranged to diagnosis the problem but follow ups are costly and not affordable.
9. They agreed that there is a generation gap. The sea changes in the technology, culture and life styles are making them to become panic.

10. It is observed that the social change especially in the social structure like caste was welcomed by the elders.
11. They have an aversion on the cultural change especially in apparel and value system.
12. There was a warm welcome to the concept of old age home. In the changing context, the old age home is inevitable one that provides the asylum to the elders in lieu of family.
13. The lose of spouse psychologically disturb the elders more.
14. Most of them living with the memories of past.

Conclusion

In countries like India, the ageing is synonymsly viewed as wisdom and experience. Due reverence was accorded to elders. But change in social and economic setup drastically affected the status of elders. The aged are considered as burden and useless. The ageism, that is the stereotyped view, is increasing among the youngsters. Ageing is a natural process not a stigma or not a disease. On account of social and economic progress, elders are side lined. The potentials of elders should be rightly used for the progress of the country as well as preservation of our tradition.

REFERENCES

Ajaya Kumar Sahoo, Gavin J.Andrews, S.Irudaya Rajan, 2009, *Sociology of Ageing A Reader*, Jaipur: Rawat Publications.

Aijazuddin, Ahmad *etal.*, (eds), 1997, *Demographic Transition* (*The Thirdworld Scenario*), New Delhi: Rawat Publication.

Bhatia, H.S, 1983, *Aging and Society: A Sociological Study of Retired Public Servants*, New Delhi: Arya Book Centre.

Birren, James, E. and K.Warner Schaie (eds), 1977, *Hand Book of the Psychology of Aging*, New York: Van Nostrand Reinhold.

Bose, A.1982, Aspects of Ageing in India, *Social Action*, 31(1): 1-19.

Dharmalingam, B, Murugan K R, Elderly Widows and their Place in the Family, *Social Welfare*, 2001, Vol. 48, No, pp. 7-11.

Dandekar, Kumidini, 1996, *The Elderly in India*, New Delhi: Sage Publications.

Hurlock-E.B., 1993, *Development Psychology: A Life Span Approach*, New Delhi: Tata McGraw, Hill.

Panda Archanana Kaushik, 2008, *Elderly Women*, New Delhi: Concept Publication Co.

4

CHAPTER

Modernization and Perception of Youth on Elderly People

Dr. C. Gobalakrishnan

Asstt. Professor, Department of Sociology, Periyar University, Salem-636 011

G. Phary

Research Scholar, Department of Sociology, Periyar University, Salem-636 011

Introduction

In India, the attainment of the age 60 has been mostly considered for the purpose of classifying aged persons, where as the U.S.A., U.K. and other western countries, it is from 65 years. India is becoming an aging country. The 2001 census has shown that the elderly population of India accounted for 77 million. While the elderly constituted only 24 million in 1961, it increased to 43 million in 1981 and to 57 million in 1991. The proportion of elderly persons in the population of India raised from 5.63 per cent in 1961 to 6.58 per cent in 1991 and to 7.5 per cent in 2001. According to the population projections by the Registrar General and Census Commission of India, the 60+ population of India will grow from 56 million in 1991 to 71 million in 2001, 96 million in 2011 and 113 million in 2016. However, India at the moment is not well-equipped with a social security system that will protect the elderly.

In the Indian society, the social and cultural values and along with the traditional practices emphasize that the elderly members of the family be treated with honour and respect. Its ethics pay homage to respect for older people. Its mottos, such as "the elder is a treasure in the family", are strongly emphasized. Older people, therefore, are presumably accorded the highest position in the family hierarchy and are entitled to be respected and honored by the younger generation. From a young age, Indian children are taught to hold positive attitudes toward their elders and to converse with them in a formal and polite style.

On the other hand, economic and social changes may have an impact on the status of older people and consequently on one's attitudes toward older people. Modernization and urbanization are believed to promote value systems that either equalize age groups or result in lower status for older people (Cowgill, 1975). Therefore, it will be of interest to investigate if one's perception toward the elderly people and the present study was conducted among the youth in Omalur Taluk of Salem District.

Methodology

The present study was conducted in the Kottakoundamapatty Village Panchayat in Omalur Taluk of Salem District. This village panchayat comprises of eight hamlets with a total population of 4368. Among the total population, 2257 are male and 2111 are female. In order to understand the attitude of the youth towards elderly people, there were 100 respondents selected from these eight hamlets by adopting convenience sampling method. The concept 'youth' defined in this study as the person who is belonging to the age between 18 years and 30 years. A structured interview schedule was used as a tool of data collection for the present study. The interview schedule consists of personal profile of the respondents and their attitudes toward elderly people. There were 20 statements used to measure the respondents attitudes toward the elderly people and all the statements were measured with five-point scale. The data collection was took place in the month of December 2010. For data analysis the percentile score, mean, standard deviation and chi-square test were used in the present study.

Results

In the total sample, 58 per cent were males and remaining 42 per cent were females. While consider age, 39 per cent of the respondents were belonging to the age group of 18-21 years (young age group), 26 per cent of the respondents were belonging to the age group of 2-25 years (middle age group) and remaining 35 per cent of the respondents were belonging to the age group of 26-30 years (old age group). The mean age of the respondents worked out to 23.76 with a standard deviation of 3.62. With regard to education, 38 per cent were completed up to primary school (low education group), 42 per cent were completed up to high school (middle education group) and remaining 20 per cent were completed higher secondary and above (high education group). The mean years of schooling worked out to 5.82 with a standard deviation of 2.68. There were 29 per cent of the respondents from a three-generation household (joint) family, and remaining

71 per cent from a two-generation household (nuclear) family. There were 32 per cent of the respondents working as construction workers, 23 per cent of the respondents working as labourers in the power loom, 20 per cent of the respondents working as labourers in silver anklet making enterprises, 14 per cent of the respondents working as agricultural coolies, and remaining 11 per cent of the respondents doing their studies in various colleges. Around one-third of the respondents (34%) had a monthly family income of Rs. 6,000 or less (low income group), one-fourth of the respondents (26%) had a monthly family income between Rs. 6,000 and Rs. 8,500 (middle income group) and remaining 40 per cent of the respondents had a monthly family income of more than Rs. 8,500 (high income group). The mean monthly family income worked out to Rs. 7,847 with a standard deviation of 2,438. Among the total respondents, 43 per cent were married (31 female and 12 male).

The respondents' attitudes toward the elderly people were measured with 20 statements and these statements were measured with five-point scale. The minimum and maximum score for these statements worked out to 33 and 91 respectively. The overall mean score for these 20 statements worked out to 58.26 with a standard deviation of 12.57. On the basis of the mean score the respondents were classified as positive as well as negative attitudes toward the elderly people. Those who secured a mean score between 33 and 58 were categorized as the respondents with negative attitudes toward the elderly people. Similarly, the respondents who secured a mean score between 59 and 91 were categorized as the respondents with positive attitudes toward the elderly people.

The respondents' positive and negative scores on attitudes toward the elderly people were compared with their age, sex, education, type of family and family income and the chi-square (x^2) test was used for this purpose. Compared to young and middle age respondents, the old age respondents have positive attitudes toward the elderly people. With regard to sex, the female have positive attitude toward the elderly people than the male. While considering education, the respondents with high education group have positive attitudes toward the elderly people than the low and middle education group respondents. There is no significant relationship between the respondents' family type and their attitudes toward the elderly people. But compared to unmarried respondents from nuclear family, the married respondents from nuclear family have positive attitude towards the elderly people. As far as the family monthly income is concerned, the respondents from high income group have positive attitudes toward the elderly people than other two categories. There is significant relationship between the respondents' marital status and their attitudinal score on the elderly people. But compared to the married respondents without children, the married respondents with children have positive attitudes toward the elderly people.

Conclusions

In light of socio-economic transformations in India, the notion of disrepute has taken on new meaning. As a result, the traditional network of support for old people embedded in the family system only needs to be reconsidered. Family is no longer the universal remedy for future elder care. The decreasing family size and job mobility have added to the segregation and isolation of family. To continue the deeply rooted tradition of elder respect, intergenerational activities should be encouraged when children are young. Therefore, various programs should be set up in the school setting to facilitate intergenerational interactions.

REFERENCE

Cowgill, D. O. (1975). Aging and Modernization: A Revision of the Theory. In: J. Gubrium (Ed.), *Late life: Communities and Environmental Policy*. Springfield, IL: Charles Thomas.

5
Chapter

Ageing
A Reason for Exclusion

E. Meera
M.Phil Scholar, G.T.N. Arts College, Dindigul

Introduction

Ageing (British English) or *aging* (American English) is the accumulation of changes in an organism or object over time. Ageing in humans refers to a multidimensional process of physical, psychological and social change. Some dimensions of ageing grow and expand over time, while others decline. Reaction time, for example, may slow with age, while knowledge of world events and wisdom may expand. Research shows that even late in life potential exists for physical, mental and social growth and development. Ageing is an important part of all human societies reflecting the biological changes that occur, but also reflecting cultural and societal conventions. Age is usually measured in full years—and months for young children. A person's birthday is often an important event. Roughly 100,000 people worldwide die each day of age-related causes. It is worthwhile to quote the following:

> *"You are as young as your faith, as old as your doubt;*
> *You are as young as your self confidence, as old as your fear;*
> *You are as young as your hope, as old as your despair."*
>
> **—Doughlas MacArthur**

Differences are sometimes made between populations of elderly people. Divisions are sometimes made between the young old (65–74), the middle old (75–84) and the oldest old (85+). However, problematic in this is that chronological age does not correlate perfectly with functional age, i.e. two people may be of the same age, but differ in their mental and physical capacities. Each nation, government and non-government organization has different ways of classifying age.

Growing Older

It is funny how everyone wants to live long but no one wants to grow old. Old Age is viewed as an unavoidable, undesirable, problem-ridden phase of life that we all are compelled to live, marking time until our final exit from life itself. Perceiving old age with fear is actually a rather recent phenomenon. It seems to increase as each day passes and the world become more complex and less comprehensible. Earlier, when life was simpler and values counted for more, those who reached a ripe old age held an enviable place in society where they could really relax and enjoy their twilight years, secure in the knowledge that they still commanded attention, respect and affection, and that though they were well past their prime, all that they had given their best for was still important – and so were they. A man's life is normally divided into five main stages namely

- Infancy,
- Childhood,
- Adolescence,
- Adulthood and
- Old age.

In each of these stages an individual has to find himself in different situations and face different problems. The old age is not without problems.

Problems of Old Age in India

In old age physical strength deteriorates, mental stability diminishes; money power becomes bleak coupled with negligence from the younger generation. There are 81million older people in India -11 lakh in Delhi itself. According to an estimate nearly 40 per cent of senior citizens living with their families are reportedly facing abuse of one kind or another, but only 1 in 6 cases actually comes to light. Although the President has given her assent to the Maintenance and Welfare of Parents and Senior Citizens Act which punishes children who abandon parents with a prison term of three months or a fine, situation is grim for elderly people in India.

According to NGOs incidences of elderly couples being forced to sell their houses are very high. Some elderly people have also complained that in case of a property dispute they feel more helpless when their wives side with their children. Many of them suffer in silence as they fear humiliation or are too scared to speak up. According to them a phenomenon called 'grand dumping' is becoming common in urban areas these days as children are being increasingly intolerant of their parents' health problems.

After a certain age health problems begin to crop up leading to losing control over one's body, even not recognizing own family owing to Alzheimer are common in old age. It is then children began to see their parents as burden. It is these parents who at times wander out of their homes or are thrown out. Some dump their old parents or grandparents in old-age homes and don't even come to visit them anymore. Delhi has nearly 11 lakh senior citizens but there are only four governments' run homes for them and 31 by NGOs, private agencies and charitable trusts. The facilities are lacking in government run homes.

Left Alone

In the old days, most people did not go very far from their birth place and thus families usually stayed together. The family unit is strong and practical. Today the family unit is breaking apart as young men and women travel widely in search of better jobs. So the chances are that the old folks will be left alone and neglected. Sometimes they are not wanted by their children at all. The luckier ones may have a child or two staying with them. The less fortunate ones may have to pine their lives away in an old folks' home or in their now empty house that once was filled with the sound of children's laughter. This neglect is a very real problem in our society and it is what the old dread most-being wanted and uncared for in the time of need.

Indifference and Neglect

There are other problems old folk's faces, but none can be as bad as the indifference and neglect of the young. The young have no time for the old even though the old have virtually no time left. Soon they will die and the young will take their place.

Socio-economical: An elderly person beyond 65 years or more is likely to face, either himself or along with the spouse, a situation which can be described as lonely and no body to take care of them or to interact with, in view of the dwindling joint family system. If the economical resource is inadequate then the problem would be compounded. In such an event the elderly could cause strain to the society and the State. However, the elderly people could be looked upon as an asset to the society and the Government, if they are looked after properly both in terms of economics and health. This brings in the other two dimensions.

Rural Areas: In India the situation is far more complex. An overwhelming number of people live in rural areas but migration from rural to urban areas is substantial, which creates problems for the ageing at both ends. If children go to urban areas leaving behind the aged in the rural areas, that creates one set of problems, and if the old are taken along, it creates another set of problems. The growth of the urban population and urban centres has been haphazard, and there are acute shortages of housing and other facilities. The health care system is woefully inadequate and there is hardly any specialised agency focusing on the old. There are no programmes available to train people taking care of the aged. In other words, the entire responsibility of taking care of the old continues to be with the traditional institution of the family.

Urban Areas: In urban areas the problems get further accentuated. Community support is weak and the kin network is diffused over a large area and relatively ineffective. The entire responsibility of support and care of the ageing falls on the male children with whom the ageing live. The composition of the family in urban areas is becoming nuclear and smaller, as a result of which there are fewer people available in the house to provide care and comfort to the ageing. Those who are available are torn apart by the stresses of urban living. Women too in the urban areas are now working outside the family. They have fixed schedules of work and have other pressures on them. Children are loaded with their studies, competitive examinations and concerns for making their careers.

The authority that the ageing exercised on their children in the past as a result of greater experience has almost vanished, and the aged are now told, 'You don't know'. There are several reasons for this admonishment. First, the children of the ageing are not in the same profession. Second, the quantum of information which their children claim to have makes the ageing look almost primitive. Third, the whole techno-economic situation has now completely changed, which leaves the ageing bewildered and redundant. When paucity of accommodation, high cost of living, general stress and tensions at all levels are added to these, the problems of the aged are extremely serious.

Political: For a number of reasons ageing has not become an issue of serious consideration for the Government in our country until recently. However, it has become now since the State has realized that unless some measures are taken the problem may go out of proportion.

Indeed the Govt. of India has announced its national policy recently. It seeks to assure older persons that their concerns are national concerns and they will not live unprotected, ignored or marginalised.

Medical/Biological: While it is true that the advances made in medical sciences resulted in improved longevity of people, medical research is still struggling to provide adequate coverage for old age dependent ramifications. As already mentioned, in the scenario of demographic ageing, that segment of population which is above 70 years would be bulging in the years to come. This means more and more people in the stages of "terminal ageing" would be seen in the society. Therefore, any Government or the society has to take two major precautions. One is to ensure that such terminally ageing individuals do not suffer from the ailments that are usually associated with that age. That means one should have a healthy ageing period devoid of major debilitations. Otherwise the whole purpose of prolonging the life span would be an unnecessary and meaningless exercise. Ageing, by itself need not become the cause of death but one could have a comfortable old age until death ensues due to the failure of a vital function. In other words, the morbidity period must be decreased to a minimum. How to achieve this? From the available information, mainly there are five killer diseases that would inflict an ageing person. These, are bronchitis and asthma, heart attack (cardiovascular problems), paralysis, cancer and TB of lungs. About 60 to 70 per cent of the older people die due to these diseases while the rest of the percentage dies due to a variety of other reasons. It is therefore important that the State should promote research and community activities leading towards prevention and better management of these diseases.

Rights of the Elderly

- Parents cannot be evicted from a house without due process of law if they have been staying there from before. There are three enactments that can be applied.
- Under section 125 of the Code of Criminal Procedure, a magistrate can order a child to maintain his old parents under the Maintenance of Parents Act.
- The Hindu Adoptions and Maintenance Act say an aged parent can demand maintenance from children in the same way that a wife can demand it from her husband.
- The Domestic Violence Act too provides parents with the right to seek relief from any kind of abuse.

A National Policy on older persons was announced in January 1999 which identified a number of areas of intervention-financial security, healthcare and nutrition, shelter, education, welfare, protection of life and property for the well-being of older persons in the country. A National Council for Older Persons (NCOP) was constituted by the Ministry of Social Justice and Empowerment to operationalize the National Policy on older persons.

Tips for Treating Elders

One should look to the elderly as really wise people who knew so much about the world. They were the ones who could be relied upon to provide a history lesson of what life used to be like in "their day". But things have changed so much in just a very short space of time. We are now more likely to hear of elder abuse within the family, residential home or a mugging that took place, involving an elderly victim. It is sad to see the elderly being abused and disregarded so much in a society that they once contributed so much to. Here are some suggestions on ways in which one should treat the elderly.

Give Them a Call

Many elderly people do not hear from people as much as they used to in their youth. Just a brief phone call to see how they are getting along can really lift their day and make them feel valued. If one lives far away from grandparents, this may be the best option. It can also help alert one to any problems if one make the effort to call.

Visit the Elderly

Many elderly people are housebound due to illness or immobility, so they might not be able to get out and about as much as they would like. One will be surprised to see the joy on their faces as they welcome their children into their home, just because they have made the effort to visit. Even if they can only spare a few minutes of time, one should try to visit and let them know that they are thinking of them. Growing older does not take away a person's need to socialize and have a friendly chat. The need for companionship actually seems to increase, rather than lessen, with age. Elderly people often admit that they are very lonely, especially if they are widowed and are living on their own. Just imagine spending year after year alone with hardly any visitors. It's a dreadful thought.

Treat the Elderly with Respect

Do not assume that a person who is elderly has lost all their faculties and needs to be treated as a child. They have lived a lot longer than the younger generation and they deserve our utmost respect. Even if one do not know of anyone elderly within one's own family, treat elderly people who are strangers with respect. One can do this by holding the door open for them to enter a shop before and giving up one's seat to them if they need it on the bus or train. A younger person tends to be fitter and stronger, whereas elderly people are more likely to have health problems and will need to rest more. This is a simple, but courteous act that will be appreciated.

Take them Out

An elderly person may not have the use of a car any longer if their eyesight has deteriorated or because of some other reason. So think about practical ways that one can help them, such as taking them shopping. If they are unable to go with them, ask them to make a shopping list and shop for them. Also, consider doctor's visits. Many elderly people need to visit the doctor more so than when they were younger. They will need help to go to the doctor's and then to pick up their prescription afterwards.

Conclusion

These are all practical ways that one can help someone who is elderly. They may seem like insignificant acts, but to a person who is old and frail, this can be seen as great acts of kindness. Elderly people are not useless. They still serve a useful purpose in society and do much to enhance one's own life as well. The elderly make a valuable contribution to society and as such they deserve to be treated with respect and kindness.

As far as the ageing of people is concerned, apart from giving them specialised attention through nursing homes and mobile health units, family members will have to be trained in their care. It is to be borne in mind that care cannot be given by mere emotions and a sense of obligation. There has to be proper understanding of the problem and of the remedial measures which can be provided by modern knowledge of health and medicine. Thus a combination of modern knowledge and intense feeling for those who are non-productive can provide physical and emotional comfort to the old.

Thus the answer to the question "Is ageing a reason for exclusion?" is "NO". Ageing should not be a reason for excluding people from the family or society. Because,

"Without young people, there could be no NATION;
But without old people, there could be no GREAT NATION".

6
CHAPTER

Social Exclusion and Crisis of Governance
A Perspective in Manipur

Sonkhogin Haokip
Asst. Professor, Dept. of PS&DA, Gandhigram Rural Institute, Gandhigram

Introduction

Manipur is a plural society consisting of three major ethnic groups. The 'Meitei' (Manipur Hindus), 'Naga', and "Kuki-chin' (both tribal groups) with various migrant communities and the 'Pangal' (Manipur Muslims). Thus, social-cultural pluralism is the core of the social fabric of Manipur. The Meiteis were converted to Hinduism and accepted the caste system while the Nagas and Kuki-chin groups were social converted into Christianity. The Muslim community while accepting Meitei language constitutes a distinct social and cultural group based on religious profession. Therefore, social pluralism has led to the perpetuation of the various groups as distinct entities. Though there was no traditional social disharmony among these groups, it has failed to evolve an integrated social formation in Manipur. With the coming of democracy in Manipur in the post independent period, social pluralism has been harmonized to some extent by the power sharing of the various cultural groups in a democracy. However, the problem of inter-ethnic conflicts and inter-societal hiatus continues as assertion of ethnic-identity becomes formidable (Gangumci Kabui, 2004).

The process of ethnic 'identity formation in the North-East region of India was based on the idea of large group formation. Attempts were made to bring several smaller groups together to project a unified identity. Ethnic consciousness leads to identity expansion by merging together several groups and expand their identity.

In this process of identity expansion, they also develop a belief in common origin as the Nagas and Mizos have done (Achary, 1990). This argument, however, may not hold valid in the case of Manipur where (as Rajesh Dev, 2004 argued), groups that had once identified with a particular ethnic name or group is reconstructing its identity independent of its parent body and legitimating the process through reification of alleged 'indignity'. For instance, 'Zalengrong', a conglomeration of the ethnic groups like the Rougmei, Leangmei and Paomei, is asserting its own identity (ethnic) independent of the parent body *i.e.,* 'The Naga'. Similarly, the Zome Re-unification Organisation (ZRO), a conglomeration of the ethnic groups like the paite, simte, vaiphei, zou, etc. is asserting an identity independent of the parent 'Kuki' tribe.

Thus, continuing quest for 'independent ethnic identity' has reproduces images of otherness that is exclusionary, insular and ethnocentric. This has cascading effect in such a multi-ethnic region, where exclusive ethnic identities are being continually constructed thereby initiating ethnic contests between dominant and non-dominant ethnic groups. The contests reflects in the form of 'dominant meitei ethnic groups versus non-dominant Kuki and Naga ethnic groups' where the former submerges and excludes the latter from social, political and economic advantages. It (*i.e.* the contests) could also be seen to be taken place within the Kuki ethnic groups and Naga ethnic groups in the form of major-ethnic tribes versus minor ethnic tribes.

Replacement of colonial political structures by people-centric ones not only sharpened this inter-ethnic divides but also created new divides within ethnic groups as the flow of money from central governments contributed to the emergence of alternative and competing elites (Partha S. Ghosh 2005). Thus, loyalty to group identities and the formidable assertion of ethnic identity eventually crystallized into "ethnic insurgencies" based on ethnic terms.

Insurgency

At present there are about 30 insurgent groups operating in Manipur some of which have an ideology whereas majority of them are allegedly purely extortionist groups that use the underground façade to their own advantage. Hill-based insurgent groups in Manipur are the off shoot of ethnic politics based on demographic domination and power politics, which have led to the process of ethnic domination of the majority over the minority (Shimray, 2004). This ethnic politics was based on false ideology. For instance, the Naga insurgent organization-NSCN-(IM) has been actively working towards the process of forcefully assimilating the smaller indigenous tribes of Manipur into Nagahood. Smaller tribes which have been identifying under their indigenous tribes name are lured into a false promise of greater power and assertion under the banner of Naga Nationalism. Smaller tribes which were once considered to be old-Kukis such as Aimol, Anal, Maring, Kom, Purum, Chothe, Koirang, etc. have started identifying themselves as Nagas. In the process, they have lost their original identities.

The Naga insurgent elements have coerced the smaller tribes into Nagahood in a bid to expand the Naga domain and any exposition regarding the de-nagaisation of the smaller tribes are dealt with in a very violent way by the NSCN (IM). Ethnic conflicts in the hills of Manipur are a direct consequence of such hardened ethnic identities and exclusive claims. The Naga-Kuki conflict in 1992 in Manipur was the consequences of the stiff-opposition to Naga-expansionism in the hill areas of Manipur, by the Kukis.

Interface between Civil Society and Governance in Manipur

Both state and militant violence have contributed equally to the shrinking of the democratic space in the State of Manipur today. Manipur is under the veil of numerous black laws and is used in the heart of a conflict situation that had raged in the region for the past two decades and had claimed hundreds of lives. Rampant violation of basic human rights has been experienced over the years in both the hills and the plain of Manipur. The unarmed and innocent civilians (human beings) have long been sandwiched from both ends of armed forces. All the legal parameters of determining crime and punishment are being abused here without any human consideration. Extra-judicial killings of persons in custody, enforced disappearance, and torture and rape by police and other security forces, and fake-encounters are the permanent headlines in the (Manipur's) local dailies of Manipur. There is a general lack of accountability permeating the government and security forces throughout the state, creating an atmosphere of impurity, officials used special anti-terrorism legislations to justify the excessive use of force while combating terrorism and several regional insurgencies. There are several instances in which some elements of the security forces acted in dependently of government authority. Today, Manipur, which is under the veil of numerous black laws, is in the heart of a conflict situation and usably the most volatile state in India. A closer look into the trends in Manipur, would clearly illustrate some of the serious erosion of the civil society space.

Just like state violence, militant violence too has contributed largely towards the shrinking of the democratic space and in silencing the voice of the civil society. There is no scope for any democratic space in the very organizational structure and mode of functioning of the insurgent groups and the average citizen has nowhere to appeal to in case of insurgent violence.

The basis for good governance is a well-functioning democratic political system that ensures representative and honest governments responsive to the needs of the people. This involves more than simply the holding of regular, free and fair elections. It also implies respect for human rights in general, and notably for basic civil liberties such as freedom of expression and of association, including a free and pluralistic media. These are fundamental conditions for the development of a vibrant civil society that reflects the full diversity of views and interests.

The state and civil society are complementary not alternative to each other. The state performs certain indispensable functions and if those are subverted and under-mined, civil society would wither in the bud. On the other hand civil society cannot perform the crucial function of holding the state accountable and responsive unless it itself is democratized. To make the various institutions of governance accountable and responsive to the people and the society, space has to be created wherein the state, institutions of governance and the civil society work in partnership. A partnership between civil society and governance has brought to the surface, the various roles that civil society took on, in strengthening or weakening the institutions of governance (Chandhoke, 1995).

Of the hill tribes in Manipur, Nagas are united on the overall issue of Naga identity and interest. The more than 50 years of insurgent violence and wide-scale killings of leaders of civil society organizations as well as political organizations has the resulting consequences of militarizing the entire Naga society to such an extent that today, civil society groups in the Naga society have been forced to work in close liaison with the militant organization. The hold of NSCN-(IM) over the entire Naga society in Manipur is so deep-rooted that no organizations (civil society or otherwise) can afford to disregard the dictum of NSCN (IM). Ahead of February elections to the 9th Manipur Legislative Assembly, five sitting MLAs of Naga in Manipur resigned from the Manipur State Assembly. The resignations came in the wake of the campaign by the United Naga Council - which worked as per the "command from elsewhere"—against Naga candidates set up by any "political party", referring to political parties recognized by the Election Commission of India, ECI. The resignations of the MLAs can be treated as an open surrender by a good section of the political establishment in the hills, to "extra-political organizations".

Regarding the Kukis, they are dispersed in Senapati district (Saikul and Sadar Hills), Ukhrul, Chandel, Churachandpur and Tamenglong district. They are not so well organized and the recent threat from the Nagas (NSCN-IM) is the only unifying force and motivation for their identity as a tribe. Kuki militant groups like KNA (Kuki National Army), KNF (Kuki National Front),

UKLF (United Kuki Liberation Front), and KLA (Kuki Liberation Army) are operating in Kuki dominated areas of Manipur. They do not have any ideology, nor the capacity to defend the Kuki dominated areas and being fragmented, they can only perpetrate sporadic violence and thus escalate inter-ethnic as well as intra-ethnic conflicts in Manipur. Worst is the fact that, these militant groups of the Kuki have been bought by political establishments and literally, have been converted into a private armed groups of the Kuki political elites. Since political elites amongst the Kuki's are competing to gained support of the militant groups, situation has arisen where there is a necessity to buy these militants and once blood is tasted by one group, other groups mushroomed (Partha S. Ghosh, 2005) in no time and money flows into their hands relatively easily.

Virtually, there is no space for civil society to play its important role in holding the state accountable and responsive to the needs of the people especially when it is caught in the cross-fire. The state has become so soft, civil society so weak. Civil society has been silenced at the barrel of the Gun. Everyone talks of the killing of innocent people by these groups or about the inter-group violence but violence is the only method through which they can communicate and that alone would give them legitimacy as insurgents to extort money from the politicians, bureaucrats and businessmen.

Therefore, governance in the hill areas of Manipur can be equated to "Laws of the Jungle" where "might is right" has become the principle means of governance. Misguided youths who are recruited in large number in these militant groups have become a potential threat not only to civil society but to civilization as well, since these groups stands on the margin of society, culture, and civilization.

In the valley, Meitei militant groups consisting of major factors of PLA (People's Liberation Army), UNLF (United National Liberation Force), KCP (Kangleipak-Communist Part), and PREPAK (People's Revolutionary Party of Kangleipak) are all operating in Imphal valley is disjointed fashion. All have areas of interest in Imphal town and greater Imphal with PLA extending its area of operations to Thoubal and Bishnupur district. RJC (Revolutionary Joint Committee), a front organization embracing PLA, PREPAK and KCP is a recent development. Like the Kuki insurgent groups, for these meitei extremists, insurgency has become both an occupation and business and thereby control of activities in the valley to establish their writ, resulting in total erosion of government's authority and ineffective functioning of administration and law enforcement agencies. Meitei population, irrespective of status and position, are captive and subservient to the will of these insurgent groups, most pay taxes and some even actively support them.

(Manipur Governor's Report to the President of India, about the crisis in Manipur- No. GSM/LA18/93 Dt.Sep.5, 1993).

As Ajai Sahni and George have argued, the progressive 'withdrawal' of civil governance and the network of collusive arrangements with militant factions are compounded by the emergence of widespread patterns of illegal economic activity that become the mainstay and motive of all insurgencies after what may be called their early 'ideological' state. These include a thriving economy of extortion, smuggling, gun-running, narcotics, and an oligopolistic control over government contracts. Indeed, the various 'ideological' factions and rivalries within militant movements in the state of Manipur are often thinly disguised 'turf wars' to retain or gain control over lucrative 'areas of influence', especially important routes of (illegal) cross border trade, including the drug trade. For instance, 'Moreh' a small Indo-Myanmar town in Chandel district, Manipur which is the main corridors for drug and heroin smuggling, is a bone of contention for all the militant groups in the state. In so far as the Moreh entry point in Myanmar is concerned, the nearest point on the other side is Tamu, which is few km. away. The Moreh-Tamu trade is small in quantity and it is primarily a smuggling trade in Chinese, Korean, and Thai goods. However, the market in Imphal, the capital of Manipur thrives on this trade. Both Moreh and Tamu are predominantly inhabited by the Kuki-Chin groups.

The growth of this underground terrorist economy, backed by the disruptive power of the militants, distorts and inhibits the processes and growth of legitimate economic and developmental activities. The civil society along with a wide variety of economic activities that were integral to the lives of the people of Manipur have been 'criminalized', forcing otherwise law abiding citizens into a collusive relationship with militants within their areas of influence (be it the meitei militant group, the Nagas or the Kukis). Moreover, militant groups gradually usurp a wide range of governmental functions, including the (albeit conditional) perfection of life and property, and the provision of 'justice' to local communities. Militancy in Manipur can, in fact, fruitfully (though only partially) be examined as a conflict to defend or expand monopolistic control over critical functions – economic and administrative – against all 'intruders', including the government, with militant groups taking on the character of a 'primitive state' in a situation of widespread anarchy.

Government officials, especially of the engineering departments are on a routine basis, being taken into captivity by sundry organizations, all for huge ransoms. (Pradip Pahnjoubam, 2008) and there seems very little that the state can do either, for its adversaries seems to be everywhere having penetrated many of the government's own institutions. There seems very little that the militant organizations themselves are able to keep the semblance of an ideological struggle to the protracted turmoil in the land either because there is a constant mushrooming of new militant or else, semi-militant organizations. Sometimes these take the route of an organization splintering endlessly into numerous small factions, each of these units in the process acquiring a clout of its own through violent and intimidatory means. They also often come to face with each other, taking a tragic toll of collateral damages from amongst the ordinary citizenry.

Thus, Manipur with a population of 30,23,141 (2002 census) is perhaps, the state with the highest per capita "terrorist organization" not only in India but the whole world. (Of the 28 militant organisaions branded as "Terrorist" in India under POTA, ten are from the North-East region out of which again six are from Manipur). Fratricidal fighting among these different insurgent groups has seriously eroded the civil society space; and as conflicts within the society increases, the state has passed new emergency legislations. A number of "National Security Laws" are passed and operated upon in Manipur to curb insurgency. Such as:

(1) AFSPA (Armed Forces Special Powers Act), 1958,
(2) The prevention of seditious meeting Act, 1911,
(3) The Punjab Security of State Act, 1953,
(4) Foreigners Protected Areas Order, 1958,
(5) The Unlawful Activities (Prevention) Act, 1967,
(6) The National Security Act, 1980,
(7) The Code of Criminal Procedure (Manipur Armed) Act, 1983, and
(8) The terrorist and Disruptive Activities (Prevention) Act, 1985.

However, with these fairly comprehensive legal institutional and administrative arrangements to safeguard and protect "National Security" interest in Manipur over the year, the people are increasingly feeling insecure and getting all alienated from the authority. The impunity enjoyed by the Armed Forces under the various black laws requires no additional laws as they can get away with almost anything and everything they do. The special power given to them under these laws is routinely used by a large number of armed force personnel stationed in Manipur. Hundreds of suspected militants as well as ordinary civilians have been reported to be arbitrarily arrested, tortured, extra judicially executed, involuntarily disappeared; while women are raped and sexually harassed. Manipur which is under the veil of numerous black laws is in the heart of a conflict situation that had raged the state for the past two decades and had claimed hundreds of lives. Rampant violation of basic human rights has been experienced over the years both in the hills and the plain of Manipur.

The unarmed and innocent human beings have long been sandwiched from both ends of the armed groups – militant groups at one end and security forces at the other. Civil society is suffering the outcome of the spillover of the counter – insurgency military operations. As the security of the state beefed up with the government constantly increasing the strength of the armed forces in Manipur, there was an immense increase in insecure constituencies that has become a concern in the security radar screen for the Government of Manipur as well as the Centre. All legal parameters of determining crime and punishment are being abused without any human consideration.

Added to the phenomenon of insurgency, numerous civil-society protests in the form of bandhs and strikes, partial or total at the slightest provocation, have become frequent phenomenon. The federation of industries in the N.E region has estimated, and published recently in a local newspaper, that one-day's strike causes the loss of Rs.50 crores due to disruption of economic activities. Such disruptions being frequent in Manipur, one can well imagine the extent of direct annual loss to the state economy and its negative impact on the economic environment.

Crisis of Governance

Against this background, governance becomes a huge challenge for the State. The biggest impediments to good governance in the present state of affairs are the unresolved questions of insurgency and economic stagnancy moving in a vicious circle. The economic stagnancy that impedes employment and income growth serves as fertile ground for fortifying and sustaining insurgency (Sharma, 2005). On the other hand, the growing militancy and the subsequent growth of the underground terrorist economy, backed by the disruptive power of the militants, distort and inhibit the processes of growth of legitimate economic and developmental activities. Throw into this mix the question of governability and we have the enduring challenge that the state of Manipur face today.

To complicate matters is the half-hearted and unsystematic arrangement of the system of self-governance in the state. Although small population is in question, two systems of local government are in operation in Manipur and that too sometimes in contravention of the broad theoretical premise that dictated the criteria (Partha S. Ghosh, 2008). The two systems are: Autonomous District Council under the Manipur Hill Areas, District councils Act, 1975, but not under the Schedule VI of the Indian Constitution, and the Panchayati Raj Institutions as per the 73rd Amendment of the Indian Constitution.

The Question of Autonomy and Social Exclusion

Autonomy within the state's administrative set-up and autonomy movements evolving a more (militant, secessionist ideas of political and geographical demarcation of territory) marked the political discourse in Manipur for the last decade. The genesis of autonomy movements in Manipur could be traced to the post-Independent reorganization of the Northeastern States of India when, the various hill ethnic groups were brought under different territorial-administrations and the concept of state territorial politics and segmentation was imposed on them. This so-called 'administrative convenience' divided many ethnic groups into different political administrators.

The process of ethnic identity formation in the region was based on the idea of large group formation. Attempts were made to bring several smaller groups together to project a unified identity. One important formation, emergent of ethnic identity, is the development of generic terms/ names in the contiguous geographical territory. Ethnic consciousness leads to identity "expansion" by merging together several groups and expand their identity.

The northeast is a region that encompasses tremendous social heterogeneity and complex (traditional) political organizations. Numerous cultural groups with relatively autonomous histories, conflicting claims and different stages of development constitute the socio-political matrix of the region. Estimates maintain that there are nearly 75 major ethnic groups and sub-groups with 400 languages and dialects. Some of these groups were granted statehood at various moments of post-Independent history in deference to claims for (ethnic) autonomy and difference. In this way, the autonomy of 'collective life-worlds' of some of the ethnic communities residing in the region were 'recognized and protected' by legal and structural mechanisms, while majority of the ethnic communities still remained marginalized socially, economically, culturally and politically. The reorganization of states in the northeast on ethnic lines has triggered a continuing 'quest for identity' which reproduces images of 'otherness' that is exclusionary, insular and ethno-centric.

The constitutional guarantees provided in the form of 'protective discrimination' or even ethno-linguistic states meant for providing equal opportunities to marginalized ethnic groups has proved to be counter-productive in many of these states. Because in almost all these states, it is group identity that has become primary for deriving state entitlements and social rights leading to a social condition where premium is placed on ethnic identity. Thus in a social and political condition, where differential privileges were supposed to supplement citizenship rights, the result has been the contrary, i.e., differential privileges itself becoming a source of social closure. The consequence has been that in the region, an increasing process of contrasting and comparing of cultural markers that redefines ethnic identity and claims have germinated. This has a cascading effect in such a multi-ethnic region, where exclusive ethnic identities are being continually constructed. Groups that had once identified with a particular ethnic name or group is (re)constructing its identity independent of its parent body and legitimating the process through reification of alleged 'indignity'. These claims to authenticity and autonomy of group identity are often relativists to the extent that it involves denial of similar claims by 'others' thus initiating ethnic contests between dominant and non-dominant ethnic groups where the former submerges and excludes the latter from social, political and economic advantages.

In this context it may be noted that as in other parts of India, the linguistic/ethnic demarcation of states in the north east helped to consolidate the margins of group identity. State structures are now obviously identified with a particular group or groups. However, unlike the other parts of the country, in the north-east, the identification is rigidly ethno-centric to the extent that any legal or political recognition of the 'marginality' of the group and the redress of the same is considered a political game that would undermine the claims of the dominant ethnic groups. Thus group identity and the state structure are so inter-wined in most of these states that 'claims' or 'recognition' of claims of non-dominant groups are seen as belligerent, oblivious of the fact that many of the communities seeking such 'recognition' may have been residents of the state for generations. This implies that in the determination of the justifiability or legitimacy of claims by non-dominant groups it is not residency but 'indigenity' that determines a group's claim and inclusion as full social and political actors in the state. But even 'indigenity' claims of a minor ethnic group are often contested by the dominant ethnic groups who control the political apparatus of the state. An instance is the conflict between the Kukis and the Paites in the state of Manipur where the claims made by the Paites for constitutional recognition of their 'indignity' is being challenged by the dominant group on the claim that the Paites are essentially Kukis and therefore, recognition of their 'unique collective life' would undermine Kuki identity to the extent that "at one point of time there may not be anything called the Kukis.

This intertwinement of state boundaries and ethnic identity is also deepened by ethnic insurgencies in the region that undertake surreptitious eviction of 'ethnic others' from their 'imagined homelands' (Rajesh Dev, 2004).

Conclusion

The ultimate power of the state resides in the penalties it can enforce and among these penalties is that of depriving an individual of his citizenship rights leaving him completely unprotected as far as law and judicial remedies are concerned. It is the state who has the legitimate possession of coercive instruments of power and these instruments in all their ferocity are used against those who do not abide by the rules of the public sphere. Civilized behavior is rewarded and uncivilized notions are punished (Chandhoke, 1995).

At the same time, a state that takes little account of the conflicts and alliances in society can behave neither purposefully nor can it measures its own actions or modify them. The state no matter how immense the power at its command has to be responsive to the shifting balances of social forces and new social meanings generated in society, otherwise it becomes irrelevant, it in effect, becomes a state without society (*ibid*). On June 14, 2001, a five point cease-fire agreement was signed between the Government. of India (GOI) and the National Socialist Council of Nagalim (Issac), (NSCN-IM). (NSCN emerged in 1980 is an underground insurgent group based in Nagaland State (India) and spread across the North East India. It has two factions: Khaplang group NSCN (K) and Irak-Muivah group (NSCN-IM) split in 1958).

Article-I of the agreement provides extension of the cease-fire without territorial limits – the operational understanding of which means the extension of the cease-fire to the so called "Naga inhabited areas" of Manipur, Assam, and Arunachal Pradesh. It also reflects the fact that the GOI implicitly concedes to the demand of NSCN (IM) to recognize the "Naga Inhabited Areas' of Manipur, Assam and Arunachal Pradesh as territories of Nagalim.

The historic, and the unfortunate decision shows that the GOI bows to the threat of a handful of underground outlaws rather than respecting the wish of the lawful and democratic people of Manipur, Assam and Arunachal Pradesh. By submitting to the sectoral demands of the NSCN (IM), the GOI had sent up all of the North East in Flames, Manipur was paralyzed Assam was infuriated and Arunachal was angered, Tripura was incensed and there was no joy in Mizoram.

By negotiating with the insurgent and extra-constitutional bodies, the State has made the civil-society completely irrelevant and by prioritizing the louder voice in the region (NSCN-IM being the mother of all the insurgent organizations in the North East), the GOI was also sending a wrong and a very dangerous signal to the entire North East region in general and Manipur in particular. The infamous event had spurred the resurgence of ethnic violence and mushrooming of insurgent groups based on ethnic lines. Civil society as the area of democratic dialogue and contestation is in profound danger. There is little space left for the undoubted merry, but occasionally creative politics of critical consultation and dialogue. Individual has come to be engulfed by influences from two extreme spheres that flank civil society. On the one hand are the influences that emanate from particularistic loyalties as tribe, ethnicity, and linguistic affiliations, on the other flank of civil society is the state, a state which constantly seeks to speak directly to the individual and calls upon to commit himself to great cause, such as war, national honor and prestige of defending the sanctity of national boundaries. This is where Indian Nationalism comes into conflict with Ethnic nationalism of the Meitei, Kuki and the Nagas.

REFERENCES

Bhaumik Subir and Jayanta Bhattacharya, 2005. "Autonomy in the Northeast: The Hills of Tripura and Mizoram." In *The Politics of Autonomy: Indian Experiences*, Ranabir Samaddar. New Delhi: Sage Publications.

Baruah Sanjib, 2003. "Protective Discrimination and Crisis of Citizenship in North-East India." *Economic and Political Weekly*, April 26.

Chandhoke Neera (1995), State and Civil Society: Exploration in Political Theory, Sage Publications: New Delhi.North East Sun, *Fortnightly*, January 16-31, 2007, Vol.XII, No.12.

Dev Rajesh, (2004), "Human Rights, Relationism and Minorities in North-East India", *Economic and Political Weekly*, Oct. 23.

Ghosh Partha S. (2005), Challenge of Governance and Globalization: A Case Study of India's North-East, *Spring*, Vol. II, No. I.

Lokendro Abraham, 2006. "Indo-Manipur Armed Conflict: Need for Public Debates on Conflict Resolution." *Eastern Frontier*, October.

Manipur Fact File 2001, AMCTA (All Manipur College Teachers' Association).

Prabhakra, M.S. (2004), "Is North East India Landlocked?" *Economic and Political Weekly*, Oct. 16.

Sarin Vik, 1980. *India's North-East in Flames*. Vikas Publishing House Pvt. Ltd. New Delhi.

Sarma Atol (2005), Why the North Eastern States Continue to Decelerate, *Spring*, Vol.II, No.I

SECTION–II

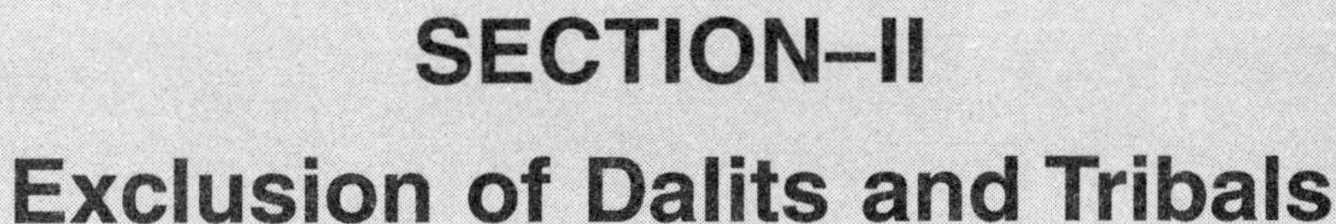

Exclusion of Dalits and Tribals

7
CHAPTER

Social Exclusion and Dalit Identity in Tamil Nadu

Dr. K. Suriyan

Asst. Professor (SS), Deptt. of Sociology, Annamalai University, Chidambaram

Preamble

Dalit ("oppressed" or "broken") is not a new word. Apparently it was used in the 1930s as a Hindi and Marathi translation of 'Depressed Classes', the term the British used for what are now called the scheduled castes. The word was also used by B.R. Ambedkar 'broken men', an English in his Marathi speeches. In The Untouchables; published in 1948, Ambedkar chose the term 'broken men', an English translation of 'Dalit', to refer to the original ancestors of the untouchables for reasons which must have been self-evident because he did not explain them. The term 'Dalit' in Sanskrit is both a noun and an adjective. As a noun, dalit may be used for all three genders, masculine, feminine, and neuter. It has been derived from the root "dal" which means to crack, open, split, and so on. When used as a noun or adjective, it means burst, split, broken or torn as under, downtrodden, scattered, crushed, destroyed.

The present usage of the term dalit goes back to the nineteenth century when a Marathi social reformer and revolutionary Mahatma Jyoti Rao Phule used it to describe the out castes and untouchables as the oppressed and broken victims of the Indian caste midden society. Weaker sections, backward classes. Scheduled castes and tribes and a plethora of similar concepts currently used in India, as descriptive terms to indicate a group of people in fact are blanket terms. Even their counterpart Indian concept like "Bur Bat or Dalit Varg" hardly enables one to know the implications and they are not by any means self-explanatory either.

However, going by the spirit of the meaning and the conventions that have developed around these concepts over the years, under, weaker sections. I am inclined to include such groups of people who are economically, politically, and educationally very backward and suffer social-religious discrimination on account of the hoary traditions of caste-outcaste based on ritual purity and pollution.

The former untouchables who largely fill the present day scheduled castes known as Harijans and Girijans approximate to the description given above, although there are some exceptions.

The Constitution and Dalits

The Constitution of India has in addition to others singled out there groups for political representation at various levels starting from the village to the Parliament and State assemblies in between. Such political representation is envisaged to create political awareness and help to develop leadership at gross-roots level. The assumption is that by a system of deliberate reservations and 'Protective discrimination' the depressed and suppressed communities who have remained like dumb cattle for centuries may gradually be drawn into the main stream. Once there is political awakening, the matching socio-economic and educational measures go a long way in fessening the evils and hardships caused by the snobberies of caste and untouchability. While political representation at upper levels is fully exploited with the tacit support of political parties at lower levels, especially villages, far from developing grass – root leadership it has often created cleavages among S.C. and to the advantage of upper castes.

Social scientists have highlighted the Aryan conspiracy in India to subjugate the dalit bahujans by attempting to construct the Indian nation on the basis of purity of blood, language and culture. With Hindu revivalism, a fascist culture centred on the purity of the Aryan race, superiority of Sanskrit over other languages and brahmanic culture are imposed on the country.

Now dalit is a widely used category in our Indian society. Are they differentiated in categories? Are they unified and integrated community? Are there any divisions among them? Are there any inequalities among them? By nature it is not so! By way of performing occupations and vested interest of the politicians these divisions have crept in. Caste identity as a dilemma appeared even before the independence of India. After independence they are being called as scheduled castes that are listed in the constitution in various states with different sub-castes.

As a democratic country which consists of 75 per cent of rural population with the conclusion of 25 per cent of dalits who involved with their traditional occupations. Owing to their tradition, they are somewhat different among themselves in their local social, economic and cultural background and mostly depend on the higher caste landholders for their survival.

Life Style of Dalits

The Constitution has made caste illegal and abolished it in 1950. Affirmative action programme was introduced to bring the unequal to the level of equality. Regardless of official policy, the system still permits Indian life and culture. "When we are working, they ask us not to come near them. At canteens, they have separate tea tumblers which have to be cleaned by the dalit himself after use. They cannot enter into temples. They cannot touch ropes of temple car while the upper caste pull. They cannot use upper caste water taps. In schools the dalit children are not treated as the children of the other castes. They live in colonies of their own"—is a testimony of a scavenger in India especially in Tamilnadu. Caste still has limited social advancement, job and marriage choices.

In the recent years the dalit had shown a lot of interest in education. Some of them got government jobs. Their life style has improved a bit. Ultimately they have planned to stay outside their traditional village living in towns or cities. But their aged parents are never interested in staying in towns as they are accustomed to village cultural practices. On the eve of pongal festival or any other family ceremonies the educated people come to their village to attend such functions. When they bring their colleagues/ friends of other caste, they have to face some embracing on account of some unwritten rules of upper caste such as folding umbrella, removing of chappals. Added to this they cannot take bath in the tanks/wells/taps as the upper caste use them; they should worship the god outside the temple, and cannot enter temple and will not be given any respect, all rituals can be followed by themselves alone with all humiliations losing their self respect in front of the fellow colleagues (guests); even a small boy of upper caste will call the man in disrespectful terms. They can tease their family members to any extent; especially the women and girls are subjected to so much harassment. There are incidences as system hereunder. They are systematically excluded for normal society. It is a process which follows under.

Social Exclusion as a Process

It involves a systematic denial of entitlements to resources and services, and the denial of the right to participate on equal terms in social relationships in economic, social, cultural or political arenas. Exclusionary processes can occur at various levels – within and between households, villages, cities, states, and globally. This is an actor-oriented approach which is useful because it points to who is doing what and in relationship with whom. It also provides information for international development agencies to identify those dynamic processes already extant which they could aim to strengthen or minimise. In a situation where there is a disparity in social power relationships, the question of who has the prerogative to define, who is the definer and who is the defined, becomes a site of conflict.

(a) *settlement:* As per the traditional norms governing life in rural India, dalit settlements were to be located on the side of the sun sets. There are several villages where dalit houses have traditionally been located on the west. However, in a majority of the villages, dalit houses were indeed constructed on the outskirts of the main village settlement.

(b) *Occupations:* In village community most of the dalits are depending upon the upper caste landholders. The lower caste (dalit) people are supposed to work in the fields of upper caste lands as coolies or traditional care takers of the land as well as the livestocks. Perhaps, some of the other categories among them are involved with dead cattle, scavenging and other polluted occupations.

(c) *Land watcher:* In the olden days there were no pump sets. For the irrigation purpose the lower caste people have to stay at the fields. They depend upon the river or pond water. They shared the water among themselves taking turns. When the landlords' turn came, the dalit subordinate has to attend the work on behalf of their landlord both day and night. They have to stay on the river bed or tank shore. By the time the caste hindu man will have sex with dalit women.

(d) *No entry to upper caste houses:* The restrictions on dalit's entry into the upper caste houses has been one of the most strictly observed practices in most of the rural areas. They were permitted only through back ways that to upto cattle-sheds to get old food and during some festivals occasions they may be given some special food after the landlords eat.

(e) *Drinking water sources:* The sources of drinking water have been another area where the upper castes used to be very touchy. Traditionally dalits and upper castes had different sources of drinking water. While all the upper castes could take water from the wells, dalits could never do so. They had to depend exclusively on their own wells.

(f) *Untouchability in religious places:* Practice of untouchability has been most pronounced in the religious sphere. The upper caste people restricted the dalits in religious life. They denied access to the classical religious traditions and scriptures. The can not enter temple to workshop. They have to be in out side and can not participate in the temple activities like pulling of temple car rope as the upper caste people did. (Ex) Kandadevi Temple festival in Ramnad Distict.

(g) *Untouchability in provision of services:* The most traditional practice of the upper caste is that dalits should not take dead bodies through the upper caste streets and also should not use the same burial ground which the upper caste people use. But all the burial ground works such as digging a pit, taking the dead body and covering it with a clothe and/or cremating the dead body should be done by the dalits only.

(h) *Untouchability in access to village streets:* In the streets of upper castes the Dalits were not allowed to walk along with slippers, upper covering, and towels on the shoulders. Not only the men and also the women. When the women work on their fields they have to fold up their sarees exposing their thighs and chest. While seeing them the upper caste men passess sarcastic comments towards them like 'the land shows up well and need to be ploughed'.

(i) *Untouchability in secular institutions:* Dalits experienced untouchability while accessing services of post office, PDS and PHCs.

(j) *Untouchability in Political institutions:* In political activities the dalits have not been given seats in the open constituencies both Lokshaba and state assembly elections. There are some reserved panchayats that have not accepted dalits as Panchayat Presidents where the upper castes also live in those panchayats.

(i) *Tanjore – Keelavenmani:* The dalit people demanded only quarter padi of paddy in addition to their coolie for extra work. The higher caste landlords put the 42 dalits in a room and burnt them alive.

(ii) *Sivagangai – Oonchanai:* There was an Ayyanar temple celebration at Oonchanai village. During the celebration the horse statue has to be taken as god. The dalits were prevented to got right and they were under murder.

(iii) *Madurai – Melur – Chennakarampatty:* A couple of dalits named as Ammavasi and Velu got the land for lease to cultivate foodgrains. The intolerant caste hindus felt how come the dalits can get land. If they get it they will not obey our order. With this they wanted to threaten the dalits taking action against those two by plucking their eyes and killing them.

(iv) *Madurai – Melur – Keelavazhavu:* A dalit man named Murugesan won the Panchayat election against the Mukkulathor caste. They were intolerant towards the victory of a dalit man. So they planned to kill him and did it along with another four of the dalits who traveled in the city bus.

(v) *Madurai – Usilampatty – Pappanayackanpatty:* While the dalits discuss their family matters with their wives the upper caste landlord gets possessive and penalize the dalit by sending him to take care of the land, thus preventing dalit man from enjoying the conjugal relationship. After sending him to field the higher caste man would stay at the dalits' house and force the wife of dalit man to have sex with him. Thus they practiced domination. Even when the dalit husband knows of this he would not raise his voice against this. This had been practiced for several decades in rural areas. In some of the states in India incidents are still worse for dalits who get loan from the upper caste man; he has to pawn his wife till he repays the loan. The upper caste man will make use of her for all purposes including sex.

(vi) *Cuddalore – Cidhambaram:* A dalit lady named Padmini was rapped at Annamalainagar police station where the famous Annamalai university is located while she went to take her husband on bail. Both of them were killed.

(vii) *Tiruchy – Thinniam:* There was an incident when a dalit lady got some loan from the money lender. Due to failure of monsoon she was unable to repay the amount within the stipulated time. For that the money lender's wife tied the dalit lady to a tree and made her to eat human faeces.

(viii) *Tuticorin – Kodiankulam:* There was an inhuman activity at Kodiankulam due to caste rivalry between dalits and mukkulathor. With a view to supporting the mukkulathor a private security force at Chennai was initiated along with police and attacked the dalits with the support of the political leaders and their friends who belonging to the mukkulator. During such regime the particular caste people were appointed particularly in police constable and sub-inspectors of police. They all acted against the dalits.

(ix) *Tirunelveli – Thamirabarani river:* The dalit people raised their voice against the wage discrimination of the Manjolai Tea Estate owner who belonged to Mumbai. Even after the court verdict they failed to follow the implementation of plantation act to provide minimum wage and other regulations. For that the workers, dalit leaders and dalit trade unions undertook a rally to focus such issue before the public and give a grievance petition to the District Collector. At that time there was a inhuman activity was practiced by the police personnel i.e when the rally was going on the bridge the police dumped the dalits and subjected to brutal beating. With a view to escape such beating the dalits jumped into the river which has the depth of 100 fts. Some of them died. Those who were still alive the police again subjected to brutal beating. Again pathetic incident women tried to escape through an attempt to cross the river to the other side with their children. They were beaten up finally a one year old girl child also killed by the police. It is also a female infanticide. Which police was arrested for such incidence and dismissed? none of them. It seemed to be heavy loss of human resources.

(x) *Jakkaian – A Dalit Panchayat Vice-President:* Jakkaian is a dalit man who is residing in a village nearby Sankaran Koil, elected as Vice-President. Due to the intolerance of Caste hindu Village President murdered Mr.Jakkaian.

(xi) *Kayathar – Panchayat Union : A dalit lady Chairamn:* A dalit lady was elected as Panchayat Union Chairman for the Kayathar Union (Where Veerapandia Kattapomman was hanged), Tuticorin District. Till date she is not permitted to sit in the chair which is allotted by practicing untouchability.

(xii) *Both Central State government employments:* Both at the central and States the reservation positions and specific courses have never been given to dalits. They are kept vacant or people are played all transferred according to their whims and fancies. Even in Gandhian institutions like Gandhigram Rural University the dalit reserved positions were given to non-dalits. Some victims made an attempt to rectify it instead of being given justice they were thrown out and subjected to torture through public rowdies, professors and police. In Delhi and Chennai IITs the dalits are only 2 per cent.

(xiii) *Penalisation attitude towards I.A.S & I.P.S officers:* Even while the dalit come up to I.A.S & I.P.S officers' grade tolerating all of social and mental pain they can not be in appropriate positions. If they come and try to attain such position the caste conspiracy will play a vital role and keep them back or suspend or at least to keep them waiting for responsibilities for a prolonged period.

(xiv) *Universities:* There are nearly 15 universities and deemed universities. Here, the administrative positions such as Vice-Chancellor, Registrar and Controller of Examinations under tenurial, appointed by His Excellency Vice-President of India and the Governor of the states. We can not find even a single dalit as in the above positions. If the dalits are in the next positions they were tortured and made them to resign by all threatening. It proves that at what extend the dalits are neglected and suppressed. If they feel the dalits are not qualified for such positions how come the former President of India His Excelleny K.R.Narayanan attains at the highest level and became Presidet of India. He also spoke in an independence speak India is like this it will face an internal war.'

In spite of 64 years of independence can one still believe that the SC/ST representation in teaching jobs at the level of higher education is a mere 2 per cent especially in Central Government institutions like IITs, universities and deemed universities even in Gandhian institutions. Then how can we expect such reservations in aided institutions.

(xv) *SC/ST Commission:* When the dalits go for reporting against such incidents there is no proper action but it boomerangs towards petitioner. Such authorities who misappropriate the dalit vacancies and dalit development funds. Behind it is the Commissions; (Central/State Government) meant for them is headed by the Dominant caste people. Even at the SC/ST commission the officials belong to higher caste man. Instead of taking action against the higher caste man who practice untouchability and caused injustice to dalits by dropping the files and writing false reports against dalits and doing all favour for the support of higher caste people. It is just like a 'Cats placed for watching dry fishes.' In general can we believe any police will take action against himself? No public can file FIR against such incidence. With these evidences how can we expect a genuine action from the higher ups?

(xvi) *Encroachment of dalit lands :* *The panchami lands (Dalit lands) were encroached by the upper caste people and politicians. For example the Sirudhavur dalit lands were encroached by an individual with the support of political leaders. Now, the dalits are forced to vacate the place. It is in the High Court of Madras for Prociquisition.

*With those experiences even among the literates how can we expect the ruling power to the dalits in appropriate positions especially in dalit panchayats.

(xvii) *Madurai – Pappapatty, Keeripaty and Nattamangalam :* *First, they prevented Dalits from filling nominations. Later, fearing the wrath of the administration, 'community leaders' fielded Dalits of their own choice as candidates, helped them win, and then made them resign soon after assuming charge. This has been the case in Pappapatti. The caste Hindu standpoint was that a Dalit cannot be accepted as panchayat president. If they become presidents, we may have to show respect to them in village festivals and public functions. This we cannot do is the common refrain.

*No nominations were received in Pappapatti, Keeripatti, Nattarmangalam and Kottakachiyendal panchayats for the president's posts in the 1996 elections. In the past, both districts have witnessed caste-related violence involving Dalits and Mukkulathors, the pre-dominant caste Hindu community. The caste Hindu majority of the villages was intolerant of a Dalit heading their panchayat and they warned Dalits of serious consequences if they dared enter the fray. Apart from this, the murder of the Dalit president of Melavalavu village panchayat in Madurai District within months of his election in 1996 also deterred Dalits in the four villages forced Dalits out of the fray. In the subsequent elections held along with 'casual elections', Pappapatti and Keeripatti opted to participate in the process, but only to make a mockery of it by forcing the winners not only to resign but also to plead with the state government to de-reserve their panchayats.

*Twelve years have passed since the 1994 Act came into force. The act was promulgated in the wake of the 73rd Amendment to the Constitution, which Parliament approval in 1993 with the objective of strengthening democracy at the grassroots level. The 73rd Amendment, together with the 74th, made it mandatory to establish strong, decentralized, democratically elected local bodies in rural and urban areas to achieve the twin objectives of 'economic development and social justice'. A three-tier panchayati raj structure-village panchayats, panchayat unions and district panchayats – and regular meetings of gram sabhas, in which all the electors are members, to involve people in the planning process are major features of the 1994 Act. While one-third of the total number of seats has been reserved for women, representation of Dalits will be in proportion to their share in the population. The Act also ensures regular elections to the local bodies. But these things unable to practice in the specified panchayats.

*There some chairs were created in different universities by the government like Rajiv Gandhi Chair on Panchayat Raj. Some crores of money was also allotted to give training for the Panchayat leaders. The Chairs are headed by the upper caste people particularly panchayat elections are not to be conducted. Some of them are the relatives of those panchayat upper caste. How come is money will be used for genuine reasons.

* Endogamy is another feature of both. Marriages are rare and few among different caste groups. There are stratifications, a hierarchical ordering of social categories, supported by social institutions. Inequality is intergenerational transmitted in caste. Prejudice and discrimination are both part of caste. They have to be abolished.

* There are mechanisms for reviewing, reporting and correcting distortions and monitoring the implementation of reservation for dalits to make them to aware of these rights; if not, such bodies should make them aware through education.

* There are economic and social disabilities which prevent them from getting education and there is a need to senitise the dalits on the need for educating the rising generation, among other things, to remain "socially fit" in the fast evolving competitive labour market.

* Other social groups, as for instance the upper castes of Usilampatty taluk have resented reservation for dalits in panchayat electios. So the State needs to create social awareness among all the concerned groups-officials, dalits, and the rest of the society about the need and justification for such reservation. This cannot be done by merely teaching the constitutional provisions in classrooms.

* The state should generate adequate employment every year to meet the dalit requirements. If the numbers are reduced to percentages and the quotas are filled only when vacancies arise and the dalits have to remain unemployed or wait for the state's mercy till doomsday that will be a deception on the Constitution.

* Globalization has been inviting high quality of effectiveness. Education to the dalits should enable them to equip to themselves for employment in the highly competitive labour market, so that their dependence on State employment will be much less.

* The election commission is able to conduct election at all levels in India with the government machineries why not in those dalit panchayats of Madurai and Virudhunagar districts. Is the election commission incapable of conducting elections in those areas?

No, because the vested interested political parties one not ready to lose the upper caste vote bank. So the political parties should take a stromg stand to conduct such elections.

* If the political parties/governments are not very serious in this regard the dalits should get ready to fight for their rights. The political decision will alone could provide a permanent solution to the stalling of the democratic process in the elections.

*The reserved panchayats like Pappapatty, Keeripatty, Nattanmangalam and Kottanchinenthal should not be dereserved by the election commission/govt. until the dalits hold the posts for a full term. Otherwise, democracy is meaningless to dalits as well as the oppressed communities. In this the government machineries should take a strong stand to withdraw the ration card and supplying of other public services to those areas.

Conclusion

The overview of the dalits till 60th independence is a comprehensive one; though there are some constitutional provisions in the form of reservation for at least 60 years since independence, contrary to expectations, while sections of the OBCs have made rapid progress the dalits haven't. The bureaucracy does not been address dalits but support the upper caste people in the form of non-implementing any constitutional provisions and a lot of formalities while availing their own rights in either getting loans or contracts or license for running any business like petrol bunk, schools, colleges or any other service institutions. There are so many educational, employments, political and economic institutions that violate the norms of reservation while admitting, appointing, allocating and offering such constitutional provisions. The politicians, bureaucrats and judicial machineries should be very genuine to protect and safeguard the rights of dalits in the constituent India. Otherwise the nation will face the internal war as spoken by the former President of India His Excellency K.R. Narayanan. So the law makers and the rulers should take necessary steps to keep India in peace.

8
CHAPTER

Social Exclusion of Tribal Community
A Study

Dr. A. Rethinapandy
Associate Professor, Deptt. of Economics, Sri S.R.N.M. College, Sattur-626 203

K. Vanitha
Project Fellow, Deptt. of Economics, Sri S.R.N.M. College, Sattur-626 203

Introduction

This chapter deals with exclusion of the tribals in general and factors for their exclusion in particular and suggestions for improving their conditions. A tribe is a group of people in a primitive or barbarious stage of development acknowledging the authority of a chief and they usually consider themselves as having a common ancestry. Tribe is a social group with territorial affiliation, endogamous with no specialization of functions, ruled by tribal officers hereditarily or otherwise, united in language or dialect recognizing social distance with other tribes or castes. A tribe is a group of bands occupying a contiguous territory or territories and it has a feeling of unity derived from numerous similarities in a culture and frequent contacts .India's population of over a billion includes 70 million tribal people (8.6%). They are scattered throughout India. Tribals are small in scale and restricted in the spatial and temporal range of their social, legal and political relations. They possess a morality, a religion and world view of corresponding dimensions. Characteristically too tribal languages have no written form.

Conditions of the Tribals

As the human society advanced, the accruing fruits of such advancement did not reach all sections of the society. Certain sections of humanity were deprived of them. In course of time, they were marginalized. Even in a developed country, this happens. The tribal is the very symbol of deprivation.

Even while mankind is stepping on into the twenty first century, this sect languishes in the 'Stone Age'. Governments come and governments go. Administrations change. But there is little improvement in their lot.

Due to the treachery of unscrupulous money-lenders, forest-contractors, police officials, officials of forest department, traders and middle-man, the tribals have been reduced to the level of sub-human beings. In their society, education is not adequate. So, superstition and religious bigotry are high. They are largely at the periphery of civilization and outside the main-stream of life. Governments now and then come up with welfare measures to alleviate their sufferings. But nothing substantial reaches them. Sri. Rajiv Gandhi, the late Prime Minister, once observed that for every hundred rupees spent by the government, only six rupees reach the real beneficiaries for whom the welfare measures are meant. But what the tribal society gets is even less.

The tribals are victims of ruthless exploitation and deceit and the women particularly, of lust. These people are pushed to an almost total dependence on nature for living. But even the natural wealth—the forests and lands are being taken away from them either by coercion or by deceit. Their social alienation is yet to be rectified in full.

Features of Tribes

Following are the features of tribes in Indian context:

- It should be economically backward (i.e. primitive means of exploiting natural resources, tribal economy should be at an underdeveloped stage and it should ave multifarious economic pursuits).
- Absence of strong, complex, formal organization. Tribes should be politically organized and community panchayat should be influential
- Communitarian basis of land holding.
- Segmentary character.
- There should be a comparative geographical isolation of its people.
- Kinship as an instrument of social bonds.
- A distinct psychological bent for enjoying life.

Geographical Location of Tribes

Tribals in India live in the following five territories:

1. ***The Himalayan belt:*** (Assam, Meghalaya, Arunachal Pradesh, Nagaland, Manipur, Mizoram, Tripura, hills of Uttar Pradesh and Himachal Pradesh).
2. ***Central India:*** Bihar, West Bengal, Orissa, and Madhya Pradesh. Fiftyfive per cent of the total tribal population of India lives in this belt.

3. ***Western India:*** Rajasthan, Maharashtra, Gujarat, Goa, Dadra and Nagar Haveli.
4. ***The Dravidian region:*** Karnataka, Andhra Pradesh, Kerala and Tamil Nadu.
5. Andaman, Nicobar and Lakshadweep islands.

It is also important to point out that those tribals who belong to different language families live in distinct geographical settings.

Concept of Exclusion

The term 'social exclusion' is ambiguous and contested. Definitions range from little more than a re-naming of poverty to more broad based concepts or inability to participate in society. Exclusions of tribal community which include, 'exclusion from goods and services', 'labour market exclusions', 'exclusions from land', exclusion from education and 'exclusion from security'. Discussion of social inclusion and exclusion also relates to citizenship debates, particularly in terms of the dichotomy between individualism and collectivism. "[Social exclusion is] the process through which individuals or groups are wholly or partially excluded from full participation in the society in which they live."

The exclusion of tribes, on the other hand, is based on a set of economic and cultural factors that have little to do with caste ideology. Scheduled Tribes have traditionally lived in more remote areas of the country and in closer proximity to forests and natural resources. The remote and difficult geographical terrain inhabited by the tribes has isolated them from mainstream Indian society. This has afforded them a measure of cultural autonomy and economic independence. Traditional Scheduled Tribe communities value their close relationship to nature and make optimal use of the natural resource-base for their daily sustenance. However, modernization and accumulative processes of production have resulted in massive encroachment into their natural habitats. This has in turn resulted in displacement, poverty and heightened levels of exploitation through a system of bonded labour. The term 'double disadvantage' has been used to characterise the socio-economic and spatial marginalisation of the tribes in India.

Social exclusion has to be seen as an institutionalized form of inequality, the failure of a society to extend to all sections of its population, the economic resources and social recognition which they need in order to participate fully in the collective life of the community.

Social exclusion denotes the following characteristics:

(*i*) Inability to participate effectively in economic, social, political educational and cultural life.

(*ii*) Distance and alienation from a so-called mainstream society.

(*iii*) Isolation from major societal mechanisms which produce or distribute social resources.

Social exclusion is a broader concept. It is a related concept with education, unemployment and poverty. It is said that exclusion and poverty are mostly interrelated. Tribal people are more likely to have lower income, poorer physical living conditions, less access to health care, lack of education, and a range of other services, worse access to labour, land and capital markets and worse returns to work as well as weaker political representation. The poverty and social exclusion experienced by the tribal people are largely due to discrimination at social and institutional level during colonial and post independent era.

Exclusion of Tribal Community

For ages, tribals are considered as primitive segment of Indian society. They lived in forests and hills without any contact with civilized society. During British rule they consolidated their position. The British introduced the system of landownership and revenue. Annual tax levied on them was beyond the paying capacity of the tribal cultivators. Many non-tribals began to settle in the tribal areas offering credit facilities. Initially it provided relief to tribals but gradually the system became exploitative. Over the years the tribal population faced all types of exploitation. This aroused the tribal leaders to mobilize the tribals and start agitations. The following are the factors for exclusion of tribal community:

- Indifference from administrators and bureaucracy in dealing with tribal grievances.
- Harsh and unfriendly forest laws and regulations.
- Lack of legislation to prevent the passing of tribal land into the hands of non-tribals.
- Lack of credit facilities.
- Ineffective government measures to rehabilitate the tribal population.
- Delay in the implementation of recommendations of different committee
- Discrimination in the implementation of reform measures.

Land Alienation

The history of land alienation among the tribes began during British colonialism in India, when the British interfered in the tribal region for the purpose of exploiting the tribal natural resources. Coupled with this, tribal lands were occupied by moneylenders, zamindars and traders by advancing them loans etc. Opening of mines in the heart of tribal habitat and even a few factories provided wage labour as well as opportunities for factory employment. After the British came to power, the Forest policy of the British Government was more inclined towards commercial considerations rather than human considerations. Some forests were declared as reserved ones where only authorized contractors were allowed to cut the timber and the forest -dwellers were kept isolated deliberately within their habitat without any effort to ameliorate their economic and educational standards. The expansion of railways in India heavily devastated the forest resources in India. The Government started reserving teak, Sal and deodar forests for the manufacture of railway sleepers. Forest land and its resources provided the best means of livelihood for the tribal people and many tribes including women engaged in agriculture, food gathering and hunting. They were heavily depended on the products of the forest. Therefore, when outsiders exploit the tribe's land and its resources the natural life cycle of tribal ecology and tribal life was greatly disturbed.

Poverty and Indebtedness

Majority tribes live below the poverty line. The tribes follow many simple occupations based on simple technology. Many of the occupations fall into the primary occupations such as hunting, gathering, and agriculture. The technology they use for these purposes belong to the most primitive kind. There is no profit and surplus in such economy. Hence, their per capita income is less than the Indian average. Most of them live under abject poverty and are in the hands of local moneylenders and zamindars. In order to repay the debt they often mortgage or sell their lands to the moneylenders. Indebtedness is almost inevitable since heavy interest is to be paid to these moneylenders.

Health and Nutrition

In many parts of India, tribal population suffers from chronic infections and diseases out of which water borne diseases are life threatening. They suffer from deficiency diseases and snake bite is also a permanent problem. The tribes suffer from goiter due to lack of iodine. Leprosy and tuberculosis are also common among them. Infant mortality was found to be very high among some of the tribes. Malnutrition is common and has affected the general health of the tribal children as it lowers the ability to resist infection and leads to chronic illness. There are no hand pumps and wells in many hamlets. Tribals depends only on ponds or streams for their drinking water which is usually contaminated. The ecological imbalance due to cutting of trees have increased the distance between villages and the forest areas thus forcing tribal women to walk longer distances in search of forest produce and firewood.

Education

The tribals were also educationally quite backward as compared to the non-tribals. Only 27.89 percent of them were recorded as literates as against 64.31 per cent in the general population. The literacy rate among tribal males was 35.25 per cent and among females 20.23 per cent. The gap between the tribals and the non-tribals goes on widening in respect of the higher educational attainments. The educational backwardness of the tribals is due to many reasons. All the tribal settlements are situated in hilly and jungle areas. Tribal villages are smaller as compared to non-tribal villages. Further, the tribal settlements are approximately villages (schools). So, it is extremely difficult for tribal children to attend the primary school situated in a particular non-tribal village.

The second reason for educational backwardness among the tribal children is the poverty of the tribal households. High influence of poverty compels the tribal children to help their parents in gainful employment even at the age of 10 and even children below 10. They have to take care of their younger brothers and sisters. They also take care of livestock like cows, sheep and goats etc., and do some household work. Therefore, the tribal children are not able to go to schools.

Thirdly, language is another important factor for the illiteracy of the tribal children. The Palliyan tribals in this study area uses their own dialect. They do not follow the standard Tamil that is used in written books. Further, the tribal children do not go to school, because of the fear of the non-tribals.

Fourthly, the cultural isolation of the Tribals is another factor for their illiteracy. The Tribals stand culturally separated from the non-tribals. Most of the tribal parents have inferiority complex about their economic backwardness, food and dress etc. The tribal children find it more difficult to study the prescribed text books, lessons and concepts.

Finally, the tribals have general fear over the non-tribal teachers. They are afraid of coming to towns because of the fear of crossing the roads. They think that they are exploitated by the non-tribals. They feel that they are harassed because of the ill -treatment of the non-tribals.

Educationally the tribal population is at different levels of development but in general the formal education has made very little impact on tribal groups. Earlier, Government had no direct programme for their education.

But in the subsequent years, the reservation policy has made some changes. There are many reasons for the low level of education among the tribal people. Formal education is not considered necessary to discharge their social obligations. Superstitions and myths play an important role in rejecting education. It is not easy for them to send their children to schools, as the children are considered extra helping hands. The formal schools do not have any special programmes for the tribal children. Most of the tribes are located at interior and remote areas where teachers would not like to go.

Cultural Exclusion

The tribals have thin framed body structure. This is mainly because of malnutrition. The Palliyan male is seminude in nature. i.e., he has a cloth only around his waist. The female wears normal dress with a saree and a blouse. Almost all the ladies wear the same dress daily until it becomes useless. They do not have additional saree or blouse. The children below the age group of seven years wear no dress. Most of the people have no proper house to reside. Also the younger people never care for the older ones. They sleep on the rocks and stream sands during night time, only with the cloth around their waist without minding the seasonal changes.

Regarding their marriages they do not adopt any fixed procedures like the non-tribals. Their marriages are usually non-customary. They do not care for 'auspicious' day, or time. If a male tribe likes to marry a female, then he 'marries' her simply in the presence of the tribal leader. Sometimes, if a male and a female like each other, they join together and go into the interior forest without informing their families for two to three months. If any problems arise between the married couple, they separate themselves and live with their parents. The process of divorce or any other formal way of separation is not found in this group. The separated male and female if they want to join again, they come together without any condition or process. The practice of polygamy (one man marrying two or more women) is also found in this group. The practice of dowry is not found in any form—cash or kind. Except their own brothers and sisters, they marry any one they like. *Thali* (Holy Thread), new cloths and garlands are not worn at the time of their marriage.

The Palliyan tribes living in Varusanadu Hills worship Lord Muruga, Palliyan, Pallichi and Karuppasamy. They do not take to fasting to please their deities. The purpose of worship is just to protect them from evils and wild animals. They start their work after worshipping their Gods and Goddesses. In the Andipatti region, a tribesman is the "pusari" for the "Mavuthu Vellappar Temple" in which Lord Muruga is the presiding deity.

Suggestions for Overcoming Exclusion of Tribal Community

- Giving protection to their distinctive way of life.
- Protecting them from social injustice and all forms of exploitation and discrimination and bringing them on par with the rest of the people so that they may be integrated with the national life.
- Improving educational facilities.
- Offering opportunity for employment.
- Offering subsidies to improve the economic conditions.
- Abolition of bonded labour.
- Protection from social injustice and all forms of exploitation.
- Reservation of seats for the tribes in Lok Sabha and Assembly, atleast in local bodies.
- Increased grants from central government to the states for the welfare of the Scheduled Tribes and raising the level of administration of Scheduled Areas.

Conclusion

The discouraging features the tribals of are abject poverty, low standard of living, illiteracy, and ignorance, small size of land holdings, low income, natural calamities, primitive farming practice, inadequate irrigation facilities and lack of housing. These factors have reduced the tribals to lead a life of 'hand to mouth existence'. And also, most of the tribals are living in thick jungles, hills and inaccessible forests. This isolated living in these hilly regions is the main reason for the social exclusion of the tribals.

REFERENCES

Baruah Sanjib, *Durable Disorder, Understanding the Politics of Northeast India*, (Oxford), 2005

Constituent Assembly of India, Volume no. IX, Monday, the 5th September, 1949.

Dena Lal, *'Hmar-Dimasa Ethnic Conflict: 1988-2004'*, Unpublished work.

Elwin Verrier, *A Philosophy for NEFA*, (Shillong: Published by Sachin Roy on behalf of NEFA), 1959, p. 54.

Guha Ramachandra, 'The Absent Liberal, An Essay on Politics and Intellectual Life', *Economic and Political Weekly*, December 15, 2001, pp. 4663-4670.

Ghurye,G.S, Conceptualized tribes as 'the backward Hindus'. In G.S. Ghurye, *The Schedule Tribes*, (Bombay: Popular Prakashan), 1963.

Rustomji Nari, *Imperiled Frontiers, India's North-Eastern Borderlands*, (Delhi: Oxford University Press), 1983, p. 47.

Sonntag Selma K., 'National Minority Rights in the Himalayas', *Heidelberg Papers in South Asian & Comparative Politics, Working paper*, No. 21, ISSN 1617-5069, www.hpsacp.uni-hd.de, June 2004.

Taylor Charles, 'Democratic Exclusion (and Its Remedies?)', in Rajeev Bhargava, Amiya Kumar Bagchi and R. Sudarshan (ed.), Multiculturalism, Liberalism and *Democracy*, (Oxford University Publication), 1999, pp. 139-141.

Thakur, Devendra and Thakur, D.N, Tribal Life in India – 1 and 8, Tribal Life and Froests. Deep & Deep Publications Pvt. Ltd, New Delhi, 2009.

Xaxa Virginius, 'Politics of language, Religion and Identity: Tribes in India', *Economic and Political Weekly*, March 26, 2005, pp. 1362-1370.

9

CHAPTER

Social Exclusion of Arunthathiyars in Tamil Nadu

S. Basil Xavier

Asstt. Professor, Arul Anandar (Autonomous) College, Karumathur-625 512 Madurai (Dt), Tamil Nadu

Arunthathiyars, the dalits of the dalits, are suppressed, deceived and thus socially excluded in education, employment, politics, literature, religion, language and media not only by the so called upper caste people but also by fellow dalits. By these complex processes, they are denied full participation in society. This paper elucidates how social exclusion is multi-dimensional and argues the excluded (dalits) becomes sometimes excluders!

Introduction of Arunthathiyars

Arunthathiyars (Chakkliars) are one of the sub-castes of the dalits in Tamil Nadu. Other names of Arunthathiyars are Sakkilliyars, Maadiga, Pagadai and Maadhaari. In the present socio-cultural situation, they have the status of being the dalits of the dalits. In a caste society they have traditionally been allotted the menial tasks of sweeping and scavenging the streets, cleaning the sewers, etc. They are also specialists in tanning animal hide and making shoes, etc.

Historical Backdrop of Arunthathiyar Movements in Tamil Nadu

A bird's eye view of recent history of Tamil Nadu shows that different socio-political movements emerged on behalf of different socially excluded groups. When non-Brahmins in Tamil Nadu felt that they were excluded in education, employment and in politics, the Dravidian Movements (formerly as Justice Party) came into existence.

Under the vociferous leadership of E.V.R. Periyar, they fought tooth and nail against Brahminism (A simple definition of Brahminism is to move away from others and to exclude others!) and got reservation for Non-Brahmins in education and employment.

But unfortunately as mostly backward caste communities (*œudra jãtis*) were benefitted by this Non-Brahmin movement, dalits felt that they were excluded. They started their own dalit movements and still they are fighting for their rights. But unfortunately Arunthathiyars, dalits of dalits, are excluded by their own fellow dalits namely Devendirars and Adi Dravidars in the dalit movements. That's why Arunthathiyars founded their own movements for their concerns. After a long struggle, with caste people and with their own fellow dalits, they have now got inner reservation in dalit quota. What are the concerns of Arunthathiyars, in other words, how they are socio-politically excluded is discussed below.

Social Exclusion of Arunthathiyars in Different Spheres

1. ***Education:*** Arunthathiyars are not fully benefitted by dalit reservation. The following sample statistics brings the truth. According to 2001 census, illiteracy rate among Adi Dravidars is 6.6 per cent only, Devendirars 10.7% only but among Arunthathiyars is 12.7 per cent. In the last eight years (2000--2008), total seats for dalits in medical colleges are 1796. But only 126 (7% only) seats are given to Arunthathiyars. Total engineering seats for dalits in Anna University for two years (2006–2008) are 582 but Arunthathiyars got only 37 (6.3%) seats. Similarly in law colleges, for the past seven years (2000–2007), among the total 2926 dalit seats, Arunthathiyar students got only 180 (6%).
2. ***Employment:*** Although there is 18 per cent reservation for dalits, there has been not even a single Arunthathiyar Supreme Court Judge. There has been a very few Arunthathiyar Vice Chancellors, I.A.S and I.P.S. officers. Here in India, there is 100% reservation only in Sanctum Sanatoriums (for Brahmins) and Sanitary works (Arunthathiyars)!
3. ***Politics:*** Arunthathiyars are not given proportionate representation in Tamil Nadu politics too. Updating the statistics already given by Ezhil. Ilangovan, R. Adiyaman claims, "572 Dalit M.L.A.s were elected from the reserved constituencies in the past 13 assembly elections held so far. As Arunthathiyars form one third of dalit population, 190 Arunthathiyar M.L.A.s should have been elected but only 25 were elected. Similarly, 91 dalit M.P.s won in the parliament elections held so far. Among them at least 30 should have been Arunthathiyar M.P.s but only 3 were elected so far."

4. ***Literature and Arts:*** When dalit literature appeared in Tamil literary scenario in the last decades of 20th century, it was argued philosophically and proved that only dalits can write dalit literature such as poems, short stories, novels, etc. But as only non-arunthathiyar dalits (few exceptions like M. Mathivannan) wrote these, life of Arunthathiyars is not well represented in dalit literature too. Still there is not even a single novel written by an Arunthathiyar. Even in "Dalit Cultural Nights" Arunthathiyars were sidelined. Therefore they are now conducting their own "Arunthathiyar Cultural Nights".

5. ***Religion:*** In Tamil Nadu, the Christian missionary contribution for the betterment of dalits is very significant. But unfortunately they too seem to have ignored arunthathiyars, although there interested in converting other dalits namely Adi Dravidars and Devendirars in large numbers. Only in 1930s they were trying to convert a few arunthathiyars in north western parts of Tamil Nadu. But it was vehemently opposed my caste Hindus. There were even violent agitations by high (?) caste people. That's why, although Tamil Nadu Churches are dominated by dalits (more than 50%), there are only a handful of arunthathiyar Christians. They form only about 1 or 2 per cent. There is not even a single Catholic Christian Arunthathiyar priest and not even a single Arunthathiyar Bishop in all Tamil Nadu Churches. Consequently it is evident that arunthathiyars could not even benefit from Christian institutions such as schools, colleges, hospitals, etc.

6. ***Language:*** Arunthathiyars are socially excluded in the name of language also. Apart from Tamil, arunthathiyars also speak Telugu or Kannada. This does not mean that they are either Telugus or Kannadigas because in Tamil Nadu what arunthathiyars speak is entirely different from what is spoken either in Andhra or Karnataka. Arunthathiyars use these languages only as spoken and they do not know how to read and write Telugu or Kannada. Ezhil. Ilangovan, R. Adiyaman have proved that arunthathiyars are ancient Tamils. Very well knowing this scenario, with vested interests, even dalit movements reject arunthathiyars in the name of ideologies such as Tamil Nationalism or Tamil Buddhism.

7. ***Media:*** Arunthathiyars are also rejected by media too. Newspapers, Magazines and Television do not give importance to Arunthathiyar Movements and their leaders which they do it for other dalit movements and leaders such as Thiruma and Krishnasamy. For

example, recently Arunthathiyar movements staged demonstrations, rail rako, etc. demanding the abolition of human scavenging. It was completely ignored and rejected by popular media. No newspapers or TV channels gave this news item.

To Conclude

The complex process of social exclusion is studied with a special reference to arunthathiyars. They are being put at a disadvantage and their rights are denied to participate on equal terms in social relationships in economic, social, cultural and political arenas. As Alan Touraine puts it, exclusion is an issue of being in/out or of the excluders/the excluded. Dalits, who are the excluded by the large caste society as untouchables, in turn exclude arunthathiyars, their fellow dalits. Thus arunthathiyars are *doubly excluded.*

REFERENCES

As dalits arts were ignored and rejected by media, etc., dalits themselves organize whole night cultural shows in order to bring out the treasure of dalit arts and to assert their identity (for example, by beating simultaneously 100, 200 drums, *parai,* on stage).

Devendirars also claim that their concerns are not well depicted in dalit literature.

Ezhil. Ilangovan, *History and Culture of Arunthathiyars* (in Tamil) (Coimbatore: Adi Tamizhar Peravai, 2002) and R. Adiyaman, *Call of Adiyaman* (in Tamil) (Coimbatore: Adi Tamizhar Peravai, 2007.

For a detailed statistics refer M. Mathivannan, *We, the Arunthathiyars ...* (in Tamil) (Coimbatore: Adi Tamilar Peravai, 2008).

P. Muthaiah, "Dandora: The Madiga Movement for Equal Identity and Social Justice in A.P." in *Social Action*, Vol. 54, April-June 2004. How madigas, a sub-caste of dalits in A.P. fought for categorization in reservation is discussed elaborately in this insightful article.

Philosophical tools such as Phenomenology, Existentialism, Hermeneutics, Postmodernism and Poststructuralism were employed.

R. Athigamaan, *War Voices of Ancient Tamils* (in Tamil) (Thoothukudi: Maadiyar Publications, 2007).

Same is the case with Ph.D. researches in the universities. For example, in Madurai Kamaraj University, among the 80 dalits who get Rajiv Gandhi Fellowship just one scholar is Arunthathiyar.

10
CHAPTER

Social Exclusion
A Study with References to Dalit Community in Tamil Nadu

Dr. R. Subburaman
Associate Professor, Deptt. of ACE&E, GRI

M. Suresh
Research Scholar, Deptt. of ACE&E, GRI

Introduction

There is, however, one category of exclusion, vital in the Indian context among the Hindus, that is fixed at birth and that is caste. This is a category that sociologists typically study, and economists tend to ignore, but the importance of this category can hardly be overemphasized. There are several aspects of exclusion which cannot be characterized by a person when he is described as being simply poor or unemployed. For example, untouchables in many parts of India are prevented entry into certain temples; there are certain villages where members of the Scheduled Caste (SC) are forbidden use of certain village wells that are the exclusive preserve of the upper caste members. This is because to be in contact with a schedule caste person is polluting.

The notion of exclusion may also be widened to incorporate the notion of rights. Eradication of caste-based exclusion is, however, a much slower and yet more daunting task. We look at a dimension of social exclusion that is of central importance in India. This has to do with exclusion of the basis of caste. This is in some sense the most potent form of exclusion because this sociological characteristic is fixed at birth and is hence completely inflexible. A number of other forms of exclusion from certain basic rights deserve careful consideration.

One may identify several other important dimensions of exclusion like exclusion from education, exclusion from housing, exclusion from property ownership, exclusion from democratic participation, exclusion from access to health services, exclusion from public goods, to name but a few.

In addition to these one may think in terms of gender-based exclusion, exclusion of the old age and infirm, exclusion of widows, and exclusion of the physically handicapped.

Defining Dalit

If Dalit is to be seen in a maxi a sense, it has to be a class emerging from the dissolution off all classes, a class in civil society and not as class of civil society. Such a class has a universal character because its sufferings are universal; the wrong done to it is general and not a particular wrong. Such a class has no traditional status but only human status. It is a class which seeks to total emancipation from the chains of dominations and control. This particular class is the class of proletariat. Although consciousness is determined by existence and not *vice versa* consciousness becomes a means of uniting and mobilizing the proletariat. In such collective consciousness commensurate with the existing conditions of the proletariat, lukas puts this point as follows.

Untouchables

The degrading term "untouchables" was changed by the British administration in to depressed classes". Gandhiji called them Harijans. The British government defined them as the scheduled castes; finally it was left for the untouchables" themselves to coin new name for themselves Dalits. They think of themselves as Dalit panthers (wounded) Tigers that remind them of the Black panthers of the United States. The term 'Dalit' is no more another name for "untouchables".

The Concept of Untouchability

The Hindu society insists on the segregation of untouchables and does not allow them live inside their own residential areas. They were generally required to live at a distance from the main village. Residential segregation was somewhat strictly enforced; Prabhu mentions that untouchatbility refers to dyeing even human status to a group of human beings this group is not even allowed the consideration, which may be shown to creatures like animals. Hanumantha Rao says that untouchables is a feeling of pollution defilement of contamination entertained by non-scheduled castes towards scheduled castes and is caused by: (*a*) touch; (*b*) sight; and (c) or bymena physical proximity of the scheduled caste persons.

The pollution concept is institutionalized in the Hindu society through caste system. Manusmriti mentions. Wine, urine, spittle, pus or blood, etc, as objects causing pollution. In the same category maitri Upanishad places bones, skin, sinews, marrow, flesh, seed, eyegum, dung, gall, phelgom, etc. Fears of pollution are extended by many Hindu to even be owns saliva. G.Hanumantha Rao feels that low social-status attached to certain occupations, is the cause of untouchability. It relates to impure occupations, such as removal of carcass, shimmering, tanning, scavenging, etc. Max Weber, while describing the rituality impure occupation states, "the lower caste stratum was considered to be absolutely defiling and contaminating".

First the stratum comprised a number of trades, which are almost always despised because they involve; physically dirty work, street cleaning and others. Furthermore the stratum comprises services with Hinduism considered rituality impure, which is tanning, leatherwork etc. Lower castes, because they are segregated together on the basis of untouchability, they are often pushed to live in a distant part of a village or ghettos of a city, it is an accepted phenomenon that the scheduled castes are still lagging behind in almost all fields and undergoing hard ships, suffering and oppressions.

Statement of the Problem

Socio-economic status and problem of dalit is an important problem for socio economic development of our country. Attempts have been made by government through all of laws to fulfill the constitutional obligation of providing protection to dalit and to abolish untouchables. Though amply the government of India to uplift the status of dalit people formulates number of welfare programmes and schemes, they are still living under poverty and occupy the very low status in the society.

There are several studies that highlighted the kind of caste problem such as land holding, land distribution economic development programme for schedule caste, indebtness, dalit movement that prevail in India. It appears that there are only few attempts have been made to test their problems; the present study is a modest attempt to fill the gap, though we realize some of the weakness of it.

Pilot Study

Pilot study is preliminary study conducted before the original studies are carried out. In order to gain some primary information on the basis of which the main project would be planned and formulated. The primary survey or study of the universe in question helps to acquire a general knowledge about the problem, which ultimately helps to know the nature and different aspects of the problems. In the pilot study, the few respondents of specified situation are approached with free mind and collected information about their background, reasons of admission and their problems.

Objectives

1. To study the socio-Economic status of dalit people.
2. To identify the social problem of dalit.
3. To find out the economic problems of dalit.
4. To understand the political problems of dalit.
5. To investigate the health status of dalit people.
6. To analyze the nature of relationship between sub caste people among dalit.

Research Design

To interpret the primary data collected from the study centers; the descriptive research design was opted.

Major Findings Suggestion

Major findings suggestions and the final conclusion draw out from this study are given in this chapter. The major findings are as follows:

- The majority 98 per cent of the respondents are married.
- The majority 82 per cent of the respondents follows nuclear Family system.
- The majority 90 per cent of the respondents has electric facilities and has not electric facilities.
- The majority 74 per cent of the respondents still now also follow the practice of untouchability.
- The majority 68 per cent of the respondents are not allowed the higher community house.
- The majority 76 per cent of the respondents or accepted in common temple for the worshiping.
- The majority 90 per cent of the people have accepted and rejected the identification of dowry problem.
- The majority 100 per cent of the respondents says that there is not malnutrition problem.

Suggestions

- Skill training programmes should be given to the self-helps groups and prepares them to start their own business or trade.

- Animal husbandry also offers promoting opportunities for increasing rural employment. There are no reliable estimates of total employment in animal husbandry since many cultivating household under take it as an allied activity.
- Promote diversification of agricultural into high-value crops and agro processing.
- The quantity of the public distribution system items should be increased. Because majority of the people are suffering through getting grocery from the private shops.
- Various steps must be taken to provide awareness about the government welfare measures allocated especially for the scheduled caste people.
- Providing employment opportunity to the Dalit people for improving their standard of life for that they must be organized and trained in economic generating activities.

Conclusion

The present study has attempted to evaluate "Social Exclusions A study with some references to Dalit community in Mullipadi Panchayat". Dalit are the descendants of the Dravidians, the original inhabitations of the Tamil Nadu. Nevertheless, they are living under poverty and low Socio-economic status they face lot of problems in society. The Government of India creates various commissions for the welfare and upliftment of the Dalit people. However, it deviated from its goals and objectives.

The problem of unemployment, illiteracy, and caste discrimination are the main reasons for the low socio-economic status of Dalit and problem of Dalit. Through bringing attitudinal changes among Dalit, the self respect, self esteem of them could be achieved and that may reduce the prevalence of low socio economic status and discrimination against dalits in India in general and Mullipadi Panchayat in particular.

REFERENCES

Ambedkar : *Communal Dead lock and a way to solve it in his writing and Speeches*, Vol. 1, Bombay, Government of India, 1981, pp. 15-30.

Ambrose, "Dalit in Gulbarsa upper caste hold in Police", *Economic and Political Weekly*, Vol. XXXVI, No. 3, March 2000, pp. 10-23.

Mishra P.K., *Harijans in Hindu and Tribal Social Structures*, Discovery publishing House, New Delhi, 1992, pp. 15-32.

Sing, R.B. *Scheduled Caste welfare myth or Reality* A.P.H. Publishing Corporation, New Delhi 2003, pp. 16-39.

Sharma Mangal, G.C., *Caste class and Social in equality in India* Vol. II, Deep Publications, Jaipur (India), 2003, pp. 123-132.

Journals

Ambruse, "Dalit in Gulbarga upper caste hold in Police", *Economic and Political Weekly*, Vol. XXXVI, No. 3, March 2000, pp. 10-23.

Das, B., *Untouchability, Scheduled castes and Nation building, Social Action*, 1982, pp. 15-20.

Harsh Mader, "Dalit Status Agenda for State Intervention." *The Administrator*, Vol. XII, January-March, 1997, pp. 101-121.

Satyanarayana, "Dalit protest Literature in Telugu", *Economic and Political Weekly*, Vol. XXX No. 3, December 1995, pp. 171-173.

11
Chapter

Land Issues and Agitations of Dalits and Tribes in Kerala
A Review

Praveen, C.S.
Research Scholar, Pondicherry University, Puducherry

The tribal people were once in possession of large tracts of forests in the State, especially in areas that are now in Palakkad, Wayanad, Idukki, Pathanamthitta, Kollam and Thiruvananthapuram districts. To a large extent, post-Independence governments were responsible for the Adivasis losing their lands. Non-tribal settlers made their plight worse as the pressure on land increased in the plains. The land-people ratio is very high in the State. In the majority of cases, the ignorance and innocence of the Adivasis were used to the hilt by the non-tribal settler "farmers". Either by using force or inducements such as a bundle of tobacco, or by offering a low price, they made the Adivasis part with their "ancestral land". In most cases there was no document validating such transfers and some tribal persons were even forced to sign on blank sheets of paper. The non-tribal people who got possession of the lands gradually became the virtual owners.

Over the years, alienation from their land of birth pushed the Adivasis into poverty and dependence and forced them to search for other forest land for food and shelter. However, the same process was repeated in the new stretches of forest land, and these too became the farmlands of non-tribal settlers. Political parties and successive governments turned a blind eye to the process, as more settlers meant more votes. (The Adivasis, who number 3.21 lakhs, account for only 1.1 per cent of the population of the State.) The social and ecological implications of this were serious.

Wayanad was once a tribal majority area. In 1942 the tribal population here was around 61,000 out of a total of about 74,000. But the large scale migration of farmers, especially from the southern districts, changed the demography of Wayanad. Now the population is 7,80,619, out of which the tribals are around 1,37,000, i.e. a mere 17 per cent (source: Census 2001). Prior to the colonial period, there was no private land ownership among the tribal people. The land was a community asset. During the British period, tribes were forcibly displaced for building large scale tea and coffee plantations. Widespread alienation of tribal lands to settler farmers resulted in the high level of landlessness among tribes.

According to government data, at present, 7,893 tribal families are landless in Wayanad; another 14,000 families have inadequate land. Both are entitled to get land up to one acre since the LDF government declared to provide minimum one acre land to all landless tribal families.

The socio-economic condition of tribal people in Wayanad is pathetic. They are mainly poor, landless and unskilled workers. Alarmingly, life expectancy among the largest tribal group, called Paniyas, is only 40 years. Alcoholism is widespread among them, along with poverty and unemployment. Genetic disorders like sickle cell anaemia are widespread among certain tribes. It is painful to note that some of the primitive tribal groups are facing extinction.

P.R.G. Mathur, tribal expert and former Director of the Kerala Institute for Research Training and Development Studies of Scheduled Castes and Scheduled Tribes (Kirtads), says that money-lending is the major factor for alienation of tribal land in Attappady. In the absence of any savings, the tribal people have no option but to borrow to meet expenses in connection with social obligations. Indebtedness is widespread among them, many taking loans from their own patrons, besides moneylenders, petty traders and other unscrupulous exploiters. They are unable to repay within the stipulated time. Consequently, they have to transfer the land by oral lease mortgages or oral usufruct agreements. (Prabhakaran 2001)

There are three types of credit system among the tribes of Attappady — "Kuthakapattam," "Bogikaraya" and "Chalaku." Under "Kuthakapattam," people of the Irula tribes lease out land to the settlers for three to five years on a nominal rent. The debtor receives the rent in advance for one year or the entire period. At the end of the term, the land is to be restored to him. Thus, under this system, usufruct of the land gets adjusted against the contract rent advanced to the debtor. Under the "Bogikaraya" system, widely prevalent in Attappady, the land is mortgaged for securing loan. In this mortgage too, the usufruct of the land gets adjusted against the interest on the loan. "Chalaku" refers to a local unit of eight "paras" of grain to be measured by the debtor at the creditor's house for the loan. The rates of interest are 400 per cent, 650 per cent or even 900 per cent.

Unless the tribal people get rid of indebtedness and the accompanying evil of land alienation, it is unlikely that any legislation will prevent them from transferring their land whether by sale mortgage, gift or lease. Under the existing system, there can be hardly any opportunity for effective control of money-lending in tribal areas.

The Kerala Land Reforms Act, initiated by the communist government in 1957, in spite of the amendments and dilutions made in it by the subsequent right wing governments, helped to end landlordism in Kerala and the *jenmam* (ownership) rights of *jenmis* (landlords) on land were legally vested with the state government as on April 1, 1964. Ceiling limits on the land to be owned by individuals and families were stipulated. The Act conferred ownership rights upon more than 26 lakh peasant families in the state on the land they had leased. In 1967, the Left led EMS government again enacted a law to provide ownership right on 10 cents of land and homestead lands occupied by poor and landless agricultural workers and peasants. Nearly 5.5 lakh families benefited from it.

Problems Faced by Aboriginal Tribes of Kerala

(a) *Extinction:* Aboriginal tribes of Attappady who have been here since the Vedic time, seem doomed to extinction due to major health problems like infertility, sickle cell anaemia, tuberculosis and thrombo angiitis obliterans (TAO). A recent survey conducted by the Health Department found that among 3,600 young married tribal couples 30 to 40 per cent are facing infertility problems.

b) *Land issues:* In the last 100 years, over one million acres of land are believed to have been grabbed from Kerala's tribal population. Their long agitation to regain the forests and lands where their ancestors have lived for generations was intensified after the starvation deaths of 32 tribal last year. Tribal people are also facing many socio-cultural, economic and health problems.

Land Issues and Agitations

After independence, though many laws were enacted especially to address the landlessness among tribes, not much progress was made in solving the problem. The Kerala Land Reforms Act, too, did not specifically address the landlessness among the tribes. The central Tribal Land Act of 1975 purported to retrieve the alienated tribal lands and redistribute the same among the tribals, but it was not implemented due to sharp resistance from the settler farmers who were occupying tribal lands. When the 1975 Act got the presidential assent in November that year and was subsequently included in the Ninth Schedule of the Constitution (which ensured that the Act would not be challenged in any court of law), it seemed a dream come true for the Adivasis. But it was not to be. Successive governments allowed more than a decade to pass (during which the encroachments continued, especially in the tribal areas of Palakkad and Wayanad districts) before framing the rules to implement the Act. When the State government finally formulated the rules in 1986, it specified that the Act would come into effect retrospectively from January 1, 1982.

The rules made all transfer of property "possessed, enjoyed or owned" by Adivasis to non-tribal people between January 1, 1960 and January 1, 1982 "invalid" and directed that the "possession or enjoyment" of property so transferred be restored to the Adivasis concerned. However, the Act required that the Adivasi return the amount, if any, they had received during the original transaction and pay compensation for any improvements made on the land by the non-tribal occupants. The government was to advance this amount to the tribal people as loans and recover it from them in 20 years. Only about 8,500 applications seeking restoration were received from the tribal people, because most of them were either unaware of the new law or afraid to accept the offer of loans or were cheated by the corrupt encroacher-official nexus. Hence, even after the framing of the rules, the general atmosphere helped only to encourage the encroachers to continue to occupy tribal land and successive governments took no action to implement fully the 1975 Act.

This triggered the second important phase of the Adivasi struggle. In 1986, Dr. Nalla Thampi Thera, a non-tribal person from Wayanad district, approached the Kerala High Court seeking a direction to the State government to implement the 1975 Act. It took five years for the court to give a verdict - a favourable one - on the public interest petition. In October 1993, the court ordered the government to implement the Act within six months. Yet the case dragged on for two and a half years with the government continuing to seek extensions of deadline to implement the Act. Finally, in 1996 the court fixed a final deadline of September 30, 1996 to evict the non-tribal occupants, if necessary with the help of the police, and threatened the officials concerned with contempt of court proceedings if they failed to implement the court directive. However, the government responded with yet another controversial act of amending the 1975 Act.

Meanwhile as the non-tribal settlers where getting entrenched in the alienated land of the tribal people, the tribal people themselves were getting increasingly disillusioned with the ability of the government and the courts to find a remedy for their plight. Hence, although government programmes had helped improve the lot of many tribal people, the majority of them continued to be landless, had no means of livelihood, and became more dependent on the non-tribal settlers for work and wages. As a large section of the landless tribal people had not filed applications and were hence outside the purview of the 1975 Act, they were ineligible for a piece of land even if the Act was implemented in toto. By the early 1990s, the first signs of discontent were already becoming evident in the Adivasi-inhabited areas, especially in Wayanad district, where some extremist groups had been active for a long time.

On the other hand, most of the land from which the settlers were to be evicted under the 1975 Act had by the 1990s been in their possession for 15 to 30 years. They were cultivating the land and had constructed buildings and other structures on them. In several cases, the next generation of the original encroachers were in possession of the lands. When the State government could get no more extensions of the deadline from the High Court, the politically and economically powerful settler-farmers activated their organisations and raised the demand to amend the "impractical provisions" of the 1975 Act.

To the consternation of the tribal people, successive governments started to give in to the demands of the settlers. Two ordinances seeking to amend the 1975 Act, introduced by the United Democratic Front government during early 1996 and later by the Left Democratic Front government, which came to power in May 1996, did not get the Governor's approval. As pressure from the court mounted on the government to evict encroachers by September 30, 1996, the government hastily introduced an amendment Bill in the State Assembly. Whatever may have been the justification for it - the impracticality of the provisions of the 1975 Act perhaps being the most important one - it must have been an eye-opener for the mushrooming tribal organisations in Kerala to see the 140-member State Assembly pass the Kerala Scheduled Tribes (Restriction on Transfer of Land and Restoration of Alienated Lands) Amendment Bill, 1996 almost unanimously (there was only one dissenting vote).

The 1996 Amendment Bill dashed all hopes of the Adivasis. Most important, it made legal all transactions of tribal land up to January 24, 1986. In other words, the government made the need for the restoration of alienated land (as per the 1975 Act) unnecessary. According to the government, it was the only practical alternative, given the turmoil and the political repercussions that would have been created had it tried to evict the non-tribal settlers. However, the tribal people felt that the government was trying to give legal sanctity to the alienation of their land. The agitation in front of the State Assembly, with the Adivasis, led by their leader from Wayanad C.K. Janu, trying to enter the State legislature, supported by a group of

Communist Party of India (Marxist-Leninist) volunteers, was perhaps an early indication of the gradual transformation of the agitation.

This was soon followed by one of the best known incidents in the struggle. On October 4, 1996, a so-far unknown extremist group named "Ayyankali Pada" (named after a Dalit leader from Kerala), stormed the Palakkad Collectorate and held Collector W.R. Reddy hostage for over nine hours. The incident invited a strong response from the government against growing signs of radicalism among Adivasis and also in a way prevented the agitation from taking a turn for the worse. Later, the President refused to give assent to the 1996 Amendment Bill passed by the State Assembly on the grounds that the 1975 Act had been included in the Ninth Schedule of the Constitution. However, to bypass this difficulty, yet another Bill was passed unanimously by the State Assembly in 1999. The Kerala Restriction on Transfer by and Restoration of Lands to Scheduled Tribes Bill, 1999, defined "land" as "agricultural land" (a State subject) in order to try and get over the need to send it for presidential assent. The new Bill also had a controversial provision to repeal the 1975 Act.

As per the 1999 Act, only alienated land in excess of two hectares possessed by encroachers would be restored, while alternative land, in lieu of the alienated land not exceeding two hectares, would be given elsewhere. The thinking was that the number of applicants claiming land in excess of two hectares would be negligible, making restoration unnecessary. The new Bill also had a provision to provide up to 40 acres (16 hectares) to other landless tribal people - a new set of beneficiaries - within two years. The government said that it estimated that there were about 11,000 such families in the State. However, the High Court rejected both the 1996 and 1999 Amendment Bills and declared the provisions under them illegal. The State government, in turn, went on appeal to the Supreme Court and obtained stay orders. Several appeals against the stay orders are pending before the Supreme Court.

It was in this context that starvation deaths were reported from the Adivasi-inhabited areas in the State from July 2001. The outside world came to know about it only after a group of tribal people, supported by some naxalite groups, waylaid a mobile store run by the State Department of Civil Supplies and took away its contents. They distributed the foodstuffs and encouraged the tribal people who gathered there to take home the rest of it.

In 2001, Adivasi agitators led by Janu pitched their tents outside the Chief Minister's official residence in Thiruvananthapuram. They were organised under the banner of the "Adivasi Dalit Action Council", which claimed to have the support of all Adivasis in the State. Despite two rounds of discussions with the government, the tribal people refused to withdraw their agitation. The main demand of the Adivasis was five acres (2 ha) each to all landless tribal families in the State. Although the government's offer to prepare a master plan for the tribal people was welcomed by the agitating Adivasis, they refused to withdraw the agitation until their demand for land was met. The tribal people have lost their faith in promises and court cases. They were sure that running after alienated land was a futile exercise which, even if it succeeded in the long run, would benefit only a few among them. The protestors demanded restoration of at least 5 acres of land to each tribal family in order to sustain themselves, allotment of 2.25 lakh acres of land to 45,000 tribal families in the state and inclusion of tribal areas under Schedule V of the Constitution so as to make them autonomous regions. They also demanded enforcement of the provisions of the Panchayats (Extension to Scheduled Areas) Act of 1996.

Finally, an agreement containing following points was reached between the government and the agitators:

(*i*) Allotment of 5 acres to each landless Adivasi family wherever possible and to guarantee a minimum of one acre each;

(*ii*) Five-year livelihood programme to be implemented till the land becomes fully productive for the families to sustain themselves;

(*iii*) Enactment of a law to prevent any further alienation of land;

(*iv*) State cabinet resolution to declare Adivasi areas as scheduled areas under Schedule V;

(*v*) Implementation of a master plan for the development of adivasis and to prepare it with the involvement of Adivasis;

(*vi*) Maximum possible land will be found in Wayanad district, at least 10,000 acres, where Adivasis are concentrated;

(*vii*) Promise to abide by the decision of the Supreme Court regarding the appeal.

Yet, for the present, the most significant factor is the shifting focus of the demands raised by the Adivasi leaders who are in the limelight. They are no longer asking for alienated land, at least not as emphatically as they used to in the past. Instead they demand mainly five acres of other land each for all landless tribal families. Another demand is the inclusion of tribal areas in the Sixth Schedule of the Constitution in order to make them autonomous regions.

The AKS and KSKTU have provided leadership in the struggle to establish the tribal people's right on the wasteland and surplus land under HML in Wayanad. Around 800 landless tribal and agricultural worker families have erected huts on these lands as a part of the agitation.

On February 15, 2008, the High Court ordered reclamation of the land from illegal occupation and its distribution among the landless tribals. Even after two years, however, the district administration has not initiated action to get the stay in a lower court vacated and repossess the land. This is the background in which the AKS initiated a land struggle in Krishnagiri village. The centre of another land agitation is the 67 acres of land at Vellaramkunnu near Kalpetta, the headquarters town of Wayanad. Around 340 landless tribal families entered the land on February 8, erected huts and have been living there since then. In November 2007, District administration, submitted a report on this land while the present sub-collector of Wayanad, Prasanth, IAS, submitted another on February 8, 2010. Both reports clearly pointed out that 179.81 acres of land at Vellaramkunnu belong to the state government and legal proceedings under the IPC need to be initiated against the scam perpetrators who forged fake records for the said land and even sold 50 acres out of it to the state government for establishing an industrial park.

Background in a Nutshell

1. The Debar Commission instituted by Central Government in 1950s suggest restoration of alienated Tribal lands back to Tribals with effect from January 26, 1950.
2. Two-and-half decades later, following outbreak of unprecedented starvation deaths in early 1970s, a meeting of State Revenue Ministers called by then Prime Minister Indira Gandhi at New Delhi on April 1, 1975, recommends passing of legislation in tune with Debar Commission Report.
3. April 1975 : The Kerala Assembly, with C. Achutha Menon as Chief Minister and EMS Namboodiripad as Opposition leader, unanimously passed the Tribal Land Act which assures restoration of all the lands lost by Kerala tribals from January 26, 1960, instead of 1950 as suggested by Debar Commission. Moving the bill, the then Revenue Minister, Baby John, proclaimed on the floor of the Assembly that "the Government treats all the alienated tribal lands as 'stolen property'" and assured that the Government is fully committed to restore it to its traditionally rightful owners the Tribals.
4. July 1975 : As part of the then Emergency measures, Prime Minister Indira Gandhi proclaims 20-Point Programme, including restoration of alienated tribal lands back to the tribals, after banning a total of 14 CPI-ML (Naxalite) groups who were actively waging armed struggle in tribal belts throughout India.
5. November 11, 1975 : The Kerala Tribal Land Act gets the mandatory assent of Indian Presient and was also included in the 9th Schedule of Indian Constitution.

6. 1975-1986 : Absolutely nothing was done by all the successive UDF-LDF Governments of Kerala to implement the Act.
7. 1986 : Rules were formulated to implement the Act with retrospective effect from January 1, 1982 (bypassing 1950 fixed by Debar Commission and 1960 by the parent Act).
8. 1988 : Dr. Nalla Thampi Thera of Mananthavadi, Wayanad, moved the first writ petition before Kerala High Court pleading to instruct Kerala Government to implement the Tribal Land Act of 1975.
9. October 15, 1993 : Kerala High Court directs Kerala Government to implement the the Act within 6 months.
10. April 1996 : An attempt by the UDF Government led to bring an Ordinance amending the 1975 Act was rejected by the Governor on the ground that it was violative of the election code.
11. May 1996 : LDF Government led by E. K. Nayanar occupies power.
12. August 9, 1996 : Principle Secretary for SC-ST Development inform the High Court through an affidavit about the Government's inability to implement the 1975 Act due to organised resistance from the powerful encroacher-settlers in tribal belt.
13. August 14, 1996 : Rejecting the above claim of the Government, the High Court firmly gave final direction to implement the Act within six weeks ending 30 September 1996. The High Court also directed that the "RDOs should effect delivery of possession of alienated tribal lands to its original owners in cases where no appeals are pending against orders for restoration of land and where no compensation is payable", and that adequate law and order machinery could be used to carry this out, and that the RDOs have to file affidavits by September 30, 1996.
14. September 1996 : Like its predecessor UDF Government, the LDF Government also tries to bring an Ordinance seeking to amend the 1975 Act which, too, was rejected by the Governor.
15. September 23, 1996 : With the support of all LDF-UDF MLAs, barring Ms. K. R. Gouriamma, the Kerala Assembly passes the Kerala Scheduled Tribes (Restriction on Transfer of Land and Restoration of Alienated Lands) Amendment Bill, 1996 in a hurried attempt to avoid contempt of Court proceedings on RDOs. This amendment bill scuttled the whole spirit of the 1975 parent Act. For example, it held legal and valid all transactions of tribal land between 1960 to January 24, 1986. In other words, the same Kerala Assembly, which proclaimed in April 1975 that all the alienated tribal lands since 1960 were stolen property tried to give legal sanctity for the illegal possessors to enjoy

this very stolen property through the September 23, 1996, amendment bill.

16. October 4, 1996 : The incident of Ayyankali Pada group of Naxlites holding Palakkad District Collector, Dr. W. R. Reddy, as hostage demanding withdrawal of the amendment bill and total implementation of the 1975 parent Act, drew national and international attention to Kerala's tribal land issue, and on the negative attitude of the successive State Governments towards it.

17. March 1998 : Despite a joint LDF-UDF delegation led by then Chief Minister Nayanar and Opposition leader going to Delhi seeking Presidential assent to the widely condemned anti-tribal amendment bill of September 1996, the same was rejected by President K. R. Narayanan, and notably three days before A. B. Vajpayee's NDA Government at the Centre was sworn-in. One of the known reasons for the Presidential rejection was the inclusion of 1975 parent Act in the 9th Schedule of the Constitution and, therefore, it cannot be amended by the State Assembly.

18. 1999 : The LDF Government, with due support of UDF opposition, pass the second amendment bill in the State Assembly. In order to bypass Presidential assent, the words tribal land was replaced in it with agricultural land and it secured the needy approval from the State Governor. This second amendment bill was patently meant to help the big encroachers since it sanctifies even those who own 100 acres of land in tribal areas to legally occupy an additional five acres of tribal land. On the other hand, it kept limitations on tribals permitting them to occupy land only upto one acre and, that too, as part of the rehabilitation package which is nothing but uprooting the tribals from their ancestral land to far away places wherever land is available for distribution.

19. 1999 and 2000 : The High Court rejects both the 1996 and 1999 Amendment Bills.

20. 2000 and 2001 : Kerala Government file writ appeals before Supreme Court to get stay against High Court verdicts. Petitions by Dr. Nalla Thampi Thera and Niyamavedi of Kochi against these stay orders are still pending before the Apex Court.

21. August 14, 2001 : Following unprecedented starvation deaths in Adivasi belts, a group of tribals, supported by radical Naxalite groups, snatched food stuffs from the Government-owned mobile Maveli van at Noolpuzha area in Wayanad. This took place on the anniversary of August 14, 1996, final order given by the High Court directing the State Government to implement the 1975 parent Act

before September 30, 1996, which led to the passing of Amendment bill on September 23, 1996, and the subsequent Ayyankali Pada action at Palakkad on October 4, 1996. It was this Noolpuzha incident which once again drew nation-wide attention to the unending plight of Adivasis in Kerala due to repeated State violations and which resulted in the spate of agitations by different Adivasi bodies, including the one in front of the Secretariate led by Ms. C. K. Janu under the banner of "Adivasi Dalit Action Council in 2001-2002.

Still the struggle for land continuing, but ray of hope starts blooming in the hearts of atleast in case of a minority of tribes in the form of ownership rights by the Government. In Kerala, the LDF government has in the last four years created a record by providing ownership rights to 1,11,187 landless and poor peasant families. Of these, 21,985 are tribes. However, after 4,000 tribal families got ownership rights in Wayanad alone, around 22,000 tribal families are yet to get the same.

Conclusion

It is not just the alienation of land but also alienation of successive regimes from tribal people that has led to this assertion of tribals. Tribals were forced to assert independently in view of conscious policy adopted by both UDF and LDF regimes that went against the interests of tribals. The process of alienation of land was through exploitation and cheating of tribals who were unaware of their rights, innocent and powerless. In this backdrop, political parties of all hues in the state, including both UDF and LDF gave in to the settlers argument of 'impracticality' of restoration. The tribal agitation is a reflection of a definite anti-tribal tilt in favour of migrant settlers in the state administration and of continued neglect of tribals in various parts of the state. The UDF regime has proved to be a Police Raj. Failure of the government to implement its own promises of the 2001 agreement and subsequent police highhandedness has really led to the tragic incident. The agitation is also a pronounced critique of Left movement in the state, particularly the LDF led by CPI(M), in terms of its nature, land reforms and the continued neglect of the most vulnerable section of the society. The Left movement should have given necessary protection to tribals, that too when land reforms of the state are considered to be relatively more progressive. Land to the tribals should have been the first priority of any land reform. Unfortunately, it has become the last priority for the 'architects' of land reform. What we witness today is only a fallout of the omissions of the ruling.

However, some disturbing trends have emerged in the course of the struggle. The 'Adavasi-inhabited areas have become breeding grounds for extremist organisations espousing the tribal cause and swearing to empower the tribal people in order to fight for their rights. There have been sporadic incidents of violence since 1992, when such groups encouraged the Adivasis to take the law into their own hands and forcibly occupy government land. Since the 1990s the activities of Hindu chauvinist organisations, Christian missionaries and voluntary agencies, often funded from abroad, have also increased in the tribal areas. The past decade saw the disillusioned tribal people move tantalisingly close to extremism and communalism. Such proclivities would certainly undermine their genuine struggle.

REFERENCES

Krishnakumar, R (2001), Promise of land, Volume 18 - Issue 22, Oct. 27 - Nov. 09, 2001 *India's National Magazine from the publishers of THE HINDU.*

Krishnakumar, R (2001), The Adivasi struggle, Volume 18 - Issue 21, Oct. 13 - 26, 2001 India's National Magazine from the publishers of *THE HINDU.*

Menon, C. Mukundan (Secretary General)(2001), *A Fact File on Tribal Land*, CHRO.

M.G. Radhakrishnan (2009), Kerala: The lost slogan, *India Today* October 22.

Prabhakaran. G (2001) Tribal land issue festers again, *The Hindu*, July 16

12
CHAPTER

Social Exclusion on Dalits
Problem and Prospects

M. Karuppuchamy
Research Scholar, Department of Commerce, Madurai Kamaraj University, Madurai

M. Karuppiah
M. Phil Scholar, Sourastra College, Madurai

Introduction

Dalit is not a new word. Aparently it was used in the 1930s as a Hindi and Marathi transaltion of "Depressed Classes", the term British used for what are now called the "Scheduled Castes'. The world was also used by B.R. Ambethkar in his Marathi speaches. In 'The untouchables published in 1948, Ambethkar Chose the term 'Broken men' an English translation of 'Dalit'.

Scholars also have written about the Dalits in different ways. Two views predominate. Those using a class analysis of Indian society subsume Dalits within such class or occupational categories as peasants, agriculture labour, factory workers, students and the like. This can be seen in most Marxist historical writings and to a lesser degree, in the Dalit panther manifesto. To those using a communal analysis of caste, Dalits are the people with in Hindus society who belongs to those castes which Hindus religion consider to be polluting by write of hereditary occupation.

Definition of Scheduled Castes

According to Dr. D.N. Majumdar the term 'Scheduled Castes' refers to the 'Untouchable Castes'. "The untouchable castes are those who suffer from various social and political disabilities many of which are traditionally prescribed and socially enforced by higher castes".

We can define the scheduled castes as those economically, socially, educationally and politically backward castes which are kept at a distance by the other castes as 'untouchables'. Scheduled Castes are those untouchable castes which are subject to some disability in every walk of life -social, religious, educational, economic and political.

Examples: Madiga Chalavadi gas, Billavas, Edigas, Korama, Machigars, Dhoras, Samgaras, Mahars, Mangs, Holeyas, Upparas, Ezhavas, Chamars.

The Scheduled Castes - An Integral Part of Village Life

The Scheduled Castes constitute an integral part of village life. According to the Census Report of 1971 the Harijans constitute 15.04 per cent of the total population of India. More than 90 per cent of them are living in the villages. Still they are not in majority in any part of India. About 75 per cent of them are engaged in agriculture and large numbers of them are landless labourers. They are spread over the entire nation. In fact, there is no village in India in which the Harijans are not found. Even today, they continue to render some menial services to the other caste people. Most of them live below the line of poverty.

Problems of the Scheduled Castes

1. Lowest Status in the Hierarchy: In the Caste hierarchy the Scheduled Castes are ascribed the lowest status. They are considered to be 'unholy', 'inferior' and 'low' and are looked down upon by the other castes. They have been suffering from the stigma of 'untouchability'. Their very touch is considered to be polluting for the higher caste people. Hence they have been treated as the servants of the other caste people. The Scheduled Castes have always served the other castes, but the attitude of other castes is of total indifference and contempt.They were kept at a distance from other caste people. In some instances (in South India) even the exact distance which an upper caste man was expected to keep between himself and the Harijans was specified.

2. Education Disabilities: The Harijans were forbidden from taking up to education during the early days. Sanskrit education was denied for them. Public schools and other educational institutions were closed for them. Even today majority of them are illiterate and ignorant

3. (a) Civic Disabilities, Prevention from the use of Public Places: For a long time the untouchable castes were not allowed to use public places and avail of civic facilities such as—village wells, ponds, temples, hostels, hotels, schools, hospitals, lecture halls, dharamashalas, choultries, etc. They were forced to live on the outskirts of the towns and villages during the early days. Even today they are segregated from others spatially. In South India, restrictions were imposed on the mode of construction of their houses, types of dresses and patterns of their ornamentation. Some lower caste people were not allowed to carry umbrellas, to wear shoes or golden ornaments and to milk cows. They were prohibited from covering the upper part of their body. The services of barbers, washermen and tailors were refused to them.

(b) Religious Disabilities: The Harijans also suffer from religious disabilities even today. They are not allowed to enter temples in many places. The brahmins who offer their priestly services to some lower castes, are not prepared to officiate in the ceremonies of the 'untouchable' castes. They do not even bow down to the duties of these 'untouchnble' castes .The Vedic mantras which are considered to be more pure, could not be listened to and chanted by the Harijans because of the taboos. They were only permit-ted to make use of the upanishadic mantras which are considered to be less pure. Burial grounds were also denied for them in many places.

(c) Economic Disability: The Harijans are economically backward and have been suffering from various economic disabilities also.

No Right of Property Ownership: For centuries the Harijans were not allowed to have *land* and business of their own. It is only recently their ownership to the property has become recognised. The propertied people are comparatively less in them. Majority of them depend upon agriculture but only a few of them own land.

Selection of Occupations Limited: The Caste system imposes restrictions on the occupa-tional choice of the members. The occupational choice was very much limited for the Harijans. They were not allowed to take up to occupations which were reserved for the upper caste people. They were forced to stick on to the traditional inferior occupations such as, curing hides, removing the human wastes, sweeping, scavenging, oil grinding, tanning, shoemaking, leather works, carrying the dead animals, etc. These occupations were regarded as *'degraded'* and *"inferior'.*

(d) Political Disabilities: The untouchables hardly participated in the political matters. They were not given any place in the politics, administration and the general governance of India. They were not allowed to hold any public post. Political rights and representation were denied for them. Under the British rule, they were given the right to vote for the first time. After independence equal political opportunities and rights have been provided for the Harijans also. Politically, the Harijans are yet to become an organised force.

PROSPECTS AND MEASURES

Educational Development

With respect to the educational development of SCs, the Central Government has introduced major scholarship programmes.

The other important schemes for the educational development of SCs: are:

(*i*) providing coaching facilities to students to prepare them for various competitive examinations being conducted by Union Public Service Commission (UPSC), State Public Service Commissions, banks, and so on; and

(*ii*) hostel facilities to both boys and girls for pursuing education from middle level onwards.

Economic Development

The National Scheduled Castes Finance and Development Corporation (NSFDC) established in 1989, provides financial and other support to beneficiaries for taking up various income generating activities. An amount of ₹ 388.80 crore was made available to the Corporation up to 31 March 2007 as equity share contribution against the authorized share capital of ₹ 1000 crore. The number of SC persons who received assistance during the Tenth Five-year Plan (up to December 2006) is 257901.

The scheme of grant-in aid to the Scheduled Castes Development Corporations (SCDCs) was introduced in 1978-79 as a CSS for participating in the equity share of the State corporations in a Centre-State ratio of 49:51. The SCDCs finance employment oriented schemes that cover:

(*i*) agriculture and allied activities including minor irrigation;

(*ii*) small-scale industry;

(*iii*) transport; and

(*iv*) trade and service sector. They also finance projects by dovetailing the loan component from NSFDC/Banks.

Protective Measures

Two important protective legislations in operation for people belonging to SCs are the Protection of Civil Rights Act, 1955 and the Scheduled Castes and Scheduled Tribes (Prevention of Atrocities) Act, 1989. However, despite these Constitutional provisions, atrocities and crimes on members of SCs, especially the women, continue to occur in all parts of the country in varying degrees. As per the National Crime Records Bureau Report 2005, the crimes against SCs in the last few years were mainly atrocities followed by hurt and rape. Data for the last five years are reproduced in Table 12.1.

RESENT STATUS OF THE SCHEDULED CASTES

Education

Although the literacy rate of SCs has increased considerably, from 10.3 per cent in 1961 to 54.7 per cent in 2001, till recently the gap between literacy rates of the general and SC population had not reduced. However, the Census in 2001 showed a distinct reduction in this literacy gap (see Table 12.2).

Table 12.1 : Comparative Incident of Crime against Scheduled Castes

S. No.	Crime-Head	Year					% Variation in 2005 over 2004
1	2	3	4	5	6	7	8
1.	Murder	763	739	581	654	669	2.3
2.	Rape	1316	1331	1089	1157	1172	1.3
3.	Kidnapping and Abduction	400	319	232	253	258	2.0
4.	Dacoity	41	29	24	26	26	0.0
5.	Robbery	133	105	70	72	80	11.1
6.	Arson	354	322	264	211	210	-0.5
7.	Hurt	4547	4491	3969	3824	3847	0.6
8.	Protection of Civil Rights Act	633	1018	634	364	291	-20.0
9.	SC/ST (Prevention of	13113	10770	8048	8891	8497	-4.4
10.	Atrocities) Act Others	12201	14383	11401	11435	11077	-3.1
	Total	**33501**	**33507**	**26252**	**26887**	**26127**	**-2.8**

Source: *Crime in India – 2005*, National Crime Records Bureau, Ministry of Home Affairs

Table 12.2 : Literacy Rate of General Population and SC Population, 1961-2001

Year	General			SC		
	Male	Female	Total	Male	Female	Total
1961	34.44	12.95	24.02	16.96	3.29	10.27
1971	39.45	18.70	29.45	22.36	6.44	14.67
1981	46.89	24.82	36.23	31.12	10.93	21.38
1991	64.1	39.3	52.2	49.91	23.76	37.41
2001	75.3	53.7	64.8	66.64	41.90	54.69

Source: Census of India

ECONOMIC DEVELOPMENT

Occupational Category

As can be seen in survey 45.61 per cent of SC workers population at the all-India level and 52 per cent at the rural level were agricultural labourers, compared to 26.55 and 33.05 per cent among all workers at the national and rural levels, respectively. The position is reversed when we come to the share of SCs among cultivators, which is 19.99 per cent and 23.47 per cent for rural workers compared to 31.65 and 40.24 per cent, respectively for all workers.

Access to Income Earning Assets Agricultural Land and Capital Assets

About 80 per cent of the SCs live in rural areas. In 2000, only 16.8 per cent of them pursued cultivation as an independent self-employed occupation, whereas among the non-SC/ ST this percentage was more than double (41.11%). The percentage of those employed in some kind of non-farm self-employment activities (read business) was about 12 per cent and 15 per cent, respectively for SCs and others. In rural areas, about 28 per cent of SC households had acquired some access to fixed capital assets compared to 56 per cent for other households (non SC/ST). In urban areas, also, the access to capital assets for SCs was low (27%) as compared to other households (35.5%)

Economic Status

Available empirical evidence suggests discrimination against SCs in employment, wages, credit, and so on. These factors have acted as constraints to their occupational ability. In urban areas, too, there is prevalence of discrimination by caste; particularly discrimination in employment, which operates at least in part through traditional mechanisms; SCs are disproportionately represented in poorly paid, dead-end jobs. Further, there is a flawed, preconceived notion that they lack merit and are unsuitable for formal employment.

EFFORTS TO BE TAKEN BY THE GOVERNMENT BASED ON THE ELEVENTH FIVE-YEAR PLAN :

The Way Ahead

1. The efforts made in the previous Five Year Plans have brought about some empowerment of SCs. However, gaps still exist in almost all social and economic dimensions between SCs and the general population. The Eleventh Plan provides an opportunity to restructure policies for faster, more broad-based and inclusive growth.
2. SC students also need to be encouraged to prepare for various competitive examinations. Reputed institutions charge very high fees for coaching students for competitive examinations. The existing scheme of coaching for SCs does not cover the fees charged by such reputed coaching institutes. There is a need to modify the scheme to ensure such coverage.

3. Over the last few years, higher technical and professional education is increasingly being provided by private unaided institutions. In the absence of explicit government aid, they charge high fees which SC/ST students simply cannot afford to pay. Therefore, the government may reimburse the total fee charged by such institutions.
4. The Rajiv Gandhi National Fellowship for SC students was introduced in 2005-06 to provide fellowship to 1333 SC students for pursuing higher studies leading to M.Phil. and Ph.D. degrees. The response under this scheme has been very encouraging in the last two years and this will necessitate increasing the number of fellowships. Those who cannot continue their education after schooling, or who wish to diversify, should be provided with vocational training/skill training programmes in ITIs, polytechnics, or other institutes. These institutes should have adequate seats on population basis and should be located closer to the SC dominated communities. The stress should be not merely on subject learning but also on personality development and entrepreneurship skills.
5. The unemployment rate of SCs in rural and urban areas is about 5.5 per cent as against 3.5 per cent for others. Special programmes of employment are necessary to reduce this by increasing employment among SCs. Priority needs to be given to SCs in the Employment Guarantee Scheme with proper monitoring of coverage.
6. Large numbers of SCs and STs depend on agricultural wages to sustain themselves and the State Government thus needs to revise agricultural wages every five years.
7. Elimination of caste-based discrimination and harassment in educational institutions should be ensured by institutions by establishing 'Equal Opportunity Offices.

There is a need to monitor implementation of the programmes under the SCSP and Tribal Sub Plan. A Committee meant for this purpose will be set up which will ensure that each Ministry's allocation of SCSP is indicated well in advance. Further, if any particular Ministry is not able to utilize the earmarked allocation, action should be initiated to transfer the unused fund available to those Ministries/Departments which have implemented the SCSP/TSP more effectively.

Conclusion

In many parts of our country continuously suffered by community and un-touchability problem. Every reader came to know by through various medias. It is starting from children to old aged people at the end. Many of the forward thinkers tried to solve the problem which are unfavour to

Dalits, but they had failed to perform their objectives, because of the political pressure. The politicians are very care about their seats and safeguards not in the suppressed community of the nations.

There are many violence takes place in Tamilnadu as frequently. Example of community problems at Uthapuram in Theni District, Two glass system is Virudhunagar districts, worker atrocity in Tuticorin and so on. To protect form these problems the government should handle special methods in those areas where found to be the problematic one.

REFERENCES

Eleventh Five-year Plan by Ministry of Broadcasting. Government a India.

Rao C.N. Shankar, "Sociology—Principals of Sociology with an Introduction to Social Thought".

Yadav Bibhutti, Dalits in India', p. 1.

SECTION–III
Exclusion of Disabled and HIV/AIDS

13
CHAPTER

Inclusion of Differently Abled Persons

Dr. M. Inbalakshmi
Associate Professor, Department of Commerce, G.T.N. Arts College, Dindigul

Jeyalakshmi
M. Phil Scholar, Department of Commerce, G.T.N. Arts College, Dindigul

Introduction

Nobody is unfit or disabled person. That's why the term 'disabled' has been changed as 'differently abled'. They turned out to be the greatest of men and proved that disability or handicap is not a curse. They proved themselves better than other able persons. Nobody should be denied to have full participation in society. This paper aims to analyse the concept of disability, the causes of disability, the job opportunities for the differently abled persons, etc. Definitely differently abled persons need equal opportunities and whole hearted support.

Concept of Disability

Various physical and mental impairments can hamper or reduce a person's ability to carry out his day to day activities. These impairments can be termed as disability of the person to do his day-to-day activities as previously. Let's take a note on types of disabilities here. A disability (or *lack of a given ability*, as the "dis" qualifier denotes) in humans may be physical, cognitive/mental, sensory, emotional, developmental or some combination of these.

Impairment is a problem in body function or structure; an activity limitation is a difficulty encountered by an individual in executing a task or action; while a participation restriction is a problem experienced by an individual in involvement in life situations. Thus disability is a complex phenomenon, reflecting an interaction between features of a person's body and features of the society in which he or she lives.

Types of Disabilities

Different types of disabilities are briefly explained below:

1. **Mobility:** This category of disability includes people with varying types of physical disabilities. This includes upper limb disability, manual dexterity and disability in co-ordination with different organs of the body. Disability in mobility can be either an in-born or acquired with age problem. It could also be the effect of some disease. People who have a broken bone also fall into this category of disability.

2. **Spinal Cord Disability:** Spinal cord injuries can sometimes lead to lifel-ong disabilities. This kind of injury mostly occurs due to severe accidents. The injury can be complete or incomplete. In an incomplete injury, the messages conveyed by the spinal cord is not completely lost. Whereas a complete injury results in a total di-functioning of the sensory organs. In rarest of cases spinal cord disability can be a birth defect though

3. **Brain Disability:** A disability in the brain occurs due to a brain injury. The magnitude of the brain injury can range from mild, moderate and severe. There are two types of brain injuries: Acquired Brain Injury (ABI) and Traumatic Brain Injury (TBI). The ABI is not a hereditary type defect but is the degeneration that occurs after birth. The causes of such cases of injury are many and are mainly because of external forces applied to the body parts. The TBI results in emotional dysfunctioun-ing and behavioral disturbance.

4. **Vision Disibility :** There are hundreds of thousands of people that suffer from minor to various serious vision injuries or impairments. These injuries can also result into some serious problems or diseases like blindness and ocular trauma, to name a few. Some of the common vision impairment includes scratched cornea, scratches on the sclera, diabetes related eye conditions, dry eyes and corneal graft.

5. **Hearing disability:** This is the category that includes people that are completely or partially deaf. People who are partially dumb can use hearing-aid to do away with the hearing problem. But the situation is worse if the deafness is complete.

6. **Cognitive disability:** It is a kind of impairment present in people who are suffering from dyslexia and various other learning difficulties. People having dyslexia face difficulties in reading, writing and speaking.

Who becomes Disabled?

The majority of disabled people experience the onset of their health problem or impairment during adulthood. (According to the Family Resources Survey Disability Follow-Up (in 1996/7), 78 per cent of disabled adults of working age became disabled at the age of sixteen or older).

On average, two per cent of people of working age become disabled each year (according to the definitions used in this study). Of these:

- 15 per cent have had an accident in the previous year;
- 44 per cent have experienced the sudden onset of a health problem;
- 41 per cent have had intermittent, chronic or unspecified conditions which got worse.

Acquiring an impairment or developing a serious health problem is often thought of as a random occurrence, but examining patterns of onset of disability suggests this is far from the case. People with lower educational qualifications are at higher risk of becoming disabled than those with higher qualifications. This relationship holds within each age group.

The risk of becoming disabled is also higher for individuals who:

- are not in employment;
- are in a low-status occupational group (such as plant and machine operatives, sales, or personal and protective services); or
- live on a low household income.

These factors are not independent of each other, but all indicate that the risk of becoming disabled has a strong gradient according to the individual's socio-economic circumstances.

Dependency to Independency

Dependency implies the inability to do things for oneself and consequently the reliance upon others to carry out some or all of the tasks of everyday life. Conversely, independence suggests that the individual needs no assistance whatever from anyone else and this fits nicely with the current political rhetoric which stresses competitive individualism. The differently abled persons have to change themselves from dependency to independency.

In order to develop the independency among differently abled persons our Indian Government has extended its helping hands by putting different Acts. One among them is he Persons with Disablities Act, 1995. Over and above this some suggestions are also given for developing independency among differently abled persons.

The Persons with Disabilities Act, 1995 1st in 2009)

The Persons with Disabilities (Equal Opportunities, Protection of Rights and Full Participation) Act, 1995 was enacted in 1995 to give effect to the

Proclamation on the Full Participation and Equality of the People with Disability in the Asian & Pacific Region (Beiijing 1992). The aims and objectives of the Act are:

- To spell out the responsibility of the state towards the prevention of disabilities, protection of rights, provision of medical care, education, training, employment and rehabilitation of persons with disabilities;
- To create a barrier free environment for person with disabilities in the sharing of development benefits, *vis-a-vis* non disabled persons;
- To counteract any situation of abuse and exploitation of persons with disabilities; and
- To make special provision of the integration of persons with disabilities into the social mainstream.

Blindness and low vision has been included in the definition of disability.

Obligations on Governments

In order to achieve its aims and objectives the act imposes obligations on the appropriate governments (central, state and local governments) in the following areas:

- prevention and early detection of disabilities (Section 25).
- providing equality in education (Section 26, 27, 28, 29, 30, 31).
- providing equality in employment (Section 32, 33, 34, 35, 37, 38, 39, 40, 41, 47).
- providing affirmative action programmes in providing aids and appliances to persons with disabilities and preferential allotment of land at concessional rates for housing, setting up businesses setting up of special schools establishment of research centers establishment of factories by entrepreneurs with disabilities (Section 42, 43).
- providing non-discrimination by removing physical barriers (Section 44, 45, 46).
- providing research manpower development (Section 48, 49).
- setting up institutions for persons with disabilities (Section 52).
- providing social security for the disabled (Section 56, 67, 68).

Prevention and Early Detection of Disabilities

In order to prevent the occurrence of disabilities, the appropriate government authorities have to (within their economic capacity and development):

- undertake surveys, investigations and research concerning the cause of occurrence of disabilities;
- promote various methods of preventing disabilities;

- screen all the children at least once in a year for the purpose of identifying "at risk" cases;
- provide facilities for training to the staff at the primary health centers;
- sponsor awareness campaigns and disseminate information on general hygiene, health and sanitation;
- take measures for pre-natal and post-natal care of mother and child;
- educate the public through the pre-schools, schools, primary health centres, village level workers and anganwadi workers;
- create awareness amongst the masses through television, radio and other mass media on the causes of disabilities and the preventive measures to be adopted (Section 25).

Education

In order to provide equal opportunities for the disabled in education, the appropriate government and local authorities have been entrusted with:

- ensuring that every child with disabilities have access to free education in an appropriate environment till 18 years of age.
- promoting the integration of students with disabilities in normal schools.
- promoting setting up of special schools in government and private sector in such a manner that children with disabilities living in any part of the country have access to such schools and equip these schools with vocational training facilities.
- conducting part-time classes in respect of children with disabilities who having completed education up to class fifth and could not continue their studies on a whole-time basis.
- conducting special part-time classes for providing functional literacy for children in the age group of sixteen and above.
- imparting non-formal education by utilizing the available manpower in rural areas after giving them appropriate orientation.
- imparting education through open schools or open universities.
- conducting class and discussions through interactive electronic or other media.
- providing every child with disability free of cost special books and equipments needed for his education. (Section 27).

Comprehensive schemes are to be prepared by the government for:

- transport facilities to the children with disabilities or in the alternative financial incentives to parents or guardians to enable their children with disabilities to attend schools.

- the removal of architectural barriers from schools, colleges or other institutions, imparting vocational and professional training;
- the supply of books, uniforms and other materials to children with disabilities attending school.
- the grant of scholarship to students with disabilities.
- setting up of appropriate forums for the redressal of grievances of parent, regarding the placement of disabled children;
- suitable modification in the examination system to eliminate purely mathematical questions for the benefit of blind students and students with low vision;
- restructuring of curriculum for the benefit of children with disabilities.

All educational institutions have to provide amanuensis to blind students and students with low vision (Section 30, 31).

All government educational institutions and other educational institutions receiving aid from the government are to reserve not less than three per cent of its seats for disabled persons. (Section 39) Also see: State of Kerala v. *Mary Joseph*, (2001) 3 Kerala Law Times 26.

To implement the educational rights of the disabled to the full extent the appropriate government are to set up adequate teachers' training institutions and assist the national institutes and other voluntary organisations to develop teachers' training programmes specializing in disabilities, so that requisite trained manpower is available for special schools and integrated schools for children with disabilities (Section 29). It is also entrusted with the duty of initiating research by official and non-governmental agencies for the purpose of designing and developing new assistive devices, teaching aids, special teaching materials or such other items as are necessary to give a child with disability equal opportunities in education (Section 28).

Employment

The appropriate governments are to identify posts in government establishments, which can be reserved for disabled persons and review the list of posts at periodic intervals (not exceedingly three years) (Section 32).

At least three per cent of vacancies in every government establishment are to be reserved for persons with disabilities. Out of which one per cent each shall be reserved for persons suffering from blindness or low vision and the other two per cent for persons with hearing impairment and loco motor disability or cerebral palsy. But the Central Government may exempt any establishment from the above requirements if the nature of work in such establishmentsis such that disabled persons are unable to work in such establishments. (Section 33).

If a vacancy cannot be filled up due to non-availability of a suitable disabled person, the vacancy is to be carried forward to the next recruitment year and if in that next recruitment year, a suitable person with disability is not found, the post is to be filled by an interchange of categories of disabled persons. Only if there is no suitable disabled person available for the job, can an able person be employed. (Section 37).

In order to ensure employment of disabled persons, schemes are to be formulated by the appropriate government for:

- the training and welfare of persons with disabilities;
- the relaxation of upper age limit;
- regulating the employment;
- health and safety measures and creation of a non-handicapping environment in places where persons with disabilities are employed;
- the manner in which and the person by whom the cost of operating the schemes is to be defrayed; and
- Constituting the authority responsible for the administration of the scheme (Section 38).

Government establishments are not allowed to dispense with or reduce in rank, an employee who acquires a disability during his service. (Section 47) [*Syed Sha Musebulla Alvi v. Sectionretary, G.A.D, Sectionretariat, Hyderabad,* (1999) 2 Andhra Law Times 130]. If disabled during the service tenure, the employee is not suitable for the post he was holding, he/she can be shifted to another post with the same pay and service benefits (Section 47) [*Kunal Singh* v. *Union of India and Another,* (2003) 4 Supreme Court Cases 524]. If it is not possible to adjust the employee against any post, the employee is to be kept in a supplementary post until a suitable post is available or he/she attains the age of superannuity whichever is earlier. A disabled employee cannot be denied a promotion on the basis of his disability except in conditions to be notified, where a disabled cannot perform certain functions (Sec 47).

The government can set up a special employment exchange under section 34 and direct all establishments to the employment exchange of details of vacancies that arise for person with disabilities.

Affirmative Action

The appropriate governments have to frame schemes to provide aids and appliances to disabled persons (Section 42). Special schemes are to be notified for the preferential allotment of land at confessional rates for:

- Housing
- Setting up business

- Setting up special recreational centers
- Establishment of special schools
- Establishment of research centers
- Establishment of factories by entrepreneurs with disabilities (Section 43).

Non-discrimination

In order to create a physical barrier free environment for disabled persons, the appropriate governments or local authorities have to (in their economic capacity and development) take special measures to:

- Adapt rail compartments, buses. vessels and aircrafts in such a way as to permit easy access to such persons;
- Adapt toilets in rail compartments, vessels, aircrafts and waiting rooms in such a way as to permit the wheel chair users to use them conveniently (Section 44);
- Install auditory signals at red lights in the public roads for the benefit of persons with visually handicap;
- Make curb cuts and slopes in pavements for the easy access of wheel chair users;
- Engrave the surface of the zebra crossing for the blind or for persons with low vision;
- Engrave the edges of railway platforms for the blind or for persons with low vision;
- Devise appropriate symbols of disability;
- Provide warning signals at appropriate places (Section 45).
- Provide ramps in public buildings;
- Provide Braille symbols and auditory signals in elevators or lifts;
- Provide ramps in hospitals, primary health centers and other medical care and rehabilitation institutions (Section 46).

Research and Manpower Development

The appropriate government and local authorities are entrusted with sponsoring and promoting research in following areas:

- Prevention of disability;
- Rehabilitation including community based rehabilitation;
- Development of assistive devices including their psycho-social aspects;
- Job identification;
- On site modifications in offices and factories (Section 48).

Universities, other institutions of higher learning, professional bodies and non-governmental organisations that undertake research on special education, rehabilitation and manpower development are to be provided financial assistance by appropriate governments for undertaking research for education, rehabilitation and manpower development (Section 49).

Institution for Persons with Severe Disabilities

The concerned government may establish and maintain institutions for persons with severe disabilities at such places it thinks fit or recognise any private institution (Sec.56).

Social Security

While formulating rehabilitation policies the appropriate governments have to consult non-governmental organisations working in the field of disability. Within their economic capacity and development they are to undertake rehabilitation of all disabled persons for which financial assistance shall be given non-governmental organisations working in the fields of disability (Section 66).

Insurance schemes or alternate security schemes are to be framed by the appropriate government for the benefit of its employees with disabilities (Section 67).

Schemes are also to be framed for payment of an unemployment allowance to persons with disabilities that are registered with the special employment exchange for more than two years and have not been placed in any gainful occupation (Section 68).

Implementation Agencies

The act has set up a central coordination committee at the national level to serve as a national focal point for disability matters to facilitate the continuous evaluation of a comprehensive policy towards solving the problems faced by disabled the persons (Section 8). At the state level a state coordination committees have been set up (Section 13). To assist the central coordination committee and state coordination committees, a central executive committee (Section 10) and a state coordination committee have been set up (Section 23).

The Chief Commissioner and Commissioners for persons with disabilities have to safe guard the rights of persons with disabilities and submit reports to the government on implementation of the act (Sections 57, 58, 59, 60, 61, 62, 63, 64, 65),

If there is any violation of the act, the aggrieved person can approach the head of the establishment under which he/she is employed or the Chief Commissioner or the Commissioner for Persons With Disabilities or the High court under article 226 of the Constitution of India or the Supreme Court under article 32 of the Constitution of India or even the National or State Human Rights Commissions.

Suggestions for developing independency among the differently abled persons

It is well known that many disabled people are out of work and living in poverty. In order to avoid this many of the State governments have provided breathers in the form of special job arenas for disabled. For the disabled people special places are made, besides the contemporary job market where they can find good job opportunities. Many people with disabilities, particularly wheelchair users struggle with issues of employment. According to the US Bureau of Labor Statistics, the unemployment rate for people with disabilities is at least 50 per cent higher than for able-bodied people. Some suggestions of jobs for people with disabilities are given below:

1. Turn Your Disability into an Asset

- For some companies or organizations your disability may be an asset. If you can combine your other skills with a product set you know extremely well, you may be uniquely qualified and be very attractive for a company.
- Some companies may have an interest in improving their position with disabled customers and you may be able to obtain the skills or knowledge to help them.
- Accessibility is not only about physical access. The accessibility industry is growing in many areas including technical accessibility.
- If you are disabled, you are probably already sensitized to the many issues surrounding access for people with disabilities. Your disability will give you credibility to market your services to potential employers. There are websites which will provide further information or training and help you to get started
- Another possibility is to get a degree which will enable you to mentor, teach or give therapy to disabled people. As a wheel-chair user with a degree in rehabilitation counseling, for example, you would be a prime candidate for a position as a counselor to newly injured patients in a rehab clinic.
- You do not have to limit yourself to disability related jobs. But nevertheless, consider areas where your disability would make you a more attractive candidate and give you an obvious advantage over able-bodied candidates. Instead of your disability being your weak point, your disability could be one of your best selling points.

2. Hire Yourself

- Your disability may make it difficult for you to hold a full-time position. In that case, consider becoming self-employed.
- Many companies look for so called "independent reps" or manufacturers reps. An independent rep often works for several different companies and develops business with dealers in their local territory. Independent reps are usually paid on a commission only basis. However, the plus side is that as an independent rep, you can work when you want and when you are able.
- With no real boss to answer to, you have more flexibility if your disability makes you unable to work for some time. Start by getting more information from discussion forums or networks which specialize in this topic, or visit some manufacturers' rep industry websites.

3. Collaborate with a Foreign Partner

- Many small foreign companies would like to penetrate the Indian market but may find it difficult to do so. You may be able to obtain rights for their products and launch them regionally or nationally. You may not be successful in obtaining rights easily from a large company. But with the right business plan and the right approach, you may be successful in obtaining rights to products from a smaller company.
- Representing a foreign company will help you to develop business skills and a sales network. With that in place, once you have successfully launched those products you can either find new products to represent, or begin to develop some of your own. How do you find a foreign partner? There are two ways:
  - *Contact a partner company directly:* Search the Internet or disability discussion forums for products available in foreign markets that are not available in your market. Contact the company and ask if they are interested in having you represent them. Be prepared to answer questions about how you plan to market their products. Having a solid business plan in place will have you prepared for the questions.
  - *Find help contacting partners:* Most embassies offer their businesses help in finding partner companies or representatives, very often at no charge to either party. Pick a target country (or countries) which is/are attractive to you. Perhaps you speak a foreign language or you travel frequently to that country. Contact

their local embassy and ask how you can register with their trade department.

4. Get a Government (or government subsidized) Job

- Are you interested in a government job? The governments of many countries reserve jobs for people with disabilties. For example, Indian government has given lot of reservations exclusively for physically challenged people. Government jobs are listed in two ways:
- First, there are competitive government job listings which are open to all applicants, able-bodied and disabled.
- In addition, there are non-competitive job offerings open only to People with Mental Retardation, Severe Physical Disabilities, or Psychiatric Disabilities and have documentation from a licensed medical professional. Briefly put, if you get a certification that you are disabled and you are ready to work you will receive a special consideration for a government job
- You may also find jobs for people with disabilties via government sponsored or subsidized programs.

Conclusion

The differently abled persons should be independent and whole hearted support of the environment. Every differently abled person has their own specialties or they have special qualities. These are to be identified by themselves and others. They must be properly recognized not only by the society but also by themselves. As a component of the environment, it is our duty to uplift them. They have to feel and realize that nothing is impossible.

14
CHAPTER

Social Exclusion of HIV/AIDS Infected
A Case Study in Tamil Nadu

R. Kathiravan

Research Scholar, Deptt. of Sociology, Gandhigram Rural Institute-Deemed University, Gandhigram-624 302, Tamil Nadu

Introduction

India has amongst the largest number of HIV infected people in the world, second only to South Africa. According to World Health Organisation (WHO) it is estimated that about 5.1 million people live with HIV infection in India and of them 6,00,000 cases urgently need treatment. HIV/AIDS continues to show itself to be one of India's most complex epidemics—a challenge that goes beyond public health, raising fundamental issues of human rights and threatening development achievements in many areas.

As the world enters the third decade of AIDS epidemic, the evidence of its impact is undeniable. In some regions, HIV in combination with other crises is driving even large parts of nations towards destitution. It will have a multiplier effect that would in fact affect not only individual households and communities, but also some of the benchmarks of human development like infant mortality, life expectancy at birth, school enrolment rate and health. As many as 6.10 lakh children died of AIDS in 2002 out of 3.1 million deaths were due to AIDS. Over 19.2 million women are infected with HIV and the female rate of infection is steadily rising with 2 million women infected last year. According to an estimate approximately 2.5 million people were living with HIV in India in 2006. Whilst almost 25 per cent of the country's population is between the ages of 15-29 years and this age group accounts for 31 per cent of people living with HIV, demonstrating that young people are at particularly high of contracting HIV. These statistics clearly shows that how very fasts this epidemic is expanding all over the world, and becoming a global menace threatening the very existence of human being.

As the second most populous nation in the world even a small increase will represent a significant component of the world's HIV/AIDS burden. The people who are affected by HIV/AIDS face a lot of social problems especially stigmatisation and social exclusion. Apart from physical ailments, the mental trauma underwent by the HIV/AIDS infected is much higher than this psychological trauma which aggravates their problems. This necessitates to study the problems of social exclusion of patients suffered by the HIV/AIDS.

Need for the Study

The HIV/AIDS epidemic in India varies from state to state. No state is free from the virus and among them in Maharashtra, Tamil Nadu and Manipur HIV/AIDS has spreads most rapidly. Tamil Nadu has the second highest number of zero-positives cases in India. Statistics generally indicates that the incidence of zero positives among women of antenatal clinics in Tamil Nadu had increased from 0.25 per cent in 1995 to 1.31 per cent in 1998. Namakkal, a semi urban area is considered the epic centre of the AIDS crisis in Tamil Nadu, with the infection rate among antenatal patients having towned a staggering 25 per cent in 1998, according to the TNSAC's support network of Person Living with HIV/AIDS (PLWHA).

Social exclusion is seen as covering a remarkably wide range of social and economic problems and hence, we have good reason to value not being excluded from social relations, and in this sense, social exclusion may be directly a part of capability poverty among HIV/AIDS infected. Being excluded from social relations can lead them to other deprivations as well, thereby limiting their living opportunities. For example, being excluded from the opportunity to be employed that may, in turn, lead to other deprivations such as undernourishment or homelessness. Hence it is obvious that the HIV/AIDS infected faces social exclusion in a verity of ways, and it is important to recognise the versatility of the idea and its reach. In some context their inability due to infection to get a job may be helpfully analysed in terms of exclusion. And this in turn makes their social integration that much harder. Some of the evil effects of social exclusion includes skill loss, loss of freedom, psychological harm and misery, loss of human relation, motivational loss and future work and so on. Therefore, it is a felt need that empirical studies have to be conducted to bring out the nature and domains of exclusion faced by the HIV/AIDS infected.

Objectives of the Study

The present study was carried out among the HIV/AIDS infected with the following objectives:

(*a*) To study the socio-economic conditions of HIV/AIDS infected in study area;

(*b*) To understand the circumstances led to HIV/AIDS infection;

(*c*) To bring out the various problems faced by the infected;

(*d*) To assess the pattern and extent of exclusion faced by the infected; and

(*e*) To suggest ways and means to bring the HIV/AIDS infected into the mainstream of social life.

Setting of the Study

Theni district has been purposively selected for the study since it is reported the second largest district with HIV+ cases in Tamil Nadu. Theni being a market place wherein convergence of cross-sections is frequent, accordingly there is scope for transmission of HIV+ to persons having pre-marital and extra-marital relationship through commercial sex workers. In Theni district Koduvilapatti panchayat has the high concentration of HIV/AIDS patients. Of the total population (6800) of the panchayat about 100 persons are identified as HIV/AIDS infected. Since the population of the infected is too small attempts were made to include all the infected persons. However, due to unwillingness of the infected the sample size has been restricted to 60. A structured interview schedule was prepared to collect data from the infected persons. Both for convenience and to collect systematic and unambiguous data all they were met alone to avoid interruptions. Since the sample size was too small no necessity arised to form hypotheses and accordingly to test them. To arrive at general conclusions the collected data were analysed and interpreted by applying descriptive methods like percentage, proportion, and average and presented in summary form.

Summary of the Study

Who are Vulnerable to HIV/AIDS Infection

To understand that who are vulnerable to HIV/AIDS infection, their sex, age, educational level, occupation and monthly income and the type of family are concerned. It is found that men are more vulnerable to HIV/AIDS infection in the study area. It is proved through the present study that of the total infected males constituted 90 per cent while females' proportion in the total is only 10 per cent.

The grouping of the infected-respondents on the basis of age group reveals that nearly half (48.3%) of them are in the age group of 20-29 while another one-thirds (33.3%) in the total infected belongs to 30-39 age category and 18.4 per cent inpected belongs in the age group of 40-49. The mean age for them is 31.5 Figure 14.1 evidences this.

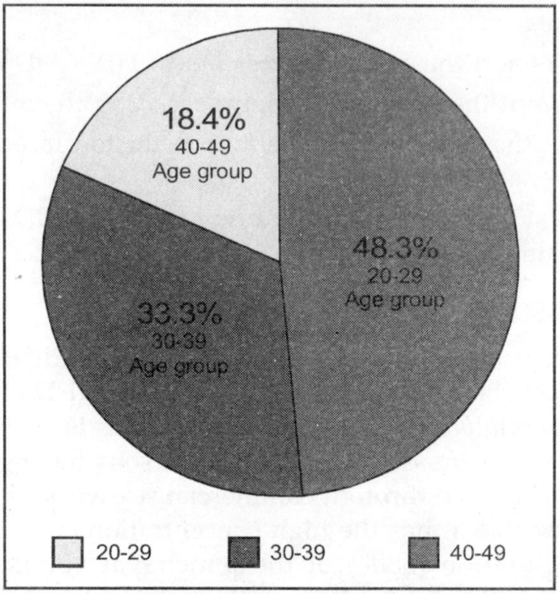

Fig. 14.1 : Age of the HIV/AIDS infected persons

It is found that the prevalence of HIV/AIDS is more among educationally poor section in the study area. About half of (46.7%) the total infected reached upper primary school stage while another 41.3 per cent completed primary education. However, about 12 per cent in the total are illiterates. Almost all they (95%) are Hindus and of them 38.3 percent belongs to Backward Castes followed by Scheduled (31.7%) and Most Backward (30%) castes. What it indicates that HIV/AIDS spread among the people irrespective of caste.

As far as HIV/AIDS infected persons' occupation is concerned of the total a half (50%) of them are non-agricultural labourers while another 28.3 per cent in the total are agricultural labourers. While considering the monthly income of the infected about three-fifths (58.3%) in the total earns ₹ 3000-4000, per month and the mean income for them is ₹ 3,533.

It is found that more than three-fourths (76.7%) of the total infected are married and all they established nuclear family. Only 23.3 per cent in the total are unmarried. It is found that almost all the (95%) infected are living in the study area from their birth.

Circumstance Led to Infection

While probing the causes for the spread of HIV/AIDS among the respondents a majority (46.7%) of them accepted that they involved unprotected sex while another 31.7 per cent in the total infected got it through commercial sex workers whereas the remaining 21.6 per cent through their spouse and homosex.

A large majority (70%) of the infected are affected after marriage. However, the remaining 30 per cent in the total are affected before their marriage, according to them. It is found that extra/pre-marital sex is one amongst the reasons for the spread of HIV/AIDS among the infected–respondents. It is observed from the study that nearly three-fourths (72.3%) of the total infected are involved extra/pre-marital intercourse, and of them more than one-fourths (28.3%) are motivated by their friends while another 23.3 per cent had during travel whereas the remaining 48.4 per cent in the total during local festival time.

It is found that about three-fifths (58.3%) of the total are affected for the past three years while another 30 per cent is for about six years. However, all they are suffering of HIV/AIDS for an average of the past 3.5 years in the study area. It is important to note that of the total two-thirds (66.7%) of them came to know about their infection while gone for casual treatment followed by while donating blood (27.7%), and during child birth (6.7%).

Table 14.1 : Mean for Some Selected Variables for HIV/AIDS Infected

Variable	Mean(N= 60)
Age (in yrs.)	31.5
Monthly income (in Rs.)	3,533
No. of years suffering	3.5

Stigmatisation and Health Status

The typology of negative emotions faced by the HIV/AIDS infected reveals inferiority complex, negative emotions of insecurity, low-level of confidence, depression and suicidal thoughts. However, more than two-thirds (68.2%) of them do not face the problems like solitary confinement, anger or sadness.

It is to be highlighted that of the total a large majority (80%) of the infected have taken treatment and among them 51.6 per cent approaches special clinics while another 41.7 per cent commutes general hospitals whereas the remaining 6.7 per cent consults the specialists.

While probing the stigmatisations experienced by the infected it reveals that of the total more than two-thirds (68.3%) of them experiences stigmatisation and of them majority (41.6%) felt depression and worries about stigmatization while the rest (58.4%) have suicidal thoughts.

As far as their physical problems is concerned majority of the infected are with prolonged illness, inability to work, lack of concentration and loss of appetite. However, they all reported that their routine works are not affected.

Social Exclusion of HIV/AIDS Infected

While analysing the family's response towards the infected it is heart worthy to mention that a large majority (83.3%) of them receives sympathy and given of support and care by their family members. Only the remaining 16.7 per cent in the total are neglected by their family members and faces discrimination in the family in terms of separate food, separate tumbler/ plate, shelter and clothing.

It is found that the majority of the infected faces the discrimination from their relatives in terms of ignoring and non-responsive behaviour. The kind of ill-treatment faces by them is either avoidance or given of no response. Only few of them are neither allowed in the relatives' house or to interact with the children of the relatives.

It is important to note that almost all the HIV/AIDS infected are kept at a distance by their neighbourhood community and moreover, fears even to speak with them. While about two- thirds (38.3%) of the infected are neglected in community functions another 23.3 per cent are expelled. Only 36.7 per cent in the total are allowed to participate in community functions.

As far as the exclusion of HIV/AIDS infected in the worship place is concerned a large majority (80%) of them are kept at a distance while the remaining 20 per cent are not allowed in the temple. During festival celebrations more than two-fifths (43.3%) of the total infected are not shared of pleasure even by their family members while another 30 per cent in the total are ignored whereas the remaining 26.7 per cent are kept at a distance. Hence, a large majority (76.7%) of the infected felt that it is hard to participate in the festivals since they are neglected by the public whereas the remaining 23.3 per cent in the total replied that their interaction with others is harmonious.

While asking the infected about their friends' reaction when they knew about the infection they replied that they are unable to believe, shocked and expressed fear and some of them exhibited mixed feeling. Therefore, more than half (55%) of their friends avoided the infected- respondents while another one-thirds (33.3%) of the HIV/AIDS infected experienced behavioural changes in them. However, 11.7 per cent in the total infected receives moral support from their friends, according to them.

It is found that three-fourths (60%) of the total infected are avoided by their coworkers while another 25 per cent expressed stigmatisation towards the them. However, the remaining 15 per cent in the total receives moral support from their colleagues. The forms of exclusion found in working place are avoidance in term of speaking (43.3%), provided of separate work place (28.3%), improper co-operation (21.7%), and avoidance during lunch (6.7%). Most of the time their co-workers are scared to work with them and keeping distance from them. It is also to be noted that almost all they are scolded by their employer and do not receives any sympathy either from their co-workers or employer. Hence, it is obvious that almost all the infected-respondents are facing problems in employment in the study area.

More than half (51.7%) of the infected are not allowed even to sit near to others in hotels while another one-thirds (34.4%) are provided of separate place. However, the remaining 13.3 per cent in the total are not allowed even to enter in to the hotel. Almost all they are provided of tea in disposable cups in tea shops.

About three-fifths (56.7%) of the infected are detained deliberately while approaching the hospitals for treatment since all they are HIV+ while another 23.3 per cent in the total are not given of proper respect whereas the remaining 20 per cent are compelled to wait at outside of the hospital premise.

It is satisfactory to note that majority of the infected reported that testing facilities, ART (73.3%) and counseling (66.7%) facilities are availed to them. However, the facilities like physiotherapy (70%) recreation (78.3%) and special food (68.3%) are not availed to the infected, each respectively. While eliciting their perception towards the availability of medical care facilities almost all (98.3%) the infected opined positively. However, all they are in dissatisfaction due to shortage of medicine and delayed issuing.

More than half (51.7%) of the infected are not allowed even in barber shop for hair cutting. However, the service is extended to the remaining proportion (48.3%) in the total with hesitation.

In case of government retail price shops all they are forced to stand away from the normal queue while purchasing things. Moreover, they are instructed to keep their bags on the floor prior to lending of things since they are considered as unapproachable. The forms of discrimination found in common place are avoidance from speaking (41%), kept at a distance (40%), humiliation (10%), and denial of using public assets/facilities (10%).

Conclusion

While concluding the present study on HIV/AIDS infected it is to be highlighted that they all faces problems of discrimination and thereby being excluded. Many-a-times they are unable to utilise the common facilities. Discrimination exists in the forms of omission from family functions, separate cups in tea shops, prohibition of using common toilet facilities, problems in sharing food in employment areas and hence, almost all they are in isolation. However, despite of such exclusion some of them reported that they are able to participate in social gathering, enter tea shops and faced no stigmatisation. However, a majority of the infected faces the problems in getting employment, stigmatisation, fear, low income, and seclusion therefore, the following would be suggested for their inclusion in the mainstream of life.

- Promotion of sex education among the adults/ student for understanding the causes and prevention of HIV epidemic.
- Creating awareness on HIV/AIDS among the village women groups, youth clubs, working place at large through HIV infected persons because that, it created natural sharing the develop the confidentiality of newly infected life.
- The HIV/AIDS awareness programme should focused on the social discrimination against the HIV infected through mass media for changing the attitude of mass towards the HIV/AIDS infected.
- The Government must implement act to producing "Free from HIV" certificate at the time of marriage for preventing the HIV transmission.
- The Government should provide free medicine to HIV infected upto the end their life.
- The NGO promote suitable income generation programmes for HIV infected persons.
- Instead of adopting safe sex, morality should be insisted.
- Counselling facilities must be enhanced for the welfare of HIV/AIDS infected who faced negative emotions like depression, anxiety, fear.
- Awareness about medical care availability must be created among HIV/AIDS infected.

REFERENCES

Cantwell, Alan, *AIDS: The Mystery and Solution*, Aries Rising Press, Los Angles; 1991.

Catrill, Kevil M.(ed), *The AIDS Epidemic*, St. Martin Press: New York, 2001.

CSIS, India at the Crossroads: *Confronting the HIV/AIDS Challenge a Report of the CSIS HIV/AIDS Delegation to India*, 2004.

Geeta Rao Gupta, "How men's power over women fucls, the H!V Epidemic" *British Medical Journal* 324, No.7331 (2002): 183-24.

Lam Fisher, "Stigma of AIDS in Ukraine" *New York Times*, Jan 23, 2002.

The World Bank, HIV/AIDS, *Treatment and Prevention in India, Modeling the Costs and Consequences*, 2004.

Murti, Chaitanga, "Media and HIV" *Social Initiatives*, 2(12), Dec.2008.

15
CHAPTER

HIV/AIDS-Related Stigma and Discrimination at Workplace

Dr. T. Sundara Raj
Assistant Professor, Deptt. of Sociology, Periyar University, Salem-11, Tamil Nadu

Introduction

HIV/AIDS - stigma represents a set of shared values, attitudes and beliefs that can be conceptualized as the result of process called stigmatization. Here stigmatization is a social process of devaluation of people living with HIV/AIDS with respect to their seropositve status. HIV/AIDS stigma is manifested in the form of behaviours, thoughts and feelings that express prejudices against people living with HIV/AIDS (PLWHA).

HIV/AIDS - related discrimination occurs when a distinction is made against a person, that results in their being treated unfairly and unjustly on the basis of their belonging or being perceive to belong to a group of people living with HIV/AIDS. HIV/AIDS - related discrimination is the result of HIV/AIDS related stigma, which conceives prejudices against PLWHA. HIV/AIDS - related discrimination is manifested as unjust treatment by others in all major social institutions (like family, education, health care system etc) and in community against PLWHA.

In the present study, workplace did not emerge as a major institution for discrimination/exclusion and stigmatization, probably because most respondents had not disclosed their HIV/AIDS status at work place. Workplace is an institution, the established procedures like hierarchies of power and duties are supplied to a group of individuals engaged in productive activities under an organization. Thus in workplaces there are a group of individuals in different strata, an organization and established procedures for the functioning of this organization.

Therefore, in this study only 52 per cent of the total respondents (PLWHA) had any kind of occupation in a workplace setting, under this working definition. Most of the respondents did not have a job, as they were less educated and economically backward

In addition, majority of them who had an occupation was working in the unorganized workplaces. A significant number of females were sex workers and for them there was no discrimination from the co-workers or clients. Therefore the dimensions of the HIV/AIDS related stigma and discrimination is manifested both organized and unorganised sectors of work places. There it is mainly explicated in two ways, viz. Discrimination by management and discrimination by co-workers.

Methodology

Thiruvananthapuram and Thrissur are the highest HIV prevalent districts in Kerala. Kannur is selected from the north region where the prevalence rate HIV infection growing dramatically. Moreover, the availability of samples from these districts is more easily as there many NGO is working in these districts. From the each area of study 25 respondents were selected through purposive sampling from the population identified through snowball technique. Thus, a total sample of 75 respondents was selected for structured questionnaire interview. Primary data were collected mainly through personal interview from people living with HIV/AIDS, relatives PLWHA, Doctors, other medical staffs, AIDS counsellors, heads of rehabilitation canters, social activities and head of corporate offices. PLWHA is identified through the networks of NGOs. The researcher has given some broad observation based on the study.

Discrimination by the Management

Management's discrimination against HIV-positive workers seemed to be due to lack of knowledge and/or the absence of protective policies. Discrimination and stigmatization from management made it particularly difficult for individual workers to have their rights respected and earn a living. This is often manifested as mandatory testing, dismissal from the job, restrictions in the workplace, forceful withdrawal of health insurance schemes...etc.

Mandatory Testing

HIV/AIDS is not a contentious issue in the work place situation, as HIV/AIDS is not a disease that spreads through the casual contacts. Still some companies asked the respondents to screen for HIV/AIDS compulsorily. 38.46 per cent of the respondents who were employed in the workplace, asked to undergo such a test in order to work in that company. Later, majority of them lost their job and thus shifted to new companies. But 61. 54 per cent of the employees in the study were never instructed to undergo mandatory screening at the time of joining or during the course of employment.

There were only few companies in Kerala, which HIV/AIDS test as mandatory criterion for the selection of employees. And most of the companies were not interested to screen their employees because the authorities presumed that their employees' higher economic and educational status would be a safety valve for non-infection. Recently some companies, especially franchises of multi-nationals and few banking industries incorporated HIV/AIDS - free certificate as an employment requirement. Moreover, the trend is moving in a positive growth.

This requirement that, an individual has to agree to an HIV - test before being offered employment contravenes international human rights standards that you might test negative today and be positive tomorrow because of the window (window period- the period where virus remains undetected in Elis test even after infection. It is otherwise known as incubation period) before the infection shows in the test and it is necessary to keep on testing to find if there is a change in ones status (Commonwealth Medical Association). The need for mandatory HIV-testing in workplace is spreading rapidly. This shows the level of HIV/AIDS stigma attached with the management people. For them PLWA were not entitled to have the universal right of employment, as they were lethally diseased, potentially infectious marginalized people. Management was not ready to accept PLWHA as potentially productive groups like that of other similar skilled general population. Instead, they were discriminated as unequal, just because of their zero positive status. Even though this study points to the lower rate of mandatory testing in workplace, a study by Bezmalinovice (1996) showed that HIV/AIDS mandatory testing was on an increase in the international arena.

Dismissal

Dismissal from the job is the worst form of discrimination that is prevailing in workplace settings. It is not only human right violation, but also it questions the sustainability of HIV-infected employees and the society as a whole. If all the potentially productive HIV/AIDS employees were dismissed, they should have to consume the part of production produced by their close relatives/friends. Moreover, this will lead to additional burden on the country's economy. Therefore PLWHA should be allowed to work during their asymptomatic stage of infection for the benefit of themselves and the whole society. But in practice the rate of dismissal of PLWHA is increasing day by day, as they were known HIV-positives openly. In the present study,

84.62 per cent of the total employed respondents were dismissed from their earlier workplaces. These points to the enormity of stigma and discrimination in the workplace. Once the identity of an HIV-patient exposed in the workplace she/he could not work there for a long period, either he/she would get dismissed by the manage/authority, or the coworkers' attitudes force him/her to resign or the co-workers force management to dismiss him/her.

The dismissal of HIV/AIDS patients from the workplace is also observed by Bezmalinovic and Jack (1991) in their studies and they suggested that effective policy formulation and implementation regarding the security of HIV/AIDS patients in employment, should be brought out nationally and internally to fight this discrimination by the management. This denial of employment based on HIV- status is an exemplification of the perceived stigma of HIV/AIDS among those who are in power. In addition, this power is exercised over the powerless marginal people who are infected with HIV ensuring economic hardship and questions the sustainability of their life.

Status of Health Insurance Scheme

As most of the respondents were working in the unorganized sector, they did not have any Health Insurance policy as such. The above table shows that 35.9 per cent of respondents had no health care insurance policies. In the present study, health insurance was not a major problem for PLWHA. Still 23.08 per cent of employed respondents said that the authority forcefully withdrew their insurance policies. While the majority of respondents about 41.02 per cent, were continuing their health insurance scheme. In the international arena, the health care insurance policy withdrawal was a great issue; this was outlined in the study of Parker in 2000. In the international arena, most of the medical treatment is done through health care insurance policies. But, that is not the case of Kerala, here these policies are not that much prevalent.

Discrimination from the Co-workers

Many respondents feared the discrimination by their co-workers. For them the sustainability in the workplace depended on the attitude of co-workers, if they would not co-operate with the PLWHA, remaining in the company for long be an arduous task. And they experience such discrimination in the earlier workplace from where they were dismissed. Therefore, majority of the respondents did not reveal their zero status to co-workers. They mentioned fear of social discrimination, isolation, lowered prestige and possible jobless as outcomes of the disclosure.

Co-workers Awareness about the Respondents' HIV-positive Status

The study shows that only 7.69 per cent of the respondents said that their serostatus was an open issue to all co-workers. While the majority 48.72 per cent of employed respondents mentioned that, they did not disclose their zero status to anybody in their new organization. Most of them experienced denial by the co-workers, when they knew about their zero positive status, in their earlier companies. Often this non-disclosure caused psychological strain among PLWHA. They often had to tell numerous lies about their poor health conditions and reasons for long absence. For them the stress created by non-disclosure was much better than the disclosure related discrimination. But 43.59 per cent of the employed respondents told that they had disclosed their HIV-positives, so for them confidentiality was not a problem. But in the cases of others, they were always under the stress, because of the fear of leakage of their HIV-positive status and possible job loss.

Reasons for Non-disclosure

Most respondents had not disclosed their HIV/AIDS status at work even those who were open at home. Many had a strong fear of social isolation and stigmatization, and they worried about losing their job it they were to reveal their status. This fear was validated by their earlier experiences. It seems that they had internalized the social stigmatization, as they were ought to be discriminated. They were also aware that they could not withstand these discriminations by the co-workers and management. Indeed, many asymptomatic individuals felt that there was no need to reveal their status at work as long as they remained physically healthy. Business and Industry largely did not have AIDS policies, and no special benefits are offered to workers with HIV (Bharat, 2001).

Thus, openness about the status of PLWHA creates more severe problem leading to self-stigmatization, social discrimination and the loss of job in the workplace. Those who were not shared their positive-status to anybody in the workplace also experienced stress, which emanated their psychological stress. Briefly, whether PLWHA were open about their sero status in workplace, or not, they were facing serious psychological disturbances.

Most of the respondents stated a number of reasons for their unwillingness to open about their positive status with their co-workers. The respondents who had disclosed their status to few close friends also feared about knowing it to all persons in the workplace. 77.78 per cent of the respondents feared the discrimination by the co-workers and management. While, loss of job and fear of isolation were quoted as reasons for non-disclosure by 66.67 per cent and 43.59 per cent of the total employee respondents whose sero status were not know to all the workplace respectively. A minority of 15.38 per cent of the respondents suggested that, it was not only the discrimination and isolation, but also, the loss of reputation in the workplace and society as the reason for non-disclosure.

Discrimination by Co-workers

In the present study, the employed respondents faced much discrimination in their earlier workplaces like labelling, avoidance, isolation...etc. In the present employment context, only 51.28 per cent of respondents revealed their sero status too few in the organization. Among them 40 per cent of respondents faced discriminations from the co-workers very often. While 30 per cent of the respondents that they had faced no discriminations from the colleagues, as their serostatus was closely safeguarded within the micro-friendship relation. Another 30 per cent respondents felt discriminatory attitudes from the co-workers often, as their zero status condition was leaked from his/her close friend circle to few other co-workers. That is some close friends were ready to accept the PLWHA as they are, but if a wider group knows it, they cannot accept the reality of his/her HIV-positive status. Discrimination by co-workers towards PLWHA in India is also studied by Bharat (2001) and suggested that this discrimination was the reasons for loss of job to the majority.

Restrictions in Movement

Restrictions in movement were primarily affected persons whose HIV-status some or all in the workplace knew. Restrictions were made mainly by management, they by co-workers. Among the respondents, whose status was an open issue 65 per cent of them experienced restrictions in movement. Most of them often confined themselves in the room/place allotted for them. They were not allowed to enter the common areas like canteen, recreation room, and were not allowed to use common latrine. In few cases one latrine allotted to these respondents, if they were using it, they had to clean it; the cleaners were reluctant to enter these latrines.

Conclusion

Employment and workplace is not an area of HIV-transmission. Still the supposed risk of transmission has been used to perpetuate discrimination and thereby inequality with respect to PLWHA. The structural manifestation of HIV/AIDS-related Stigma and Discrimination is mainly occurred as the discrimination by the management and co-workers. The management instructed mandatory testing for HIV/AIDS as a requirement for the recruitment or during employment. The positive test result often forced PLWHA to terminate their job. And if allowed to continue there, they were imposed by many restrictions. The authority forcefully withdrew Health

Insurance policies of some respondents. The management was not ready to absolve the reality of zero positive status of PLWHA. Instead, they focused only the upward growth of the company and for that, PLWHA seemed to be an impediment.

REFERENCES

Bezmalinovic, B (1996). The Private Sector, how are the corporations responding to HIV/AIDS? In: *AIDS in the World II*, ed. J. Mann and D.J.M. Tarantola, New York, Oxford University Press.

Bharat, S (1996). *Facing the Challenge: household and community response to HIV/AIDS in Mumbai, India*, Geneva, UNAIDS/Mumbai, TISS.

Bharat, S with P. J. Aggleton and P. Tyrer (2001). *India: HIV and AIDS-related Discrimination, Stigmatization and Denial.* UNAIDS Best Practice Collection.

KSACS, Report, 2003. From the office of Kerala AIDS Control Society, Thiruvananthapuram.

Karuppiah, A (2002). *Society and AIDS—A Sociological Study on HIV/AIDS patients*, Tamil Nadu State AIDS Control Society.

National AIDS Control Organization, *Country Scenario, 2001*, www.naco.nic.in

Parker, R (2000). *Administering the epidemic: HIV/AIDS policy, models of development and international health in the late-twentieth century, in Globalization, Health and Identity*. The Fallacy of the Level Playing Field, ed L.M. Whiteford and L. Manderson. Boulder, Co: Lynne Rienner Publishing.

16
CHAPTER

Social Exclusion of Physically Challenged People

Dr. A. Joseph Xavier
Assistant Professor, Department of Commerce, Ayya Nadar Janaki Ammal College, Sivakasi

M. Kaladevi
Research Scholar in Commerce, Department of Commerce, Ayya Nadar Janaki Ammal College, Sivakasi

People are excluded when they are not part of the networks which support most people in ordinary life - networks of family, friends, community and employment. Among many others, poor people, ex-prisoners, homeless people, people with AIDS, people with learning disabilities or psychiatric patients might all be said to be at risk of exclusion. This is a very broad concept: it includes not only deprivation, but problems of social relationships, including stigma, social isolation and failures in social protection.

In practice, the idea of exclusion is mainly used in three contexts. The first is financial: exclusion is identified with poverty, and its effect on a person's ability to participate in normal activities. The second is exclusion from the labour market: exclusion is strongly identified with long-term unemployment (though there is some research evidence to question whether long-term unemployed people are really excluded). Third, there is exclusion in its social sense, which identifies exclusion partly with alienation from social networks, and partly with the circumstances of stigmatised groups.

The idea of social exclusion comes from France, where it was the basis for a policy of 'insertion' or social inclusion, combining benefits with plans and agreements to integrate people into society. This policy has been widely imitated, and the idea of exclusion has become one of the main concepts in the European Union.

CAUSES FOR SOCIAL EXCLUSION

Unemployment

The causes of unemployment are complex. Some kinds are long term: technical unemployment happens when people's skills are made redundant. Some are medium term: cyclical unemployment happens because there is inadequate demand to keep production going. Some are short term: frictional unemployment happens because people change jobs or locations. Seasonal work, casual employment and subemployment are patterns of work which lead to people being employed only for short periods at a time.

Exclusion from the labour market takes many forms: some people can opt for early retirement, further education or domestic responsibility, and others cannot. If poor people are unemployed more, it is not just because they are more marginal in the labour market; it is also because they have fewer choices, and because people who become classified as 'unemployed' are more likely to be poor. The unemployment figures are an artefact; economic analyses which are based solely on the formal 'unemployment rate' are generally misconceived.

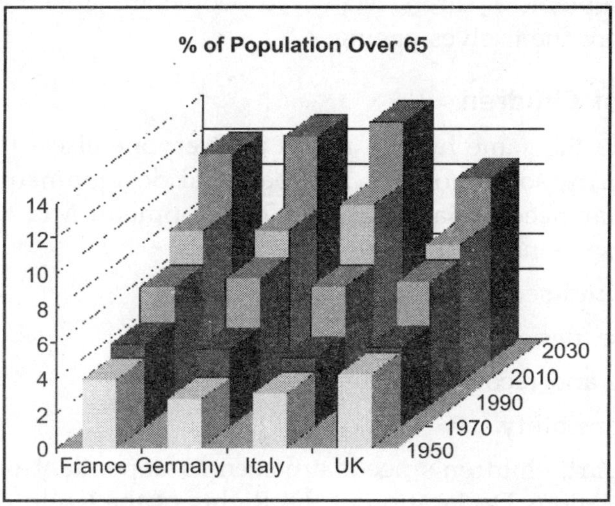

Old Age

There are increasing numbers of elderly people throughout the developed world. Many have no problems, but there is a risk of increasing dependency. The main reasons for dependency are:

(a) *Sickness:* The health of old people is often poor, not simply because of old age, but also because diet, housing, occupation and lifestyle in previous times have not been conducive to good health.

(b) *Physical disability:* At least a third of people over 75, probably more, can be classified as 'disabled'. The single most common cause of disability seems to be arthritis; the main single reason for ill-health is probably smoking.

(c) *Mental impairment:* Dementia is believed to affect about 5% of the elderly population.

(d) *Poverty:* Poverty is, for some, the result of an extended period on low incomes; for others, simply a continuation of previous circumstances.

In general, the older a person is, the more likely these problems are to occur.

Other problems may include:

- isolation, as friends and families die or move away.
- bereavement, when spouses die.
- housing: old people often live in older housing, which may be deteriorating.
- the problems of carers. Many old people are looked after by women who are themselves ageing.

The Needs of Children

Children have the same human needs as everyone else - for example, for material security, social contact, and personal development. But they also have particular needs related to their development. Mia Kellmer Pringle identifies these as needs for:

- Love and security;
- New experiences;
- Praise and recognition; and
- Responsibility.

In large part, children's needs are seen as dependent on their parents. The United Nations Declaration of the Rights of the Child declares:

'The child, for the full and harmonious development of his personality, needs love and understanding. He shall, wherever possible, grow up in the care and under the responsibility of his parents, and in any case in an atmosphere of affection and of moral and material security.

The needs of children are treated as a social issue when families fail to meet them - either because the family is unable to make provision (education and child poverty) or because the family itself is a source of problems (neglect and abuse).

Mental Illness

'Mental illness' is a broad term covering a range of conditions. The most important are:

- *Functional psychoses*, mainly schizophrenia and manic depression. Schizophrenia is itself a set of conditions rather than a single illness. It is characterised by a complex of symptoms including, e.g., a clouding of consciousness, disconnected speech and thought, variations of mood, feelings that one is being externally controlled, or hallucinations (which can be auditory, visual or tactile).
- *Manic depression leads* to severe and sometimes prolonged extremes of mood: in 'manic' phases, constantly active and extrovert; in depressed state, withdrawn and negative. Drug therapy can be used against the cycle.
- *Organic psychoses*, caused by infections, drugs, metabolic distur-bances, or brain traumas.
- ***Neuroses***, including anxiety states, phobias, obsession states, hysteria, and some depressions.
- *'Behavioural' disorders*. These are not true 'illnesses'. Probably the most important is psychopathy, which is characterised mainly by a lack of social awareness, consideration, or conscience towards others.

Mental illness can be seen as primarily a medical or physiological condition; however, because it is identified through the behaviour of the mentally ill person, it can also be seen as social. 'Anti-psychiatrists' have argued that conditions like schizophrenia and depression are best understood and responded to in social terms.

Services for Psychiatric Patients

The main thing psychiatric patients have had in common is not mental illness -their needs differ greatly - but their experience of psychiatric treatment. For many years, mental illness led to prolonged hospitalisation, often in antiquated institutions intended to isolate 'mad' people from the community. The main reasons for this movement have been

- The 'drug revolution' of the 1950s, which has made treatment possible outside hospitals;
- Disillusion with the role played by large institutions; and
- Substantial increases in the relative cost of institutional care.

The trend to 'community care' should mean, in principle, that psychiatric patients are re-integrated into the community rather than isolated. The essential services include:

- Community psychiatric support, to enable continued health care and medication;
- Social support, to counter the problems of social exclusion associated with mental illness;
- Accommodation, including access to ordinary housing, and the provision of a range of supportive residential units, including half-way houses, staffed group homes; and
- Access to income and employment opportunities.

There has been a trend to favour shorter-term psychiatric care in general hospitals, and the use of the older hospitals has been changing, for example as a base for psychiatric services rather than a closed institution.

Learning Disability

'Learning disability' refers to a state of delayed intellectual development. In the U.S. used to be called "mental retardation", and now is called 'intellectual disability; in Australia it is 'intellectual handicap'. Although it is associated with other conditions - a high proportion of people with severe learning disabilities are also severely physically handicapped - most has no physical or organic origin. (Down's syndrome, probably the best known cause, accounts for only about one sixth of all cases.) As people with learning disabilities grow older, they often become sufficiently competent to function in society.

Because many people have learning disabilities from early childhood, the problems have tended to be constructed in terms of aid to families. In practice, the main support for most people with learning disabilities comes, not from the state or even from voluntary organisations, but from families (and in particular women in the families). The effect of services is mainly to supplement the care given by the family.

Normalisation

Learning disability has always been socially rejected. In the late 19th century, mental deficiencies were seen as evidence of 'degeneracy' and blamed for poverty, madness and crime. Degenerates had to be isolated from the community, which led to the incarceration of 'idiots', 'feeble minded' and 'moral defectives' in large, isolated mental institutions. Wolfensberger argues that many of the problems of the institutions stem from a design and organisation intended to deal with residents as if they were animals: primitive, uncontrolled, ineducable, unfeeling and dirty. This may seem exaggerated, but the view it represents is supported by a long line of scandals in mental institutions in different countries.

The principle of normalisation was developed as a reaction to these dehumanizing policies. There are several different formulations, including:

- promoting independence and autonomy;
- making it possible for people with learning disabilities to have an ordinary life;
- giving people with learning disabilities the same choices and opportunities as everyone else; and
- accepting and valuing what people with learning disabilities can do.

Normalisation was a key element in movements both for education and for empowerment.

Physical Disability

Physical disability is not one problem, but a wide range of problems of different kinds. It includes people who have lost limbs, who are blind or deaf, who have difficulty moving or walking, who are unable to sustain physical effort for any length of time, and so on. The treatment of disability as if it was a single problem may mean that disabled people receive insufficient or inappropriate assistance. The problems that disabled people have in common are not so much their physical capacities, which are often very different, but limitations on their life style. Income tends to be low, while disabled people may have special needs to be met. Socially, disabled people may become isolated, as health declines, they struggle to manage on the resources they have, and they may be socially excluded.

Physically Challenged People

The World Health Organization identifies three elements in disability: problems in bodily function or structure, which they used to call 'impairment'; problems relating to activities, or 'disability'; and problems related to social participation, which they called 'handicap'. Some groups of people with disabilities have objected to the idea of 'handicap' and prefer to talk of a social model of disability, understanding disability in terms of the social norms and expectations which shape the experience of people with disabilities.

In developed societies, most disabled people are old. Policies tend to be focused on younger groups, because younger groups are politically more active, and disability in old age is seen as normal. People with a disability make up over one in ten of the working-age population.

But despite policies over the last two decades to promote employment and direct more help to those in greatest need, they remain under-represented in the workforce and over-represented among those on low incomes. This report offers detailed analysis of the position of disabled people in the labour market and in the income distribution, and how the situation has changed since the 1980s.

Part of the Work and Opportunity series, *Enduring economic exclusion* looks at:

- the economic activity of disabled people;
- transitions into work and employment retention;
- disabled people's income and expenditure;
- trends over time;
- whether Labour's policies will make a difference.

Employment Opportunities for Disable People

Consecutive governments have implemented policies designed to promote employment opportunities for disabled people and direct more resources to those in greatest need. But what impact have these policies had over the last twenty years? Tania Burchardt used nationally representative surveys to examine the past and present position of disabled people of working age in the income distribution and the labour market. The study found:

- Disabled people make up a large and growing proportion of the working-age population: between 12 and 16 per cent, depending on the definition used.
- Employment rates among disabled people are low, at around 40 per cent, and have remained stable. In 1999, disabled people made up half of all those who were not employed but said they would like to work, and one-third of those who were available to start in a fortnight.
- Of those who become disabled while in work, one in six lose their employment during the first year after becoming disabled. By implication, improving retention could make a substantial difference to overall rates of employment among disabled people.
- Getting work is more difficult for disabled than non-disabled jobseekers, and one-third of disabled people who do find work are out of a job again by the following year.
- Half of all disabled people have incomes below half the general population mean (often taken as an indicator of poverty), after making an adjustment for extra costs. Even without adjustment, two in five are found to be in poverty - an increase of one-sixth since 1985.
- The researcher concludes that many of the factors behind economic exclusion for disabled people - such as low educational qualifications

- are common to other groups in society. Inclusion will not be achieved until both the impairment-specific and more general barriers to participation are dismantled.

The Labour Government has committed itself to on-going implementation of the Disability Discrimination Act, and to applying the welfare reform principle, "work for those who can, security for those who cannot", to disabled people. Disability policy under previous administrations has had similar objectives; this study set out to examine what the impact has been on disabled people's employment and standard of living, and what the prospects are for the future.

Definitions of disability used in the research were largely determined by the data sources. Estimates of the proportion of the working-age population who are disabled vary from 12 per cent (OPCS definition) to 16 per cent (work-limiting disability), and all sources indicate the proportion is growing. The OPCS definition uses a scale of severity from 1 to 10. Broader definitions of disability make problems seem more widespread but tend to understate the barriers faced by those who are more severely impaired.

Disabled People's Employment

Participation of both disabled and non-disabled women in the labour market has grown since 1985, while for men, employment rates have been static. Overall, disabled employment rates have fluctuated around 40 per cent, about half the level of non-disabled employment.

- In 1999, disabled people made up *half* of those who were not employed but said they would like to work, and one-third of those who were available to start in a fortnight.
- Employed disabled people are disproportionately likely to be in manual occupations and they have lower average hourly earnings than their non-disabled peers - even after taking account of differences in age, education and occupation. This earnings gap appears to have grown substantially since 1985.

Characteristics associated with a greater likelihood of being in employment are similar for disabled and non-disabled people - for example, good educational qualifications - but a smaller proportion of disabled people have these characteristics. In addition, there are barriers relating specifically to impairment, particularly for those with mental health problems or a locomotion impairment.

Movements in and Out of Work

The disadvantage experienced by disabled people is also apparent in movements into and out of work. Employment rates for both disabled and non-disabled people vary with the economic cycle, but are more volatile for disabled people. Analysis of individual movements into and out of work was based on small samples, so results should be treated with caution, but it suggested:

- Each year, around three per cent of those in work become 'limited in daily activities', of whom about half also report disability the following or a subsequent year. Of these, one in six lose their employment in the first year after becoming disabled.
- The proportion of unemployed non-disabled people who get work is around six times the proportion of disabled people who do so. Even after allowing for the fact that some disabled people cannot, or do not wish to, move into employment, the proportion of non-disabled people likely to get work is still four times that of disabled people.
- One-third of disabled people who get work are already out of work again by the following year, compared with one-fifth of non-disabled people starting work.

Personal and job characteristics associated with better chances of retaining or getting employment are similar to those identified by research on other marginalised groups, but the differentials - for example between manual and non-manual occupations, or areas of high and low employment - are in many cases sharper for disabled people.

Disabled People and Poverty

Many disabled people incur additional expenditure as a result of their impairment. Specific benefits (such as Disability Living Allowance) are designed to help with these costs. Additional tiers of benefit have reached further down the severity scale, although take-up remains low. Around one-half of extra costs for those with impairments in severity categories 7 or 8 may now be covered by these benefits, up from one-third in 1985. This has contributed to a substantial reduction in the proportion of disabled people in the bottom tenth of the income distribution.

Despite these improvements, and real absolute income gains across all severity categories, disabled people remain poor relative to the general population (see Figure 16.1).

- Greater severity of impairment is generally associated with lower income. The exception are those in the top two severity categories, a greater proportion of whom receive benefits to help towards extra costs. However, the average income of this group has fallen relative to the general population since 1985.

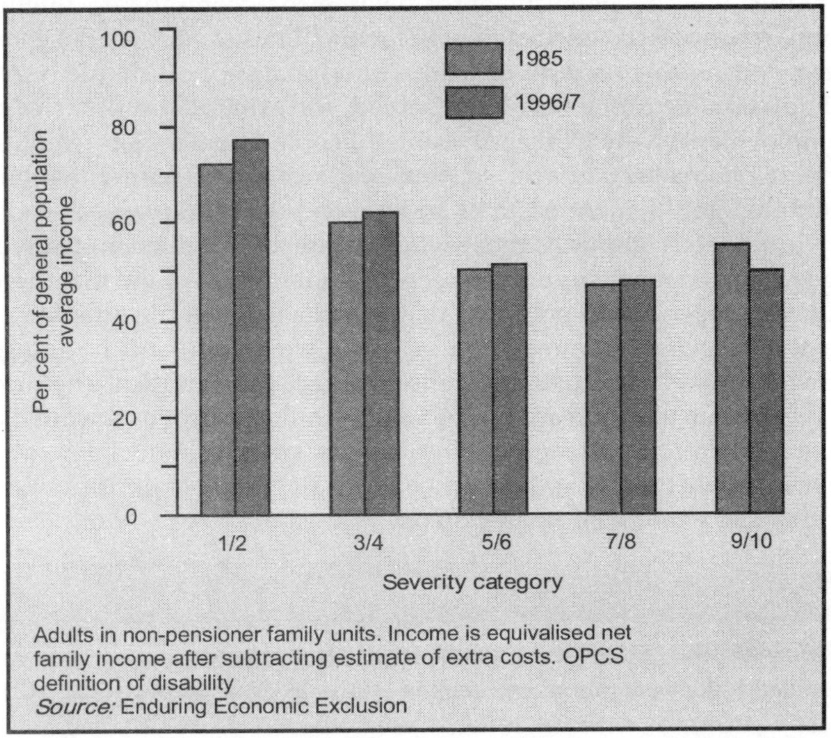

Fig. 16.1 : Disabled People's Average Income, Taking Account of Extra Costs

- Overall, half of all disabled people have incomes below half the general population mean (often taken as an indicator of poverty), after making an adjustment for extra costs. Disabled adults in families with children are even more likely to be in poverty: 60 per cent, by this measure.

Positive developments have not been sufficient to counter broader trends towards inequality, both within the disabled population and in society as a whole, fuelled by:

- growing earnings differentials for those in work;
- concentration of work in fewer households;
- widening gap between incomes in and out of work, as benefits are linked to prices rather than earnings.

By 1996/7, disabled people accounted for between one in five and one in six of the working-age population on low income (defined as below half population average).

Conclusions

Firstly, insufficient attention has been paid to transitions, between employment and non-employment, and between being non-disabled and being disabled.

Benefit rules need to be sufficiently flexible to accommodate fluctuating conditions (particularly associated with mental illness and some degenerative diseases), and varying patterns of work. Additional support should be offered to individuals when they become disabled, for example, in order to retain their employment. New Deal for Disabled People pilots on job retention are welcome in this respect, but the schemes will need to recognise that barriers to continuing employment occur at and beyond the workplace, as well as at an individual level. Similarly, those who are already disabled and succeed in getting work need more support in keeping their jobs. Keeping that discourse in mind, it is important to point out that in India's development efforts there has been no coherent appreciation of social exclusion, and no integrated approach to combat exclusion, despite the fact that political rhetoric and policy documents take into account women, ethnic groups, backward classes, scheduled castes and scheduled tribes. Issues such as civil rights, poverty, untouchability, inequality and basic needs are all related to exclusion in some ay but this fact is not well appreciated.

REFERENCES

B S Rowntree, 1901, *Poverty : A Study of Town Life*, Longman.

D Piachaud, 1981, *Peter Townsend and the Holy Grail, New Society* (Sept.) 421.

J Bradshaw, 1972, *A Taxonomy of Social Need*, New Society (March) 640-3.

SECTION–IV

Exclusion of Women and Children

17
CHAPTER

Exclusion of Women and Children

S. Rasheedha Begum
M. Phil Scholar, G.T.N. Arts College, Dindigul-5

Jeyalakshmi
Associate Professor, G.T.N. Arts College, Dindigul-5

Introduction

The state of affairs in India with regards to "inequality, power and social exclusion" is somewhat paradoxical. On the one hand, since its independence India has demonstrated a longstanding political willingness to recognize different forms of inequality and exclusion and to use constitutional and legislative measures to address them. On the other hand, there continue to be large disparities in poverty levels, mortality rates, educational attainments and access to resources between regions, social groups and the sexes. India today remains a country of stark contrasts and striking disparities. Some states and districts of India report levels of social development similar to leading industrialised countries. Other parts of India report achievement levels that are worse than the average of the poorest countries in the world. In this brief we will look at exclusion of women and children. The women varied in age, ethnic and racial background, family situation and gender roles, ability and disability, and sexual orientation. Women spoke persistently about social isolation as a central experience of living in poverty. They understood isolation to be a consequence of overlapping life situations, including material scarcity and discrimination, gender roles and responsibilities, health, disability and impairments, and immigration. In contrast, academic, political, and public discussions often frame isolation as individual experiences of loneliness and disconnection without investigating the broader systemic processes that shape women's isolation (Findlay, 2003; Fioto, 2002; Havens, 2004)

Experiences of Social Isolation

Being poor: Material scarcity and discrimination Women named material scarcity as a major reason for isolation. One woman said "it [living in poverty] puts limits on what you can do basically. There's not many things to do for free and you just have to sit there and think of what you can do. It's lonely too because when you don't have the extra money to spend to go out with friends then a lot of times you're stuck at home by yourself."

Many women felt their material deprivation led to a loss of self-esteem and increased stress and depression. These feelings in turn increased the possibility of social isolation. One woman explained that she felt "ostracized because I never had any money, and can't go out." For a younger single mother, isolation arose directly from the lack of funds and the resulting pressure: "I don't have friends, so therefore I don't have anyone who can baby sit for me. So therefore, I don't get to go out. I don't have money for recreation, so I don't get to go out the social isolation comes from the financial situation and the stress that goes along with that." Material scarcity isolated the women because they could not afford to go out and because resulting stress, depression, and low self-esteem meant they did not want to leave their homes. A new country, culture, and language Many women cited life in a new country as a source of social isolation.

Addressing Women's Social Isolation, Exclusion and Poverty

Women's multi-faceted experience of poverty and exclusion requires multiple and complimentary approaches to policy and program change. WOAW helped develop strategies for combating poor women's exclusion. Since those living in poverty could not afford community recreation programs, activities were organized at very low or no cost. Community centre recreation staff involved in WOAW became aware of how policies that required applicants for a recreation subsidy to prove poverty discouraged and humiliated, to the point of exclusion, poor women.

Women in South Asia are the most excluded and discriminated segment of the population. Patriarchy is at the core of the structural element in discriminating women. Patriarchy constrains women in all facets of life. Control of women's reproductive abilities and sexuality is placed in men's hands. Patriarchy limits women's ownership and control of property and other economic resources, including the products of their own labour. Women's mobility is constrained, and their access to education and information hindered. Over the years, it has been recognized that the experiences of the majority of women are grounded in both poverty and patriarchy. Both these feed into each other and subject women to exclusion and exploitation. Over the past three decades, theorists, practitioners and activists involved in both women's movements and women's studies around the world have also focused on the attitudinal underpinnings in the relationship between men and women.

Perceptions about men and women

Women	Men
Submissive	Ambitious
Sensitive	Rational
Gentle	Courageous
Emotional	Strong
Weak	Decisive
Sexy	Analytical
Nurturing	Manipulative
Jealous	Bold
Humble	Goal-oriented
Patient	Eloquent

The very perception of women by men is an indication of the exclusion and discrimination they are subjected to. In these ways, patriarchal structures perpetuate the enduring gaps between the opportunities available to South Asian women and South Asian men. Along with the mindset if one pays attention to the structural exclusion of women then one understands the outcome of exclusion of women in India.

Mass media is perhaps the most powerful tool in the world for creating, changing or perpetuating society's ideas about an issue or group of people. It works both overtly and subconsciously: deciding which issues are important, how to frame those issues, who to show as affected by them, and, increasingly, providing personal commentaries on the matters at hand. Because the majority of media outlets are owned by corporations dominated by white heterosexual men, many minorities are portrayed in ways that perpetuate negative stereotypes – if they are portrayed at all. Even though women have made great strides towards equality, they continue to experience both misrepresentation and under representation in the modern media.

The most significant phenomena of excluding women from their legal and economic rights: the exclusion of women inventors from intellectual property rights Property rights are subject to feminist criticism. On the one hand, patent law aims at assisting in the advancement of science, industry and technology, as a goal agreed upon by public opinion, the state, male and female inventors and by employers and by the employees. However, observing this rationale through feminist lenses reveals the severe phenomenon of the exclusion of women from the patent-field. Upon superficial observation, it would appear that the patent law seems objective and neutral. The reality, however, is different.

The Social Exclusion of Children

Europeans talk differently than Americans do about disadvantaged and vulnerable children and their governments feel an obligation to do more. A currently favored concept, "social exclusion," has become increasingly popular in policy discussions in Europe, Latin America, and Canada. Should we in the U.S. adopt the concept as the Congress, the White House, and social welfare service systems plan for the future? Would it enrich our child and family policy debates? A recently released Columbia University report explores these questions and concludes that while specifics need to be worked out and negotiated, it is urgent and timely to take the child policy discussion "beyond poverty," if we are to improve the situation of American children. As the report states, "Clearly, those engaged in the debate are not satisfied with what we now do. Our 1996 Welfare Reform chose "dependency" as its main target (how much would caseloads fall?)" As we write, there are those who want to adopt poverty reduction as the primary TANF target in the reauthorization legislation while others want to focus on marriage; and there is also comprehensive legislation in the Congress initiated by the liberal Children's Defense Fund, which would "leave no child behind." President George W. Bush borrowed the very same phrase but for a more limited education package which was enacted. What does all of this mean? Are we ready for "social exclusion" or some other summing up of disadvantage that goes beyond poverty?

Among the reasons for exploring an alternative concept to poverty, or a supplementary concept, are: (1) the growing dissatisfaction with the limitations of the conventional measure of income poverty used in this country; and (2) the apparent limits of the poverty "frame" in rallying public will to mount the policies needed to lift families and their children out of poverty. A key characteristic of "social exclusion" is the framing of the issue as social and community exclusion, rather than individual and personal culpability. It's increasingly distinguished from financial poverty and focused rather on constricted access to civil, political, and social rights and opportunities. Social exclusion is particularly devastating for children because if encountered when very young, it closes children out of the experiences they need to start right - access to health care and to preschool education

There are perfectly healthy children who enter school not yet toilet-trained. Children who cannot dress themselves, children who only know how to eat with a spoon, and have never sat around a table to enjoy a home-cooked family meal.

With 2.9 million children still living in poverty, despite the brave pledge of 1999 to have halved child poverty levels of 3.4 million by 2010, this is like so much about the now old New Labour, grimly predictable.

Amartya Sen criticized income centered understandings of poverty as incomplete. Though education is vital in securing higher later earnings he forcefully argues that it should also be considered constitutive of development, itself part ending poverty. Surely the same impulse that drove New Labour to re-imagine poverty into a relative concept concerned with social inclusion must drive it still further. A little girl unable to use a knife and fork is socially excluded. And though this may be because her parents have no time to spend with her because they are too busy struggling to make ends meet ,the exclusion consists in the fact that she can only use a spoon as well as the fact of living in a low income household. Raising income is clearly one of the most effective ways of lowering poverty, yet poorness is only part of poverty. Ward for example talks with horror of a new "poverty of aspiration".

Poverty should be re-imagined in terms of the capabilities necessary for social inclusion: to dress yourself and use a fork, to think critically and have loving relationships, to control your bladder. This is not to deny the vital role of income as a tool in poverty reduction, but simply to challenge the lack of inspiration that allowed our means to masquerade as our ends. Every act of imagination is rebellious. The truly radical understanding of poverty as social exclusion adopted by New Labour demands further change, that social exclusion be broadened beyond income as poverty was broadened into a relative concept. Nothing short of rebellion is required to resurrect Labour as a worthy electoral contender, one able to meaningfully end child poverty.

Negative Effects of Exclusion on Women

The exclusion of women may marginalize women from such valuable assets as: physical assets such as irrigation water or forest products; and human assets, such as training, credit or other benefits earmarked only for the group or organization members.

Exclusion of women from irrigation system Water User Associations (WUAs) illustrates this point. Women's participation in WUAs and the associated access to irrigation assets is always lower than men's, and where it does exist, tends to be direct, irregular, partial or decreasing over time. There are numerous examples of this from Sri Lanka, India, Pakistan, Nepal, Albania, Armenia, Mali, the Dominican Republic and many other countries. Even women heads of farming households are often excluded. Exclusion creates disadvantages for women engaged in market-oriented production of crops such as vegetables and paddy. Exclusion can also eliminate women from domestic uses of irrigation water, which would save them time and effort. In addition, some WUAs, as under an IFAD project in Armenia, receive considerable capacity-building and training in a variety of useful subjects, which are for members only.

Exclusion of women from forest management committees often results in their needs and interests in forest products being neglected. The report refers to impact of forest protection activities in Indian States of Gujarat and West Bengal. The distance that village women have to travel to collect firewood increased from as little as half a kilometer to 8-9 kilometres. The firewood collection time has increased from 1-2 hours to 4-5 hours for a head load. Wherever possible, women here are shifting to alternative fuels such as agricultural wastes, dung cakes and twigs. The report notes that the negative impact on women had more to do with women's "lack of voice and bargaining power" in the village protection committee than with availability *per se*.

Hope for Change

Development programme have experienced some success in including women in organizations for natural resource management. But it requires considerable effort and, sometimes, prolonged negotiation with village leaders, as evidenced by an IFAD irrigation project in Ghana and another in Mali. Reserving a certain number of memberships for women can result in a purely ceremonial role for women members. Women tend to be silent at WUA meetings or at forest management meetings (as in Nepal), and are rarely elected to leadership positions. But they can become more active over time. Even in the Joint Forest Management committees in Madhya Pradesh, some men are now viewing women's role as useful, seeing it as ensuring women's cooperation in forest protection efforts and as representing women's needs in the committee. Difficulties of integrating women into village organizations that manage natural resources has led some programme to establish women-only organizations,, such as women's forest management committees. Elsewhere, programmes are setting ambitious targets for integrating women into mixed-gender organizations. In both cases, women's workload needs to be kept in mind, particularly when membership brings with it time-consuming tasks and responsibilities.

In a world where approximately 113 million children are not enrolled in primary school (DFID, 2001); Lewin (2000) highlights the potential for education to reverse the negative effects of social exclusion. There are an estimated 25 million children out of school in India (MHRD 2003 statistics, cited in World Bank, 2004), many of whom are marginalised by dimensions such as poverty, gender, disability, and caste. While many educational programme have attempted to reach out to these previously excluded children, those with disabilities are often forgotten, emphasising their invisible status in a rigidly categorised society.

Conclusion

To conclude women and children are considered as most important asset of our country, they should not be excluded from the society, family, schools. Government must take essential steps to include them in all types of societal works. Todays children are considered as tomorrow's leader, so they must be given good education without any barriers. Child labour should be completely abolished. Poverty should also be eradicated. The rich must help the poor otherwise the rich become rich and the poor being the poor won't bring the country in good position, this scenario must change. Women should be given equal rights in all the fields they should not be excluded for any reason. Today they are ready and capable of taking any kind of challenges, then why should they be excluded? All the measures are taken by the government to include both women and children in the society; if we join hands with the government definitely by 2020 none of them will be socially excluded.

18

CHAPTER

Social Exclusion of Women in Unorganised Sector

A Study Based of Kerala

Jessy, K.C.
Research Scholar Deptt. of Rural Development, GRI

Mrinalini
Research Scholar, Deptt. of Sociology, GR, Gandhigram

Introduction

Social exclusion is a multi-dimensional process of progressive social rupture, detaching groups and individuals from social relations and institutions and preventing them from full participation in the normal, normatively prescribed activities of the society in which they live. Social exclusion is evident in deprived communities; it is harder for people to engage fully in society. In such communities, weak social networking limits the circulation about information about jobs, political activities, and community events. But many social workers believe that exclusion in the countryside is as great as, if not greater than, that in cities. In rural areas there is less access to goods, services and facilities, making life difficult in many respects. Social exclusion is a powerful form of discriminatory practice. In course of human development, exclusion has taken the form of segregating a group of people from the social, political, economic, cultural, educational and religious domains of societal life. Thus, social seclusion provides base for a sense of superiority and inferiority among the members of the same society or culture. Further, it also culminates into a system of domination and subjugation. All these processes ultimately lead to oppression and exploitation.

Exclusion: A Conceptual Framework

Like many social concepts, social exclusion also has evaded a neat definition. But some defining features of this social reality could be presented. According to Arjan, the concept has two main defining characteristics. First, it is a multi-dimensional concept. People may be excluded, e.g., from livelihoods, employment, earnings, property, housing, minimum consumption, education, the welfare state, citizenship, personal contacts or respect, etc. But the concept focuses on the multidimensionality of deprivation, on the fact that people are often deprived of different things at the same time. It refers to exclusion (deprivation) in the economic, social and political sphere:

1. Exclusion is the denial of ownership, access and control over resources.
2. Exclusion is the denial of right over ones labour and right over ones reproductive resources.
3. Exclusion is the denial of opportunity for education, health care, housing, public amenities, recreational facilities and spaces, basic needs etc.
4. Exclusion is the denial of social interaction and denial of access to social spaces.
5. Exclusion is the denial of right to representation and participation in social, economic, political and cultural aspects of society and polity.
6. Exclusion is the deprivation of the right to mobility, right to practice ones religion and the right to organize and mobilize.
7. Exclusion is the denial of human dignity.
8. Finally, exclusion is the denial of constitutional and human rights.

Social Exclusion: A Theoretical Framework

Various forms of exclusion, deprivation and discrimination are perceived to be and propagated to be a normal course of behaviour in most societies. But it is being realized by the social scientists, social activists and human rights activists that social exclusion is a framework for understanding deprivation, marginalisation, exploitation and oppression. Since this is a framework for analysis of the process and outcome of discrimination and deprivation, social exclusion is not a term to refer to any specific social group.

Social exclusion is the process and outcome of excluding, casting out, depriving and denying equal space to some of the citizens of a country or members of a society. This is denial of space in all senses and in all sectors; Social exclusion is closely associated with relative deprivation. In this regard it has been stated that the rising inequality in various countries has contributed to the exclusion of many social groups from opportunities; Social exclusion also has come to be seen as denial of capabilities and entitlements. social exclusion discriminates and deprives members of ones own society and nation there is lack of scope and space for solidarity among the members. Further, even among those who are poor or victimized in one way or the other, they do not come together to address the issue since they are divided due to social exclusion. This is especially true of those societies which are hierarchical, skewed and ascribe membership to people based on their origin and descent; Since social exclusion denies social integration and solidarity, the social interaction which emerges in an excluding society is conflictual in nature. Thus, conflict becomes mainstay of social interaction.

Excluded People

In the Indian context, the following are the excluded persons:

- *Social Groups:* Dalits/untouchables/lower castes, Tribals/Adivasis/Indigenous Peoples, religious and linguistic minorities, the most backward castes, especially women and children among these social groups.
- *Sectoral Groups:* Agricultural labourers, marginalized farmers, child labourers, domestic workers, informal workers/unorganized sector workers, contract workers, plantation workers, fisher communities, manual scavengers, rural and forest based.

Extent of the Unorganized Workers

Indian economy is characterized by the existence of high level of informal or unorganized labour employment. The workers in the organized sector constitute about seven per cent of the country's total work force and the rest (93 per cent) comprises of subsistence farmers, agricultural workers, fisher folk, dairy workers and those working in traditional manufacturing like handlooms are grouped under unorganized sector.

The term 'unorganized labour' has been defined as those workers who have not been able to organize themselves to pursuit of their common interests due to certain constraints like casual nature of employment, ignorance and illiteracy, small and scattered size of establishments, etc. Ministry of Labour has categorised the unorganised labour force under four groups in terms of occupation, nature of employment, specially distressed categories and service categories. In terms of occupation, it included small and marginal farmers, landless agricultural labourers, share croppers, fishermen and those engaged in animal husbandry, beedi rolling, labeling and packing, building and construction workers, leather workers, weavers, artisans, salt workers, workers in brick kilns and stone quarries, workers in saw mills, oil mills etc. In terms of nature of employment, they are attached agricultural labourers, bonded labourers, migrant workers, contract and casual labourers. Toddy tappers, scavengers, carriers of head loads, drivers of animal driven vehicles, loaders and unloaders, belong to the especially distressed category while midwives, domestic workers, fishermen and women, barbers, vegetable and fruit vendors, newspaper vendors etc. come under the service category. In addition to the above categories, there exists a large section of unorganized labour force such as cobblers, hamals, handicraft artisans, handloom weavers, lady tailors, physically handicapped self-employed persons, rikshaw pullers/ auto drivers, sericulture workers, carpenters, leather and tannery workers, power loom workers and urban poor.

The extent of unorganised workers is significantly high among agricultural workers, building and other construction workers, and among home based workers. But, the availability of statistical information on its intensity and accuracy vary significantly. Agricultural workers constitute the largest segment of workers in the unorganised sector.

According to the NSSO estimates for the year 2004-05, 52 per cent of the total workers are found in agriculture (*Economic Survey: 2007-08*). Many small and marginal farmers, because of their small and uneconomical holdings and low yield, also work on the land of others and hence qualify as agricultural labourers. Further a significant number, are engaged in rearing livestock, forestry, fishery, orchard and allied activities. Construction workers constitute the second largest category of workers in the unorganized sector.

According to the NSSO estimates, about 5.57 percentages of workers are engaged in building and other construction works in 2004-05 (*Economic Survey: 2007-08*). The construction industry covers a vast field of activity in the civil, mechanical, electrical and public health area processes. A large number of multinational, national and local companies employ lakhs of such workers. Moreover, a large number of self employed individuals are engaged in actual construction works and allied activities like white washing, painting, plumbing and fixing of mechanical or electrical fixtures etc.

Home-based Workers are those who are engaged in the production of goods or services for an employed or contractor in an arrangement whereby the work is carried out at the place of the worker's own choice, often the worker's own home. In India, there is no authentic data on home based workers. Official data sources such as Census of India do not recognise these workers as an independent category but have included them in the broad category of those working in house-hold industries. Home based workers are mainly engaged in beedi rolling, garment making, agarbati making, gem cutting, preparation of food items like papad, pickle, etc., handloom, lace and chikan work etc. The beedi rolling industry, which is generally family based, employs about 45 lakh workers out of which 90 per cent are home based workers. The major characteristics of unorganised workers could be listed as below:

1. The unorganized labour is overwhelming in terms of its number range and therefore, they are omnipresent throughout India.
2. As the unorganized sector suffers from cycles of excessive seasonality of employment.
3. Majority of the unorganized workers does not have stable and durable avenues of employment. Even those who appear to be visibly employed are not gainfully and substantially employed, indicating the existence of disguised unemployment.
4. The workplace is scattered and fragmented. The workers do the same kind of job(s) in different habitations and may not work and live together in compact geographical areas.
5. There is no formal employer-employee relationship between small and marginal farmers, share croppers and agricultural labourers as they work together in situations which may be marginally favourable to one category but may be broadly described as identical.
6. In rural areas, the unorganized labour force is highly stratified on caste and community considerations. In urban areas while such considerations are much less, it cannot be said that it is altogether absent as the bulk of the unorganized workers in urban areas are basically migrant workers from rural areas.
7. Workers in the unorganized sector are usually subject to a lot of fads, taboos, and outmoded social customs like child marriage, excessive spending on ceremonial festivities etc. which lead to indebtedness and bondage.
8. The unorganized workers are subject to exploitation significantly by the rest of the society.
9. The unorganized workers receive poor working conditions; especially wages much below that in the formal sector, even for closely comparable jobs i.e., where labour productivity are no different. The work status is of inferior quality of work and inferior terms of employment, both remuneration and employment.
10. Primitive production technologies and feudal production relations are rampant in the unorganized sector, and they do not permit or encourage the workmen to imbibe and assimilate higher technologies and better production relations. Large scale ignorance and illiteracy and limited exposure to the goings on in the outside world are also responsible for such poor absorption.
11. The unorganized workers do not receive sufficient attention from the trade unions.

12. In general, unorganized workers are observed to be large in numbers, suffering from cycles of excessive seasonality of employment, scattered and fragmented work place, poor in working conditions, and lack of attention from the trade unions.

Status of Women in Kerala

Each person occupies many different statuses. We sometime speak of the statuses or the social position of a given individual, meaning the sum total of her specific. Statuses and roles, especially in so far as they bear upon her general "social standing". The term status designate a position in the general institutional system, recognized and supported by the entire society. An example of a status in our society would be 'skilled labourer'. As defined by Secord and Bukman, "status is the worth of a person as estimated by a group or a class of persons".

Kerala's population is at 3,18, 41,374 persons which includes 1,54,68,614 males and 1,63,72,760 females. Here, the female population outnumbered males by 9 lakhs. Moreover, women constitute 51.4% of the total population of Kerala (2001). Different indicators with regard to women have shown commendable growth in the state, compared to her counterparts in other states and at the all India level her status, both economically and socially has been heads and shoulders above her counter parts elsewhere in the country. But on the other hand, despite positive trends in women development and social status, women in Kerala have been suffering on various counts.

There exists to gross mismatch between women's capabilities gained in terms of education and the opportunities that they have in terms of employment or social involvement and the aspirations they have in Kerala. This again is a paradox with regard to women development in Kerala. On the one hand, one witnesses commendable growth in different indicators of women, but on the other hand, presence of women decline sharply in the work force in the state. Studies have pointed out that, gender discrimination of labour market in terms of occupational sex-segregation contributes to the low levels of economic participation among the women in Kerala (Panda, 1996).

Economic conditions in the State have been particularly detrimental to opportunities for female employment (Eapen, 1992). Moreover, the extent of unemployment among female work seekers has been relatively much higher (Mathew: 1995). All these are indicative of the fact that there has been significant economic marginalization of women in the development process of Kerala. This difference between positive social indicators and negative economic indicators of women's role deserves special investigation. Men and women are not found equally distributed across the various types of work/employment available in the country and there is a male-female wage gap.

Table 18.1 : District-wise Sex Ratio and Work Participation Rates in Kerala – 2001

District-wise Population, Sex ratio of Kerala-2001						Work Participation Rate (%)	
District	Population	Males	Females	Sex ratio (F/M)	Female growth rate (1991-2001)	Male	Female
Thiruvananthapuram	3234356	1569917	1664439	1058	10.94	49.3	20.8
Kollam	2585208	1249621	1335587	1070	9.06	50.0	15.2
Pathanamthitta	1234016	589398	644618	1094	5.23	55.7	22.8
Alappuzha	2109160	1014529	1094631	1079	6.63	48.8	8.1
Kottayam	1953646	964926	988720	1025	7.98	42.8	6.6
Idukki	1129221	566682	562539	999	5.64	52.2	21.1
Ernakulam	3105798	1538397	1567401	1017	10.94	50.8	15.1
Thrissur	2974232	1422052	1552180	1092	8.98	55.4	17.1
Palakkad	2617482	1266985	1350497	1068	10.2	58.4	28.1
Kozhikode	2879131	1399358	1479773	1058	11.45	52.4	13.9
Wayanad	780619	391273	389346	1000	19.09	49.7	20.2
Malappuram	3625471	1754576	1870895	1063	17.76	47.6	13.2
Kannur	2408956	1152817	1256139	1090	9.11	48.5	16.7
Kasargod	1204078	588083	615995	1047	13.44	51.5	14.4
Kerala	3,18,41,374	1,54,68,614	1,63,72,760	1058	10.53	50.4	15.3

Source: Census of India, 2001

The regional variation showed that the female population topped in twelve districts with an exception in two districts viz. Idukki, Wayanad respectively. In the Idukki District men outnumber women by 4143 numbers, whereas in Waynad, only 1927 men are more than women. In Malappuram, and Kannur, more than 1-lakh women outnumber men.

Even though the share of women workers in organized sector is continuously increasing from 13.8 per cent in 1989-90 to 18.1 per cent in 2001-2002, their share is lower when compared to men's. The rest are working in the unorganized sector. In the informal sector women constitute 90 per cent of the total workers. More over unskilled workers constitute 90 per cent of rural and 70 per cent of urban women workers. In India, through there has been a slight increase in the female work participation rate from 19.7 per cent in 1981 to 25.7 per cent 2001, this is still much lower than the male work participation rate in both urban and rural areas.

Table 18.2 : Trends in Employment in Organized and Unorganized Sectors in India

(In millions)

Year	Organized	Unorganized	Total Workforce
1983	24.01 (7.93)	278.74 (92.07)	302.75
1987-1988	25.71 (7.93)	298.58 (92.07)	324.27
1993-1994	27.37 (7.31)	347.08 (92.69)	374.45
1999-2000	28.11 (7.08)	368.89 (92.91)	397.00
2005-2006	26.46 (7.54)	358.45 (92.46)	384.91

Source: Ministry of Labour and Employment, Director General of Employment And Training and Economic Survey (various years).

Note: Figures in brackets are percentages to the respective totals.

The extent of workforce in the organized and unorganized sectors, and their changes over time could be understood by the information provided by the Ministry of Labour and Employment, Director General of Employment and Training, Government of India and published in the Economic Surveys. Accordingly, the share of organized workforce was about 8.per cent by 1983, which declined to 7.54 per cent by 2004-2005. The corresponding share of unorganized workforce was about 92.07 per cent by 1983, which increased to 92.46 per cent by 2004-2005.

The Objectives of the Study

1. To know about the socio-economic condition of the unorganized women workers.
2. Attitude of the Women Workers towards their Job.

The Study Area

This study was conducted about the status of unorganized women workers in Thrissur district of Kerala. The total number of respondents for the study was 50 women, and they selected as convenient sampling method. They were engaged in various fields like cooking, cleaning in canteens, book binding, flower making, and gardening in unorganized field.

The study reveals that 20 per cent of the women are in job more than five years and rest of them are below 5 years with limited salary and selection of job by their own risk. Here, 22 workers are unmarried. They opined that they have to earn something what they can. The 50 per cent of the women workers responded that, the employers are favourable to them. Because they have received some financial help from them at needed time like during the time of marriage, education, sickness etc.

Table 18.3 : Socio-economic condition of the Women Workers

Distribution	Level of Socio-economic condition	Frequency
Age	Below 30	16 (32)
	Above 30	34 (68)
Religion	Christian	23 (46)
	Hindu	27 (54)
Marital	Married	17 (34)
	Unmarried	22 (44)
	Widow	10 (20)
	Separated	1 (2)
Education	Illiterate	2 (4)
	Below SSLC	22 (44)
	SSLC	16 (32)
	Above Higher Secondary	7 (14)
	PG	2 (4)
	Pharmacy	1 (2)
Type of family	Nuclear	50 (100)
Nature of Job	Regular	50 (100)

Note: Figures in brackets are percentages to the respective totals.

Table 18.4 : Attitude of the Women Workers towards their Job

Distribution		Frequency		
		Yes	No	
Reasons behind for selection of Job	Financial Problems	24(48)	-	-
	Alcoholism	7(14)	-	-
	Husband's Sick/Death	4(8)	-	-
	Widow	10(20)	-	-
	Safety	8(16)	-	-
	Study	1(2)	-	-
Engaged in Job	Below 5 years	40(80)	-	-
	Above 5 years	10(20)	-	-
Availability in getting Job	Direct	48(96)	-	-

...(Contd.)

Distribution		Frequency		
		Yes	No	
	Agent	2(4)	-	-
Problems in work Place	Hard work	24(48)	26(52)	52
Financial support	-	50(100)	-	-
Opinion of Family about work	Positive	50(100)		
Opinion of Worker about the work	Positive	50(100)		
Sickness	-	26(52)	24(48)	48%
Leave	-	50(100)	-	
Leisure time	-	36(72)	14(28)	28%
Financial Support	-	50(100)	-	
Satisfaction in salary	-	50(100)	-	
Knowledge regarding Minimum wage Act	-	2(4)	42(84)	84%

Note: Figures in brackets are percentages to the respective totals.

Among the sample respondents 20 per cent of the women have widows and 2 per cent of the women are separated from husband due to family problems. These women have to look after their children especially their education. Women are more likely than men to be employed in low-paid, less-secure jobs, particularly in the developing countries (Anker and Hein 1986; Lee and Nagaraj 1995; Chen et al 2006). Due to low quality and instability of informal employment, women frequently face a higher risk of poverty. Gender dimensions of poverty often gain significance from the notion that women constitute the poorest of the poor, being at the lowest rung of social and economic hierarchies. Women headed households are necessarily poorer and suffer from vulnerabilities when compared with those of men-headed households (Gangopahyay and Wadhwa, 2003).

Conclusion

Social exclusion provide space for domination, discrimination and deprivation, those who benefit out of this social formation do not want to introduce any change in this structure. Significantly, this social system becomes highly resistant to change and transformation. Interestingly, it is not only those who discriminate against those who are supposed to be 'inferior, incapable, less meritorious and lower' who resist change but even those who are victims of discrimination also are not in a position to mobilize and organize the discriminated masses to alter the existing social system. In this regard it is pertinent to state here that contrary to popular belief it is not because these social groups want to remain in the dehumanizing social order that they do not initiate change but because they fear that they may be subjected to repression if they resist exclusion and discrimination.

REFERENCES

Anupama, "Occupational Sex Segregation in the Unorganized Manufacturing Sector the case of Punjab", *Development and Change*, Vol, X111, No 2, July –Dec-2008, p. 118.

Dhas A.C *etal.*, "*Social Security for Unorganized Workers in India*", MPRA working Paper No. 9247, June 2008, Madurai.

Dhas, Albert Christopher and Helen, *Social Security for Unorganized Workers In India*, Mpra, 20 June, 2008.

Kerala State Women's Development Corporation (2008).

Louis, Dr. Prakash, *Social Exclusion A Conceptual and Theoretical Framework.*

Mathur Deepa, Women, *Family, and Work*, Rawat Publications, 1992, New Delhi, pp. 131,139.

Ramaswamy Uma, "Organizing with a Gender Perspective", in Ruddar Dutt Ed.,*Organising the Unorganized Workers*, Vikas Publishing House, 1997, p. 162.

Sharma Alakh N. *et.al.,Women and Work Changing Scenario in India,* Indian Society of Labour Economics, Patna,1992, p. 253.

19
CHAPTER

Women's Inclusivness in Local Governance
Rhetoric and Reality

K.T. Kalaiselvi
Research Scholar, Bharathidasan University, Trichirapalli

Real change in India will come when women begin to affect the political deliberations of the nation.
—Mahatma Gandhi

Introduction

Women's inclusion in local governance is a process to empower the women to decide for them to live with human dignity. The word "empowerment" is a multi-dimensional social process that helps foster the capacity to confront the issues which prevent them from empowering and gain control over their lives. Women's political empowerment refers to the process by which women acquire due recognition on par with men and participate as equal partners in the development process of the society through the political institutions. In spite of the affirmative measures taken both by Central and State governments the political participation of women has been affected severely due to various factors such as caste, religion, feudal attitude and family status. As a result, women have been left on the periphery of India's political life.

Indicators of Empowerment and the Gap

In the global perspective, Gender Empowerment Measure indicates women's participation and decision making in politics as one of the indicators of women empowerment. International agencies also insist that women's representation in policy making bodies is vital since it contributes to redefining political priorities and placing new perspectives. In India 33 per cent of seats in village councils and municipalities are reserved for women from the year 1992.

While this is viewed as a remarkable achievement for a country whose political matrix has always been male dominated through systemic exclusion of women, one cannot be blind to the realities. World Economic Forum's (WEF) latest 'Global Gender Gap Report 2010' places India in 112th position among 134 countries and ranks 23rd on the variable of 'political empowerment' of women. But the same report ranks Indian women at the 120th position in education, 128th in economic participation and 132 in health and survival. This gap should be addressed.

Reservation for Women in PRI

The 73rd Constitutional Amendment Act provided women an opportunity to take active part in the decision-making process at the local level and created space for women in political participation and decision-making at the grass root level by providing one third reservation for them in Panchayat Raj Institutions. Article 243D of the Constitution provides that not less than one-third of the total number of seats, and seats reserved for the Scheduled Castes and the Scheduled Tribes as well as offices of Chairpersons in Panchayats at each level shall be reserved for women. According to the proposed 110th Amendment to the Indian Constitution (Bill No. 99 of 2009) under consideration of the Lok Sabha stipulates that the reservation for women in Panchayats in the total number of seats, offices of Chairpersons and in the seats reserved for the Scheduled Castes and the Scheduled Tribes across three tiers should be raised from "not less than one-third" to "not less than one-half". Reservation for women belonging to the Scheduled Caste and Scheduled Tribe categories in the offices of Chairpersons in Panchayats at each level should also be "not less than one-half."

Critical Mass and the Existing Model

India is having a woman president, a woman speaker, a woman ruling party leader, a woman opposition party leader and for the first time in the history of India the representation of women in Lok Sabha exceeds 10 per cent. But these women are exceptions and do not reflect the position of majority of Indian women. History has constantly emphasized the fact that the visibility of few women in the echelons of power does not necessarily enhance the status of the mass of women. Only in this context 50 per cent reservation for women in local governance should be viewed as a means to achieve gender equality. It is important that women enter the decision-making bodies in a sizable number. If women's voice is to be heard in politics, this 'critical mass' is important. Inclusiveness of common women in politics given the patriarchal structure is an uphill task but not impossible. In Indian society it is difficult for an individual woman to negate the existing structure but as women collectives they have strength of bargaining capacity. In the process of empowering socially, economically backward women SHG model was introduced as a core strategy to achieve empowerment in the ninth plan (1997-2002) and is continued till now with the support of Government and NGOs.

Review of Related Studies

Radha in her study on 'Women in Local Bodies' (2002) reveals that an outstanding linkage to be forged in between women's movements and the political activities of women to bring out meaningful participation of women. Kerala government introduced *'Kudumbashree'* scheme and the institution of Ayalkootums to make more women participate in local governance. The study suggested the implementation of these schemes need to be strengthened and also necessary to make them statutory.

Goel and Shalini Rajneesh (2003) the authors confirmed the fact that Gram Sabhas are not generally held regularly because of many reasons such as lack of awareness among the people about the role and importance of the Gram Sabha, holding the meeting with no prior notice or very short notices, lack of initiative by elected representatives in organizing these meetings and they confirmed the fact that women's participation in grama sabha is minimal.

Poverty Eradication Mission, Andhra Pradesh (2004) in its study explains how Self-help Groups (SHG) could be a formidable social force and pressure lobby in promoting development activities in the state. The study justifies the rationale of building linkage between PRIs and SHGs as both the institutions have the same objective of ushering people-centired development and through it to empower the disempowered. It further confirmed that by providing opportunities to SHGs in to the Standing Committees of Gram Panchayats it is possible for the state government to bring out radical qualitative change in the operational efficiency of the Gram Panchayats.

A study by M.S. Swaminathan Research Foundation (2007) 'Changing Equations: the impact of SHGs on gender relations concludes that at the level of personal space, there has been expansion for women, through increase of knowledge, awareness and skills in new areas, as well the expansion of institutional space. In the public arena women became 'visible' yet there is little change in power relations. The study concludes that SHGs as such are thoroughly depoliticized and this will lead to perpetuate the existing hierarchy in terms of gender and other social relations. To challenge this SHGs should act as a collective force to enter in to the political space to bring equality in ali dimensions.

In the Indian context empowering women is a herculean task, as social and cultural moorings have established strong roots in the belief system of people. Social laws are more powerful than the constitutional laws at the community level wherever society is not democratized. So the government is unable to make the constitutional laws operational. (G. Palanithurai, 2008). Although women are enfranchised members of the political realm, actually they have remained second class citizens in terms of political participation and political power. Their rights are negated in one form or another. In this context this paper deals with the rhetoric and reality of women's participation in local governance with an analysis of empirical research on women's awareness of their civic and political rights and their participation level.

Objectives

(*i*) To find out the awareness of SHG women leaders on women's knowledge on local governance functions, rights and responsibilities of PRIs and their participation level.

(*ii*) To identify the factors which inhibit women's participation in local governance.

(*iii*) To explore what strategy could be used to enhance women's participation in local governance.

With the above said objectives, empirical data was collected from Self-help Group groups in Kanchipuram district of Tamil Nadu, using the interview schedule. Apart from their personal details, indicators like their spatial mobility, participation in federation meetings and training programs, knowledge on local governance, knowledge on reservation for women, the influencing factors on their voting decision and the inhibiting factors to participate in local governance were taken in to account to analyze the potentials of SHG women's inclusiveness in local governance. The empirical study details are given below.

Analysis of the Data

This section analyses the socio, economic profile of the women SHG leaders. Later the same is related to their voice in decision making power and mobility, areas of knowledge and information etc.

Age: Among the respondents 60 per cent of them are 40-50 age groups who have sufficient experience both in terms of family and social life.

Respondent's Age

Sl.No.	Age Category	Frequency (%)
1.	20-29	10
2.	30-39	30
3.	40- 49	60

Education: Educational qualification of the respondents, who are the SHG leaders supposed to know reading and writing, reveals the fact that only 16 per cent of them have entered high school and illiterate and semi-illiterate are more in numbers. It is to be noted that the illiteracy is the basic reason for less informative, more ignorant, and less assertive which make them voiceless in public.

Education

Sl.No	Educational Status	Frequency (%)
1.	Illiterate	32
2.	Primary	24
3.	Middle	28
4.	High school	16

Occupation: Seventiy-six per cent of the SHG leaders are agricultural coolie, 12 per cent are home makers, and 12 per cent are doing agriculture in their own land.

Occupation

Sl.No	Type of Family	Frequency (%)
1.	Agriculture-coolie	76
2.	Home makers	12
3.	Others	12

What is Expected?

Women's participation in politics can not be seen in isolation from their overall socio, economic status. It is hoped that even a slight increase in their economic independence and access to information through women collectives could influence the SHG women to come out from their private sphere to public realm to some extent. In our patriarchal structure women's spatial mobility outside the family is restricted and her contribution to the family in the form of household work is not valued. But it is expected that through roster leadership in SHG she gets spatial mobility to attend or organize meetings for the promotion of micro credit, to contact government officials, NGOs, Bank officials. This spatial mobility enjoyed by the women leaders can boost their self esteem unconsciously.

What Happens in Reality?

Federation Meetings

'Self-Help Groups in India - A study of the lights and shades' (2006) reveals that there are apparent synergies between SHGs and local politics through the membership of SHGs, or SHG clusters and federations, village women can gain experience of relevant processes (regular meetings, taking decisions, allocating money). This study reveals that Eighty four percent of the SHG leaders are attending the federation meetings and they utilize this opportunity to mingle with others, expanding their horizon, contact with various group leaders for sharing their experiences and learn new things related with only micro-credit facilities. The forum of SHG Federation is an ideal place to provide space and opportunity for open learning. In practice government and NGO officials use this forum to emphasize the importance of women collectives only to promote micro credit facilities. NGOs are reluctant to educate about civic rights justifying their stand as non participatory in electoral politics.

Training Programmes

To understand the political process and strategies and relevant trainings, education and constant interactions are required. But women SHG leaders are limited to learn about the effective functioning of SHGs focused only on micro credit components. While 70 per cent of the leaders expressed that they have participated in only micro credit oriented trainings, 30 per cent informed that they have attended a few awareness programs on women issues and none of them attended training program on local governance. Access to knowledge and information is the base for empowerment of women. This study reveals that SHG forums are not utilized to disseminate knowledge on civic rights.

Knowledge on Reservation

Knowledge level of women leaders over the reservation for women in PRI is very low. Only 28 per cent of the respondents said that they know that their panchayat is reserved for woman but do not know about the percentage of reservation for women in total and 72 per cent don't have any idea of reservation. Hence, it is imperative to educate women about the reservation and its purpose. While the reservation for women itself is not known to them claiming their right to utilize the opportunities in local governance is questionable.

Voting Decision

Voting is the most important and basic means by which women are assimilated into the political process and learn how to exercise power. Though 100 per cent of the respondents said that they cast their vote in during the election but it was very unfortunate to know from them that 53 per cent cast their vote only for money, 27 per cent are still influenced by their male members in the family and 20 per cent women vote for the people who are known to them. Surprisingly, all the respondents have said that they never discussed about electoral politics in their SHG meetings.

Knowledge on Local Governance

Most of the respondents do not have knowledge over the existence of three tier system in the local governance. They are sure that the panchayat president candidates belong to a political party. In this context it becomes a myth for them if anybody says that the panchayat president's election is not based on any political party. They are not clear about the duties and responsibilities of the elected members of PRI. Forty percent of the respondents have attended only one or two Grama Sabha meetings for all these years and even that participation was not based on any agenda or based on group decision but mere physical participation only. Sixty percent of them expressed that they do not know the grama sabha meeting dates, venue and the subject matters to be discussed. None of them have the knowledge of Standing Committees.

Desire to Contest in Panchayat Raj Institution

When analyze the respondents desire to participate in the forth coming PRI election 30 per cent of them have expressed their willingness to contest in the elections in spite of their inadequate knowledge over PRI and its role.

Role of Patriarchy

In our patriarchal society the public-private dichotomy has far reaching role in perpetuating the subordinate position of women. While social life is separated in to public and private spheres men occupy spaces in the public sphere as a matter of right and women occupy the private sphere, the family. The process of socialization legitimizes the discrimination and in turn accepts the gender hierarchy as natural. Though government is providing equal space for both men and women through affirmative measures, women hesitate to participate in politics as if it is male space. The field experiences confirm this. All the respondents expressed that their household chores demand more time and they are unable to participate in public meetings. Though they share opinions, take decisions about micro credit in SHG meetings they hesitate to speak out in public fearing that it may cause defame to the family and their males may not like it. Their identity is always associated with their husbands and it restricts their expression in public places. Though women want to express their opinions and claim their rights they keep silent because assertive women are subjected to character assassination. The patriarchal notions are expressed in different forms mentioned below:

- Male dominance and decision-making
- Family responsibility
- Lack of mobility
- Denial of expression in public space
- Character assassination
- Lack of identity
- Low access to knowledge, information
- Lack of institutional support

Findings of the Empirical Study

- Self-help Groups were not utilized to disseminate knowledge on local governance.
- Majority of the SHG women leaders limit their role in politics as voters and 53 per cent voted only for money.
- Majority of the women leaders' knowledge on reservation for women limits to their concern panchayat level.
- SHG leaders' access to information and knowledge on PRI functions is very low.
- Participation of SHG women leaders in Grama Sabha is low. Only forty percent have attended either one or two meetings with out knowing the democratic strength of it.
- There is a wide gap between the SHG leaders and the elected women panchayat representatives.
- In rhetoric Panchayat Raj election, has to be treated as non-political party election but in reality, it is not.
- 100 per cent of respondents expressed that dominant caste and political party play predominant role in PRI election. MLA of particular constituency decides the candidate through dominant caste leaders.

What is to be Done?

Networking of Various Stakeholders

The need of the hour is to develop the collective consciousness of women about their political rights, to activate collective decision making and promote collective action among the village women to be more inclusive in local politics. In this context colleges and universities should enlarge the horizon of women's struggles and use knowledge as a form of societal intervention. The linkage between research, teaching and action should be emphasized. Relevant and efficient action programs are required to make women better organized, more united and more active towards the enhancement of women's participation in local governance. Majority of women leaders (58%) do not know about the 33 per cent reservation itself. It is our foremost duty to promote networking among stake holders to propagate the importance of reservations for women. Networking provides quick access to knowledge, and enables women to share the information. Academic research on women's issues, women's perspectives and women's political participation should be clubbed with outreach programs, if research has to be translated into action.

Interventions Suggested

The practical experiences of grass roots organizations suggest multiple strategies and approaches to realigning power relationships. Organizing women for political empowerment calls for experimentations with alternative organization forms to create spaces and use these spaces for more transformative agenda (Kumud Sharma, 2004). In this context based on the empirical study the following strategies are drawn.

Workshop on voting rights and women's role in political decision making and it's implications on overall socio, economic aspects to be highlighted to the village women leaders and to the college students irrespective of their courses studying.

Inter-collegiate competitions may be organized to produce simple local language posters, slogans to exhibit women's reservation and the same may be displayed in an exhibition allied with workshops and seminars.

Encourage the Research Scholars to conduct study about women's participation in local governance and the role of SHG either in the village they live or their relatives live. So that they can able to do follow up even after completing their research.

Organize seminars in collaboration with NGOs and other civil societies on 'women's inclusiveness in politics 'and invite SHG cluster leaders to participate and reflect. Designing simple booklets on the functions of local governance in local language and distribute the same to all the participants.

Adoption of near by villages by Colleges and Universities to educate the role of women in local governance. Continuous efforts to be taken to publicize the rights and responsibilities of people, women's reservation and participation in panchayats.

The SHGs should be utilized to provide more information on participation of women in gram panchayats. This potential forum can be innovatively used to teach civic rights and in turn disseminate knowledge to a larger public. If the efforts are focused to utilize these forums to educate on women rights, civic rights and political rights there is more possibility of empowering women. SHGs as a group could extend their meaningful participation in Grama Sabha.

Participating in Grama sabha by the SHG members as a group should be made as one of the criteria to get support from Banks and other financial institutions.

REFERENCES

Bandyopadhyay, D., Amitava Mukherjee *New Issues in Pancahati Raj,* New Delhi: 2004.

Goel, S.L., Shalini Rajneesh *Panchayati Raj in India Theory and Practice,* New Delhi: Deep and Deep, 2003.

M.S. Swaminathan Research Foundation study, *Changing Equations: The Impact of SHGs on Gender Relations,* Chennai: 2007.

Palanithurai, G., G. Uma and J.Vanishree, *Networking of Elected Women Representatives at Grassroots,* Concept Publishing, New Delhi: 2008.

Planningcommission.gov.in/plans/mta/mta-9702/mta-ch13.pdf

Radha, S. Bulu Roy Chowdhury, *Women in Local Bodies,* Kerala Research Programme on Local Level Development, Entre for Development Studies, Thiruvananthapuram: 2002

'Self Help Groups in India—A Study of the Lights and Shades' by EDA Rural Systems Pvt. Ltd. in association with Andhra Pradesh Mahila Abivruddhi Society for CRS, USAID, CARE, GTZ/ NABARD: 2006.

UN Document on Women's Development 1985.

20
CHAPTER

A Study on Women Construction Workers with Specific Reference to Health

Dr. Nirmala Alex

Associate Professor, Deptt. of Social Work, Stella Maris College, Chennai

'If the democracy in India is to be moved towards a point were poor women have more voice and choice, and then they should get into the habit of seeking for their right said the (Noble Literature *Amartya Sen*).

Women constitute half the humanity and they play a very important role in the national development. *Parvin Razia.M*, 2006

Growth without Trickle Down

Construction industry is thriving thanks to IT sector boom, but workers continue to slog. Information Technology and IT-enabled Services (ITES) are recognized to be the fastest growing sectors.

Status of Unorganized Labour

The total workforce in the country as on January 1, 2000, as per the 56th Round of the National Sample Survey Organization (NSSO) of Employment and Unemployment conducted in 1999-2000, was 410 million, of which 401 million were employed. Out of the employed workforce 93%were engaged in the activities of the unorganized, while less than 7% members were reported as being employed in the organized sector.

Important Characteristics of Unorganized Labour

- Increasing size of unorganized labour.
- Increasing casualization of employment - acute poverty - hires and fire policy - no job security.

- Poor quality of employment in terms of income received and the work environment - unclean and unsafe.
- No guarantee for payment of minimum wages.
- High incidence of bonded labour and child labour.
- Absence of social security package.
- Hardly any protective - welfare legislation coverage.
- Long hours of work - nonpayment of overtime wage.
- Hardly any organized trade unions.
- Weak bargaining position - often employer - employee relationship unclear.
- Vulnerability to various occupational diseases.
- Accidents causing injury resulting in death and disablement.
- The weaker position of women labour in India is reflected both in rural participation rates as well as in lower wages. Women's real wages are 51 per cent lower than that of men's. This gives rise to lower literacy and lesser gainful employment.

Policies Concerning Unorganized Labour

There are about 8.5 million building and other construction workers in India as per the estimates of National Sample Survey (2001). These workers are one of the most numerous and vulnerable segments of the unorganized sector in India.

Construction Labour in India

Construction activities are an integral part of the Indian economy and have attracted considerable amount of finances in both the public and private sectors. In fact, investment in construction during the last thirty years is more than the total investment made during the one fifty years of British rule. It is a flourishing industry that has accumulated immense wealth in the hands of the builders resulting in the formation of a powerful builders' lobby in the country.

Status of Indian Women

India has come a long way since independence. Women, who constitute nearly half of the population, play a very significant role in the homes and outside. The future of mankind is thus linked to the development of women's potential.

Statement of the Problem

The researcher has undertaken a study on women construction workers. Having worked with various occupational groups the researcher has found that women in the unorganized sectors are facing multiple problems. They are burdened to run the family as well; they work very hard from dawn to dusk to eke their livelihood. There is no decent wage guaranteed to them by their employers. They lack job security and face gender discrimination which is more prevalent especially in the unorganized sectors.

Significance of the Study

Women in the current scenario are struggling hard to make both ends meets. They toil from morn to dusk to keep their fires burning at home. As a field worker the researcher has observed their way of life and the hardships faced by them. She had the opportunity to work directly with women in the unorganized sectors. Her constant interaction with the women at the grass roots inspired the researcher to undertake a detailed study of the women construction workers.

The author had several objectives pertaining to the overall quality of life of women construction workers. She has taken the economic aspects of the women construction workers in this chapter.

Review of Related Research

The finding of other researchers, namely Anna Mathew (2004), Balbir Soni 2007), M. Atchi Reddy (2000) Geetha Ramakrishnan (1989) Kaila, H.L (2000) and Anita Baneerji Raj Kumar Sen (2000) who have conducted in-depth studies on women construction workers have presented similar findings as those of the researcher. Some of the findings of the researcher were as follows:

- There were more illiterates among the SC/ST families in comparison to other Caste groups.
- Women construction workers were mostly rural migrants. They migrated towards cities in search of livelihood.

Women often complained of chest pain, respiratory disorders, body-ache, and fever and problems arising out of carrying wet construction materials on their head. No medical facility was provided by the employer; hence they were compelled to go to Government hospitals. Visits to hospital meant that the labourers had to forego their work as well as the wages for the day. Hence access to medical facilities was minimal. Safety rules were not practiced in construction work. The risk involved in construction carrying heavy loads. Women construction workers did not get a steady income throughout the year.

The Hindu dated April 29, 2008 highlights the struggles of the construction worker, carrying a heavy burden for Natarajan and Thangamma, a couple employed in construction work, the daily wages are barely enough for survival. They each make Rs.150 per day; their two children go to high school in Arani, where they hail from. They opined that "We get paid every week and the amount is barely enough for food and for our children's education," says Natarajan: "We can't always buy subsidized items at the ration shop, as we are never in the same place. Every time we shift to a new construction site, we have to buy rice and pulses from a shop in the neighbourhoods," says Ms.Thangamma. Their wages have not gone up in quite a while. "Since cement prices have gone up, contractors tell us that it's difficult to pay us more. Our entire family relies on this money and we cannot refuse to work for less, unless we can find jobs where the wages are higher." With Mr. Natarjan's nearly 80-year old mother taking care of their children back home, the only thing that seems to be on the couple's mind is that the children should get an education.

Women, Work and Family

The researcher will review some studies on women work and family H.L. Kaila (2005) has highlighted the occupation health problem, some of the findings have been highlight below:

> The traditional societies prevented women from entering the public domain and are given a subordinate position in the society the life of an Indian woman is like a well-defined predictable master plan. When the women liberation movement started the sociological interest in women's work changed. Since the mid-1970s sociological interest in women's employment issues has expanded rapidly. Women's status has undergone profound changes. As a result significant change has been noticed in the attitude of men and women towards women's education and employment. The traditional picture of women is very different than what it is to day. Women have played a key and largely unrecognized role in the rapid economic and social development worldwide.
>
> A proper Labour Welfare Policy helps working women have a support system and a gender - just culture. The proverb seems true that "The hand that rocks the cradle rules the world" Women are not newcomers to the working world, as some may believe, but their role is changing, as are the social values. Most women have always worked.

Research Objectives

- To study the socio-demographic details of the respondents.
- To study the health problems encountered the respondents.
- One week of rest.

Field of Study

The study was conducted in the Muffosil areas of South Chennai with specific reference to Tambaram Taluk.

Research Design

A research design indicates how the data will be collected, analyzed and reported and includes the types of sampling, methods of data collection and analysis to be used.

Sampling Design

The total population of women construction workers in the seven areas in the field of study. The researcher adopted stratified random sampling with the seven areas using probability proportional to size. The sample size (n) includes 339 while each areas list was taken into consideration for drawing the size.

Analysis

Religion

Majority of the respondents were Hindus, who constituted (94.7%), nine per cent were Muslims, while only 4.4 per cent were Christians. As per the general population scenario Hindu population were large in number which was also reflected in the study.

Caste

It was reflected from above study that 67 per cent belonged to Backward Community, 27 per cent belonged to Scheduled Caste, nine per cent belonged to Forward Caste and five per cent belonged to Most Backward Community. About 227 (67%) respondents belonged to Backward caste followed by 92(27%) belonged to Scheduled Caste/Scheduled Tribe.

Education

It was inferred from the data that about 126 (37.2%) were illiterates, 206 (60.8%) were educated at primary level only and 7(2%) had middle school education. It was significant to note that, 60.8 per cent were educated up to primary education, while only two per cent were educated up to middle school level and 37.2 per cent were illiterates.

Mother Tongue

Majority of the respondents spoke Tamil who constituted 99.4 per cent of the respondents, 0.3 per cent spoke Telugu and Urdu respectively.

Occupation

All the respondents were Chithals.

Marital Status

All the respondents were married, while 10 per cent among the married women were separated.

Details of the Health of the Respondents

Majority i.e. 99 per cent suffered from respiratory problems, while 99 per cent of the respondents suffered from chest pain. Since their nature of work was hard physical labour with constant exposure to pollution, most of the respondents suffered from health problems.

The respondents mostly had access to government hospitals which constituted 97 per cent due to their poor affordability

Majority i.e. 99 per cent had no ability to spend for medical expenses which was a hard reality, due to their poor earnings they were unable to take care for their health expenses, hence they were forced to borrow money to meet the medical expenses, 76.1 per cent borrowed from friends and 23.3 per cent borrowed from relatives.

The majority (98%) of the respondent's did not have proper sanitary facilities, 35.4 per cent opined that it was due to lack of money, while 68 per cent attributed the cause due to lack of health care facilities, although many went to government hospitals. They found it difficult to take a day off, for fear of losing their one day's wages. They were not given any medical benefits; hence if they fell sick in most cases they postponed their visit to hospital only when in chronic situation they seek medical help.

It was to note that majority of the respondents worked during the pregnancy period, (73.7%) opined that they worked during pregnancy due to lack of money, while (18%) worked due to compulsion and under forced circumstances.

It was significant to note that although there were hospitals available, there was no proper infrastructure. The respondents also had no time to undergo pre - natal test for safe delivery, as they go to hospital only at the time of delivery.

It was observed that 63 per cent went to hospital for delivery, while 18.5 per cent had home delivery, with regard to rest taken after delivery it was found that 74.4 per cent only two week of rest, while 16.2 per cent took one week of rest.

A vast majority (92%) of them were unable to take rest due to non availability of maternity welfare. With regard to practice of family planning method, a vast majority that is 91.7 per cent were not practicing family planning method.

Case Processing Summary

	Cases					
	Valid		Missing		Total	
	N	Percent	N	Percent	N	Percent
Age group no. of working days per month	339	100.0%	0	.0%	339	100.0%

Model Summary

Model	R	R Square	Adjusted R Square	Std. Error or the Estimate
1	.009[a]	.000	–.003	.956

[a]Predictors: (Constant), no. of working days per month

ANOVA[b]

	Model	Sum of Squares	df	Mean Square	F	Sig.
1.	Regression	.026	1	.026	.029	.866[a]
	Residual	308.263	337	.915	—	—
	Total	**308.289**	**338**	—	—	—

a. Predictors: (Constant), no. of working days per month
b. Dependent Variable: age group

Coefficients[a]

Model		Unstandardized Coefficients		Standardized Coefficients		
		B	Std. Error	Beta	t	Sig.
1.	(Constant)	2.596	.788	—	3.294	.001
	No. of working days per month	–.009	.053	–.009	–.169	.866

a. Dependent Variable: age group

The abov tables highlighted the age and number of working days per month among therespondents. It was found that with increase in age their frequency of working days decreases. As inferred from the data those who belonged to the age group of (18-25) had maximum of 14.1 per cent of working days per month, while those in the age group (26-35) years had 40.4 per cent of work for 15 days in a month those in the age group of (36-45) years had 34.9 per cent work for 15 days in a month, those who belonged to the age group of (46-55) years had 7.7 per cent of work for 15 days in a month. It was visible from the data that number of working days declines with age. For women in the construction industry, the opportunity to get work declines with age as productivity of labour decreases. Thus it could be inferred from the data that 75 per cent of the respondents are in the age group of (26-45) years who work for 20 days in a month proving that the productivity of labour declined wih age.

Basic Amenities

Basic amenities are vital for healthy life it is significant to note that, that 16 persons (4.7%) three per cent had access to proper water facilities, 15.6 per cent had access to electricity only on paid basis, 12.7 per cent had drainage facilities, 12.3 per cent had proper housing facilities, which they availed mostly on rental basis, while (4.7%) had access to toilet facilities, as they mostly used only public toilets.

Occupational Hazards

The majority health hazards faced by the respondents were physical ailments by which 319 persons were affected (94.1%) 293 persons (97.6%) faced respiratory disorders and 335 persons (98.8%) had chest pain due to their work nature, while 36 persons had problems of spinal cord (7.7%) faced dust allergies and 12 persons (3.6%) faced gastro intestinal problems and (2.7%) faced gynecological problems, almost all the respondents had one or the other forms of illness due to their workload.

Strategies For Social Inclusions

- Construction workers are prone to occupational hazards including loss of life, due to the dangerous nature of their job. Hence they can be brought under insurance schemes, namely the construction labour welfare schemes to safeguard their life.
- Crèche facilities need to be mandatory in all construction sites, undertaken by both public/private, sectors.
- Benefit schemes should be made accessible to the women construction workers who are pregnant. Gender disparity is highly prevalent among the construction workers, Women need to be paid counterparts to men. Voter's identity card and ration card should be ensured to every household.

- Minimum wages Act need to be sternly enforced by every authority failing which stringent action need to be taken against the defaulters.
- Safety measures at the work spot need to be enforced strictly as the researcher one see repeated fatal fall among the workers at the work site.
- Old age pension need to be guaranteed for elderly construction workers as they find it extremely difficult to work after 50 years.

Diagrammatic Presentation of the Process Approach

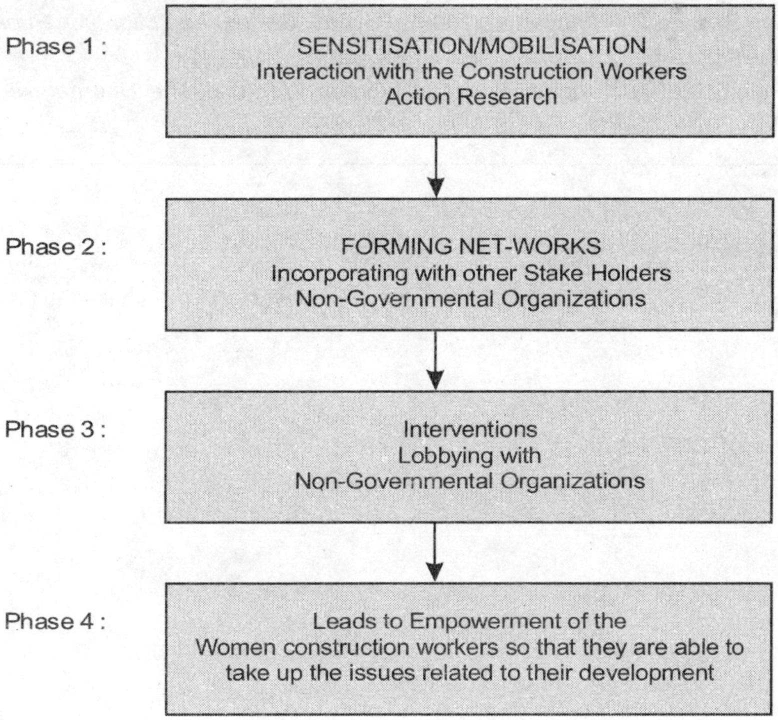

Conclusion

Let's join together in promoting the fact that women's rights are human rights and work towards creating a just humane society which nurtures equality to the most marginalized in society

REFERENCES

Anuradha, (1984) M.A. *Sex Role Orientation and Its Relation to Job and Marital Satisfaction in Women, unpublished M.A dissertation, Bangalore University.*

Bhatt. R.ELa, (2006). *Grind of Work Sewa (Self Employed Women's Association) India.*

Cockerill, John Ellison, *The construction Industry in Belfast, 1800 – 1914, (Northern Ireland).*

Jhabwala R. and R. K. A. Subrahmanya, (2000). *The Unorganized Sector: Work, Security and Social Protection,* Sage Publication, Delhi.

Kaila, H.L, (2005). *Women, Work and Family,* Rawat, Publications, New Delhi.

Malcolm Payne, (2005). *Liberal feminism* (Reynolds, 1993; Dominelli, 2002).

Pandey, A.K., (2002)—*Emerging Issues in Empowerment of Women,* Anmol Publication Private Limited, New Delhi.

Raj Anita Baneji Sen and Kumar Sen, (2000). *Women and Economic Development* Deep and Deep Publications, New Delhi.

Roy Arya Sadhna and Anupama, (2006). *Poverty, Gender and Migration Publications, New Delhi.*

Soni Balbir, (2007). *Empowerment of Women Workers, The Unorganized Sector Dominant Publishers and Distributors, New Delhi.*

21

CHAPTER

Exclusion of Workforce in Unorganised Sector, with Specific Reference to Construction Workers

J. Lohitha

Deptt. of Social Work, Stella Mary's College, Chennai

There has been intense debate in India about what constitutes work and what merits being included in the national statistics as being productive or economically meaningful. The main problem for the unorganized labour is the employer-employee relationship.

The term 'unorganized labour' has been defined as those workers who have not been able to organize themselves in pursuit of their common interests due to certain constraints, like, casual nature of employment, ignorance and illiteracy, small and scattered size of establishments, etc.

As per the survey carried out by the National Sample Survey Organisation in the year 1999-2000, the total employment in both organized and unorganised sector in the country was of the order of 39.7 crore. Out of this, about 2.8 crore were in the organised sector and the balance 36.9 crore in the unorganized sector. Out of 36.9 crore workers in the unorganised sector, 23.7 crore workers were employed in agriculture sector, 1.7 crore in construction, 4.1 in manufacturing activities and 3.7 crore each in trade and transport, communication and services.

Dimensions

Construction activities are an integral part of the Indian economy and have attracted considerable amount of finances in both the public and private sectors. A construction worker is one who contributes his/her labour to construction of structures such as bridges, houses, buildings etc. Construction labour is the second largest unorganized sector of industry employing more than two million workers.

It is one of the few industries in which operations are discontinuous making the industry a mobile one. The industry uses several types of materials – wood, bricks, cement, lime, asbestos, toxic chemicals etc. in large quantities. The origin of the construction industry dates from the origin of civilization. Rapid urbanization leads to acute need of housing and growth of industry which require massive infrastructure including roads, bridges building of factories, railways etc. due to these requirements, the construction industry stands out as one of the major activities. Construction activity is also consistently providing a substantial contribution to the national income. A large part of the unorganized and unskilled labour force in the country, both male and female, is employed in various forms of building and construction activity. Being labour intensive, it employs the second largest work-force in the unorganized sector after agricultural labour. They are mostly rural migrants either landless or share-croppers and marginal/small landowners who come to cities in search of work, being drawn from the same pool as the unorganized agricultural labour in rural areas. This labour is extremely mobile due to the conditions and problems of employment in the construction industry which is characterized by high turnover, use of contract labour, irregular employment, bad working conditions, seasonal variability and dependence on supplies of raw materials. This labour is mostly drawn from villages and is by and large illiterate, untrained, and divided along caste, linguistic and other affinities.

Some of the characteristics of construction labour are:

- High economic vulnerability due to the double combination of irregular and unstable employment and consequent high mobility on the one hand, and their utilization only in the lowest grade of job on the other.
- High proportion of child and female labour and frequent employment of whole family or couples.
- Ignorance, poverty, illiteracy, poor health.
- Lack of unionization due to mobility.
- Lack of opportunity for training, skills upgrading and literacy for employed people, and of basic education for the children.

The occupational structure of the work-force in the building construction industry is categorized into 25 occupations. These occupations are further classified as unskilled, semi-skilled and skilled. The main unskilled occupations are: weight lifting, dust lifting, digging, security, watering etc. the semi skilled occupations include centering, steel bending, concrete mixing, brick laying, glass fitting, scaffolding etc. the skilled occupations include sand blasting operation, carpentry, plastering, masonry, tile fitting, painting, plumbing, cement finishing, tile glazing, electrical fitting, black-smithy, machine operation, white washing etc.

The building construction workers are not easily identifiable as a strictly homogeneous group. They constitute essentially, an 'easily entered' and 'easily left' pool of labour force. They are to be found moving among jobs and geographical locations. Implicitly, mobility marks the mainspring of the supply side of the construction workers. This mobility is an account of people desperately struggling in abject poverty.

There is a predominance of relatively young workers in building construction work, as employers normally prefer young male workers due to the hazardous nature of work involved. The construction worker generally enters the industry at around 14-18 years.

The construction workers are recruited either from market places or directly from slums and villages or else brought from rural areas and housed on big sites. In the former case the number of days of work will be less while the payment is more, while in the big sites the wages are the lowest.

With regard to job status, one finds that young workers and women constitute a large proportion of the unskilled workers. Typically, unskilled workers are found to be illiterate, unlike skilled workers. The former comprise predominantly scheduled castes and scheduled tribes. Workers who are skilled generally belong to the upper castes. However it must be noted that SC/ST are present in all the occupations. Hence, this is suggestive of the fact that there is not very rigid occupational stratification along caste lines, as it is normally believed. Most of the construction workers are migrants to cities from rural areas. Interestingly more upper caste construction workers are migrants than the SC/ST category. The proportion of migrants with urban background is also relatively higher among the upper caste workers. They do not constitute a work-force that floats in and out of the city or between occupations within the city. The majority of them are engaged in regular work in this industry, though moving from site to site and from employer to employer. But their mobility is confined to building construction activity within the cities and their peripheral limits, despite the chequered nature of demand and the vagaries of seasonal unemployment in this industry. The males usually migrate for economic reasons while females migrate due to social reasons, *e.g.* to join husbands working as construction labor in the cities.

Problems Faced By Construction Workers

Construction workers, the builders of modern temples, have been treated as untouchables in the system of society, law and governance. The work force comprises men, women and children who are not given any fixed type of jobs. In short, they are multi-purpose workers. Their tasks range from mixing wet concrete, carrying material from one place to another, and digging and breaking stones. As far as works concerned, both the sexes are given the same type of job except scaffolding. They are exposed to rain and sun; often work late at night, with poor lighting. Very often in violation of existing rules, they are made to carry loads more than 40 kg. It is not unusual to find them carrying heavy weights to many floors and over staircases that are not properly built and over ground that is strewn with waste, like stones, nails, pieces of other building materials and so on. Additionally, they have to carry materials from one place to another continuously the whole day. All these task result in physical discomforts, like back pain, weariness and so on.

The nature of work and the long hours make the construction workers, age very fast. A little more than half the respondent interviewed was found to work more than 10 hours per day. The average no. of working hours was found to be 9½ hr per day. They do not work on Sundays and certain public holidays. But it must be noted that these are not paid holidays. There are no stipulated leave to which construction workers are entitled. Hence, even if they are ill, or injured due to injuries suffered during work, they are not given any leave.

Construction workers in Government or private sites, work under a system of contract and subcontract. They start their work by the age of term and continue till even 70 years since there is noterminal benefit or pension. They are invisible on records, not paid minimum wages on Government sites, exploited and bonded especially to big contractors. Child labour, even though banned by law, is a reality on construction sites. In spite of their right to certain welfare facilities as stipulated by various labor welfare laws, the working conditions continue to be very inconvenient and uncomfortable. For *e.g.*, drinking water supply, toilets, wash rooms, bathroom, restrooms, canteen and crèches are inadequate and poorly maintained. According to statutory requirements, construction workers are supposed to be protected from occupational hazards and occupational diseases. But contrary to the legal directives safety gadgets are rarely provided. This often leads to accident, sometimes leading to death. For e.g., one often notices construction workers working at great heights without proper safety gadgets; machinery used at the construction site are not guarded, e.g., elevated shafts are left unfenced. At times materials fall from heights where the work is going on.

Health hazards include asthma, tuberculosis and frequent respiratory difficulties due to inhalation of cement and sand dust, cancer due to paints as well as exhaustion and sever physical pain and also heat, radiation, noise, dust, shocks, toxic chemicals causing serious health problems. Further, the raw materials that the construction workers have to deal with, like sand and asbestos give rise to silicosis and asbestosis; work at heights give rise to blood pressure problems. Log and continuous exposure to heat result in problems like sun burns, cramps, sun strokes etc.

Also it is not uncommon to see pregnant women working hard till the delivery, babies in cloth curdles, and toddlers playing in sand and cement dust exposed to hazards of worksite. Accidents are every day affair while there is no speedy measure to provide medical relief or compensation.

Construction labour is poorly unionized. There are obvious reasons for it. The industry is unorganized, labor force is unstable and scattered in small numbers across the length and breadth of India, work is seasonal, and workers are migratory. Absence of bargaining capacity among the construction workers makes them vulnerable to exploitation by the contractors. Further, established trade unions in the organised sector do not show any interest in unionizing the under privileged workers in the construction industry, but these very reasons pose a challenge to union leaders.

REALITIES IN THE FIELD

Prahlad, a mason working in the name of Rajesh, in the construction site of new Secretariat complex, Chennai, earns Rs. 100 per day. His native is Orissa. He works as a Binami for Rajesh who is a mediator residing in Orissa, who initially employed Prahlad. Prahlad gets a monthly wage of Rs3000. This money is transacted by the employer to the bank account of Rajesh instead of Prahlad. Rajesh without putting in any manual labour, rips off a commission of Rs1000-Rs1500 & sends the rest of money to Prahlad. Even worser, after Prahlad receives the money, he sends a money order of Rs1000-1200 per month to his family in Orissa. Again there is a mediator involved, who takes Rs500-700 as commission and settles the rest with his family. This is the plight of just one worker and it is a realization of how wages earned by hard labour is being ripped off as commissions down the line. Many construction workers undergo the same situation, working as binamis for many gundas and mediators. Moreover, say if the mediator employs say 10-15 labourers on different construction sites, then the money he earns from commission itself is around Rs19000 per month. These problems emerge due to lack of an ID card possessed as a labourer and also due to their migration, they don't possess a Ration card or Voter's id.

It is also to be noted that in the same construction site, when men are away at work, few women and young girls who stay back in their tents get involved in commercial sex work. When encountered them, they say they are into it, as the wages they get from their labour is not enough.

Their days of work are divided as Heavy work and Light work days. Most of the days, they are scheduled for heavy work and they work not less than 9 hours/day.

Government even after passing Right to Education Act, it is shameful to accept the fact that in the construction of Government Buildings like the Secretariat itself, there were nearly 100 children below the age of 18 working on the site. Children who don't work are found to be school drop outs without any formal or informal schooling. At present, with the construction getting over in two months time, there are nearly 50 school drop outs. Children below the age of 6 are badly malnourished and live in an unhygienic condition. On the eve of this, there was a medical camp organized for children with free diagnosis and treatment. But parents showed much negligence in taking tablets for their children fearing of any danger would occur. The doctors and volunteers had to convince and educate so much on the benefit and usage of taking tablets for their children. This is the plight of their knowledge on health and medication as mostly they are used to taking self-medication.

In regard to Housing, each family is provided with a temporary tent made of asbestos, and all families reside in the labour camp, very close by to the construction site. There are just two toilets and washrooms for more than 100 families. Almost all of them use the open space for sanitary purposes. Women find it very hard in regards to sanitation and all of them bath in their tents itself, which is a normal phenomena taking place in urban slums.

SUITABLE POLICIES AND PROGRAMMES AND SUGGESTIONS FOR BRINGING CONSTRUCTION WORKERS IN TO THE MAIN STREAM OF DEVELOPMENT

Today there is an urgent need to pay attention to the welfare of the construction labour. It is the moral responsibility of the government, development al organizations, intellectuals, social scientists and every citizen of the nation to see that concrete steps are taken to regulate and protect the growing construction work-force. One step in this direction will be to organise construction workers, though it is an uphill task considering the scattered nature of construction sites, the migrant nature of the work and the contract system of employment prevailing in the industry. With a little more administrative effort, it should be possible to provide certain welfare measures to them.

As already discussed, construction workers suffer from certain common disadvantages. First, their earnings are too low, to provide even the minimum subsistence level of living. That is because they do not have the protection of unionism. In some cases, the overall earnings of workers are very low due to non – availability of work throughout the year. Second, these labourers suffer from insecurity of job and employment not only on account of intermittent nature of activities, but also on account of the lack of institutions and legislative protection. They are deliberately kept in an insecure position in order to deprive them of certain social security benefits and to prevent them from getting organised in trade unions. Third, most of the protective and welfare legislation in the field of labour is not applicable to them. As a consequence, they are deprived of regular and reasonable payment of wages and also benefits such as compensation in case of accidents, injuries and deaths, medical care, bonus, paid leave and holidays, and retirement benefits.

The Building and other Construction Workers (Regulation of Employment and Conditions of Services) Act 1988 provides exclusively legislation for the welfare of construction workers throughout the country. Proper implementation of the Act itself will cure half the problem.

It says, the appropriate government should fix hours for normal working day, day of rest, payment of wages for the day of rest, payment or overtime allowance and other welfare measures, such as facilities regarding drinking water, latrines and urinals, crèches, first-aid, and canteens in respect of building workers. The government should also take over the function of recruitment and registration of workers as well.

The existing numbers of labour laws applicable to construction workers are supposed to work on the basis of inspection – prosecution – fining, while the work itself may be over, before the end of the legal process. These laws do not protect workers against victimization thus they have become unsuited to protect the labour. Also the employer-employee relation changes and work place also shifts constantly while the existing social security laws are not suited for this changing situation.

Henceforth, in the absence of a sense of responsibility on the part of principle employers and contractors for the labourers:

- A participatory tripartite mechanism would have to pin down everyone's responsibility to protect and provide for the labourers.
- Registration of all workers and employers regulation of employment through the Labour Welfare Board should be done strictly.
- Social security measures such as crèches and proper housing to be provided by the Board.
- A levy of two per cent of the estimate cost is being collected from all constructions before plan sanction. This levy should be used for the welfare of construction workers.
- Prevailing registration procedures of labourers in the board have un-flexible renewal procedures, which have to be made simpler and flexible.

- Pension to be given to those aged 60 and above without any complex procedures.
- Compulsory registration of accidents and strict supervision of safety.
- Provision of skill training to workers especially women.
- The Board would have substantial representation of workers, with proportionate representation for women.
- The Board must be constituted to State, District, Taluk and Local levels.
- Cases of exploitation of labourers should be investigated jointly by the Board to facilitate quick remedial action.
- Special employment schemes should be taken up for women in and around their labour camps so as to prevent their exploitation by contractors and middlemen.
- Effective rehabilitation schemes should be drawn up for those labourers who have become handicapped in the course of their work and of families whose breadwinner has lost his/her life while working.
- Very important, mobile schools should be set up in order to provide formal and vocational education to school drop-out children due to migration. Also residential schools can be set up in the source area, so that only parents migrate and children continue with their education.
- A concerned effort should be made by the ministry of home affairs and the concerned state government to trace migrant labourers who are untraceable.
- Compensation has to be paid by the employer to a workman for any personal injury caused by an accident arising out of and in the course of his/her employment.
- Long working hours should be definitely reduced and those employers not abiding by the stated hours of work should be punishable.
- Social workers and NGOs should play a pivotal role in generating mass awareness and educating the labourers on the laws and welfare measures available for them.

There is need for much stringent observance of existing labour laws with deterrent penalty clauses. There is unquestionable evidence from virtually all available studies on construction workers that there is flagrant violation of statutory provision of housing, medical and other facilities, payment of travel expenses for migrant workers, compensation for accidents, sickness insurance and so on. Such violations need to be made punishable by law with strict penalties attached to them. In this context, it is necessary to provide legal literacy to construction workers, especially to women who also have special needs such as crèches, maternity benefits and toilets.

The disadvantageous position of these employees in the construction industry obviously points to the greater need of labor welfare measures for them. It has to be appreciated that the mere passing of welfare legislation for the upliftment of the downtrodden and the weak is by itself is not sufficient, though undoubtedly it is the first step in the right direction. What is important is that, every piece of social legislation enacted, particularly for the welfare of the weaker sections, must be strictly implemented in the right spirit for achieving the noble object for which such legislation is passed!

22
CHAPTER

Inclusion Socially Exclusion People Through Formation of Self-help Group

K. Anbumani
Lecturer in Commerce, Mother Teresa Women's University College, Kodaikanal

Introduction

The SHG - Blank Linkage Programme was started as an Action Research project in 1989 which was offshoot of a NABARD initiative during 1987 through sanctioning Rs.`10 lakh to MYRADA as seed money assistance for experimenting Credit Management Groups. In the same year the Ministry of Rural Development provided PRADAN with support to establish self-help groups in Rajasthan.

The experiences of these early efforts led to the approval of a pilot project by NABARD in 1992. The pilot project was designed as a partnership model between NABARD in 1992. The pilot project was designed as a partnership model between three agencies, viz., the SHGs, banks and NGOs. This was reviewed by a working group in 1995 that let to the evolution of a streamlined set of RBI approved guidelines to banks to enable SHGs to open bank accounts, based on a simple *inter se* agreement. This was coupled with a commitment by NABARD to provide refinance and promotional support to banks for the SHG – Bank Linkage Programme.

Positive Features of the SHG-Bank Linkage Programme:

The financial inclusion attained through SHGs is sustainable and scalable on account of its various positive features. The programme confronts many challenges and for further scaling up, these challenges need to be addressed.

Financial Inclusion of Poor Women

The Committee noted that more than 90 per cent of the members of SHGs are women and most of them are poor and assetless. The SHG movement has been instrumental in mainstreaming women by – passed by the banking system.

Loan Repayments

One of the distinctive features of the SHG – Bank Linkage Programme has been very high on-time recovery. As on June 2005, the on-time recovery under SHG - Bank Linkage Programme was 90% in commercial banks, 87% in RRBs and 86% in cooperative banks.

Programme Impact

The main findings reveal that the programme has:

- Reduced the incidence of poverty through increase in income, and also enabled the poor to build assets and thereby reduce their vulnerability
- Enabled households that have access to it to spend more on education than non-client households. Families participating in the programme have reported better school attendance and lower drop out rates.
- Empowered women by enhancing their contribution to household income, increasing the value of their assets and generally by giving them better control over decisions that affect their lives.
- Reduced child mortality, improved maternal health and the ability of the poor to combact disease through better nutrition, housing and health – especially among women and children.
- Contributed to a reduced dependency on informal money lenders and other non-institutional sources.
- Facilitated significant research into the provision of financial services for the poor and helped in building "capacity" at the SHG level.
- Finally, it has offered space for different stakeholders to innovate, learn and replicate. As a result, some NGOs have added micro-insurance products to their portfolios, a couple of SHG federations have experimented with undertaking livehood activities and grain banks have been successfully build into the SHG model in the Eastern Region. SHGs in some areas have employed local accountants for keeping their books, and IT applications are now being explored by almost all for better management information systems, (MIS), accounting and internal controls.

Cost Recovery and Sustainability

It is important for banks to carefully work out their actual costs for SHG lending. While the SHG portfolio is often only a small part of the total bank lending, and since the portfolio quality is good, it may be possible to reduce interest rates while ensuring recovery of costs.

In the initial phase of the SHG movement, the groups were formed by NGOs and hence start-up costs were low for banks. However, over the years, banks have also evolved as SHIPs. In the process, the start-up costs of group formation, etc. have devolved on the banks, impacting their pricing policies.

It is an accepted fact the banks will base their lending rate decisions on three important criteria their cost of funds, transaction costs and the required spreads. While the sources of funds will determine the cost of funds, the transaction costs will depend mostly on the efficiency with which the transfer of funds is enabled. Banks need to recognize the cost elements involved in the decision-making process while approving credit linkage and in maintaining the accounts of the group, throughout the repayment period.

Further, there is an element of indirect subsidy as presently NABARD supports the costs involved in formation and nurturing of SHGs up to the stage of credit linkage. This financial support is around Rs.3,000 per SHG. The Ministry of Rural Development (MoRD) has established a norm of Rs. 10,000 per group for the Swarnajayanti Gram Swarojgar Yojana (SGSY) programme, payable over four phases.

Joint Liability Groups (JLGs)

The SHGs are now emerging as an effective credit delivery channel for mid-segment clients such as share croppers and tenant farmers as their loan requirements are much larger. For developing an effective model for this group, NABARD had introduced a pilot project for formation and linking of JLGs.

A JLG is an informal group comprising 4 to 10 individuals coming together for the purposes of availing bank loan either singly or through the group mechanism against mutual guarantee. The JLG members are expected to engage in similar type of economic activities like crop production. Under the Scheme, tenant farmers cultivating land either as oral lessees or sharecroppers and small farmers who do not have proper title of their land holding will be eligible for collateral – free credit though formation and financing of JLGs.

Based on the considerations indicated above, the Committee makes the following recommendations for deepening microfinance interventions and making it an effective tool in achieving greater inclusion:

Encouraging SHGs in Excluded Regions - Funding Support

In order to further increase efforts in addressing regional imbalances, there is a need to involve State governments. In some States, the programme is driven mainly through NGOs and other SHPIs like banks, farmer's clubs, individual rural volunteers, etc. The Committee is of the view that if the programme is to reach a critical scale, the Department of Women and Child Development at the State-Level should be actively involved in promoting and nurturing of SHGs. The State Governments and NABARD may, therefore, set aside specific funds out the budgetary support and the Micro Finance Development and Equity Fund (MFDEF) respectively for the purpose of promoting SHGs in regions with high levels of exclusion.

The spread of SHGs in hilly regions, particularly in the North-Eastern Region, is poor. One of the reasons for this is that the population density in hilly areas is often low and the banking network is weak. There is a need to evolve SHG models suited to the local context of such areas.

Urban Microfinance

There have been a few instances of MFIs venturing into this area of lending to urban poor who are undertaking micro-enterprises and small business activities. Urban branches of banks, even though having manpower and technology support, are not attuned to SHG lending or microfinance. They are busy with multiple and diversified activities and generally find no time to cater to the microfinance market segment. Lending opportunities in other sector dissuade them from attempting the laborious task of micro lending. The migratory nature of parts of the low income urban population is also contributing that urban bankers are not venturing into this field.

Opening of specialized microfinance branches/cells in potential urban centers exclusively catering for microfinance and SHG-bank linkages could be thought of, to address the requirements of the urban poor BFs/BCs could be the mechanism to reach the target clientele in these areas. However, banks need to implement proper risk management practices, develop suitable models and products tailor-made to this segment. Banks can also consider associating with MFIs undertaking urban mirolending as a viable option.

Conclusion

At present, NABARD is permitted, as per its Act and Mandate, to support micro finance activities in rural and semi-urban areas only. Considering the levels of exclusion prevalent among the urban poor, the unique nature of difficulties faced by them in accessing institutionalized banking services and with a view to leveraging the expertise of NABARD in microfinance, the Committee recommends that an enabling provision be made in the NABARD Act, 1981 permitting NABARD to provide micro finance services to the urban poor.

SECTION–V
Exclusion of Transgender

23
CHAPTER

Transgender
The Struggle for Acceptance

Anitha Nallasekaran
Dept. of Social Work, Stella Marry's College, Chennai

Introduction

Transgender are individuals who were assigned a sex, usually at birth and based on their genitals, but who feel that this is a false or incomplete description of themselves.

Transgender are of two types: 'nirvana' and 'aqua'. Individuals who have castrated are called as 'nirvana' and individuals who have not gone through emasculation are called 'aqua.'

Individuals transform into transgender because of faulty pairing of chromosomes in the body that determines the sex of the individual. Apart from the biological defect, individuals who grow in an environment surrounded by females and have grown up playing with girls also tend to become transgender. Or it could be that the parents dress the child as female every time to fulfill their want to have a girl child. This has a psychological impact on the child. Thus, there is a change in the attitude and making and wanting them to change their sex. Or incidents of child sexual abuse can also play a vital role in changing the sex of an individual.

Different terms are used to denote transgender like *hijra* or *jijirat* in Arabic, *Hiz* in Persian, *Khwaja* in Urdu, *Kliba* in Sanskrit and *Hijra* and different terms in Tamil language, which is one of the oldest languages of the world, is used. In *Mahabharata* they were called as *Nabunsaki. Tholgapiyam*, which is one of the oldest literature in Tamil called the transgender as *'Pedi'*. Devaram, Thiruvasagam and other eminent poets called them *Ali.* Then later the term changed to *Aravani,* one who is married to *Aravan.* Now they are called as *Thirunangai.*

A definite structure of hierarchy prevails in the transgender community, known as *'JAMAT'*. The head of the transgender community is known as *'Nayak.'* He is the leader of the gurus. The *Nayak* has the power to formulate rules of behaviour for the entire community. Most of the transgender run away from their homes when they start experiencing changes in them and join the *jamat* system. The transgender community is a cohesive group and lives in harmony with relationships among themselves. The transgender have a special code language called the *Kaudi Basha.*

The transgender have their own set of customs and traditions. After 40 days of emasculation they have a function called as *Nirvan Pooja.* One year after the emasculation they have a function called as *Matha Pooja.* They also have different set of customs for their funerals. They have their own songs to celebrate their functions. They worship Goddess *Bothraj* who is the younger brother of Goddess *Kali,* and according to the mythology it is believed that he was a transgender himself. Religious festivals are important for this closed community. *Koovagam* festival is the most awaited festival of the transgender which falls in the month of April. *Masanakkollai* is another important festival of the transgender.

History of Transgender

The presence of transgender can be traced from the mythological period. It is believed that in *Mahabharata,* Arjuna was propositioned by the *apsara* (celestial danseuse) Urvashi. Urvashi got annoyed at this rejection, saying Arjuna has insulted her by spurning her advances. Urvashi cursed Arjuna with impotence. Later, at Indra's behest she modified her curse to last only one year, and Arjuna could choose any one year of his life during which to suffer the life of a eunuch. This curse proved fortuitous as Arjuna used it as a very effective disguise for the period of one year when he, his brothers, and their wife Draupadi all lived incognito while in exile. He assumed the name Brihannala for that one year.

Another legend about the demon Araka associates Mohini with Krishna (yet another avatar of Vishnu) rather than the god himself. The demon Araka had become virtually invincible because he had never laid eyes on a woman (extreme chastity). Krishna takes the form of the beautiful Mohini and marries him. After three days of marriage, Araka's bonds of chastity are broken, and Krishna kills him in battle.Transgender *Hijras* consider Krishna-Mohini as a transsexual, rather than a true female.

Another folktale tells of the Mahabharata hero Aravan (who becomes the Tamil god Kuttantavar), who was married to Mohini, before his self-sacrifice. Aravan agrees to become the sacrificial victim for the Kalappali ("sacrifice to the battlefield") to ensure the victory of the Pandavas, his father, and his uncles. Before being sacrificed to goddess Kali, Aravan asks three boons from Krishna, the guide of the Pandavas. The third boon was that Aravan should be married before the sacrifice so that he could get the right of cremation and funerary offerings (bachelors were buried). This third boon, however, is found only in the folk cults. To fulfils this wish in the Kuttantavar cult myth, Krishna turns into Mohini, marries Aravan, and spends the night with him. Then after the sacrifice, Mohini laments Aravan's death, breaking her bangles, beating her breasts, and discarding her bridal finery. She then returns to the original form of Krishna.The legend of the marriage of Aravan and Krishna in his female form as Mohini, and Mohini-Krishna's widowhood after Aravan's sacrifice, forms the central theme of an eighteen-day annual festival in the Tamil month of *Cittirai* (April–May) at Koovagam. The marriage ceremony is re-enacted by transgender Hijras, who play the role of Mohini-Krishna.

Transgenders are known to have performed a variety of functions since ancient times. In China, for instance, they had been political advisors in the Chen era (1122 BC- 221 BC) and retained their status under successive dynasties of rulers. In West Africa and West Asian countries they had served as bodyguards, admirals and generals. The cult of castration could have started thousands of years ago. Childless couples could have pledged their first child to the mother Goddess. If a male was born, he was dedicated to the temple and castrated to keep him under the service of the Mother Goddess. Ancient kings used hermaphrodites as servants, the Muslim kings deployed eunuchs as their slaves. Interestingly many such servants and slaves rose to positions of power and wielded great authority in their chosen professions as well as matters of state and governance. The system of employing eunuchs as servants continued till the last century, with several elite Indian homes possessing eunuch servants. Hyderabad, for instance could boast of such a practice till the beginning of the 20th century. With the system of princely states coming to an end, the eunuchs found themselves without any status or employment.

Struggle for Dignified Life

Human dignity is the quintessence of Human Rights. The word 'dignity' has been derived from the Latin word '*dignitas*' which denotes a quality of being worth or honourable. It is the society which confers dignity on the individual and it is the society that can take it away.

The Second World War paved way for the realization by the government of various countries to cherish dignity of individuals as core value in U.N.

Charter, 1945. The Universal Declaration of Human Rights (UDHR) also reciprocated the same sentiments. The emphasis on human dignity in the U.N. Charter, Universal Declaration of Human Rights and several other International Conventions as well as in Constitution of India, the concept of Human Rights has acquired new and wider meaning. Thus you can find a definite linkage between human rights and human determination. Respect for human rights is the roots for human rights and realization of full potential of each individual, which in turn leads to augmentation of human resources with progress of the national empowerment of the people through human development is the aim of human rights.

The Indian Constitution, drafted around the same time as the Universal Declaration of Human Rights (1948), captures the essence of human rights in its preamble, and the articles on fundamental rights and the directive principles of state policies. It guarantees equality, justice, liberty and fraternity to all citizens assuring the dignity of the individual and the unity and integrity of the nation.

Thus human rights are those which are available to all human beings by virtue of his/her being member of human race. They are innate, universal and inalienable and are essential for the survival and development of all human beings.

PROBLEMS AND VIOLATIONS OF HUMAN RIGHTS

Gender Identity

Gender identity is the biggest problem that the transgender face in their lives. Almost 75 per cent of the transgender experience gender identity crisis at an early age between 8 to 13 years. And their behaviour during childhood is already that of a trans-sexual.

Majority of the transgender go through mixed emotions including fear, shame, disgust and anxiety. Some even think of committing suicide.

Large number of transgender quit home due to fear of their family losing their reputation if it was known that they were going through a gender identity crisis. Some of them leave home unable to bare indifference, ridicule and neglect.

Violation of Human Rights

Universal Declaration of Human Rights (1948) Preamble begins by saying: "Whereas recognition of the inherent dignity and equal inalienable rights of all members of the human family is the foundation of freedom, justice and peace in the world."

1. **Survival:** Article 1 of UDHR says: "All human begins are born free and equal in dignity and rights. They are endowed with reason and conscience and should act towards one another in a spirit of brotherhood." The very first article itself in the UDHR is violated as the transgender community is denied their basic rights are subjected to stigma and discrimination.
2. **Health:** Article 25 of UDHR says: "Everyone has the right to a standard of living adequate for the health and well-being of herself /himself and of her/his family, including food, clothing, housing and medical care and necessary social services.

   The transgender are poor in health. They undergo emotionl stress, mainly due to health problems. More importantly, some are termed HIV positive which could lead to the dreaded AIDS. Some others are afflicted by Sexually Transmitted Diseases (STDs) and some by tuberculosis. And majority of the transgender are alcoholics and also indulge in chewing tobacco as a habit.
3. **Education:** Article 26 of UDHR says: "Everyone has the right to free and compulsory education at least in the elementary and fundamental stages. Secondary (including technical and vocational), professional and higher education shall be made generally available and equally accessible to all."

   The transgender discontinue their schooling when they start feeling uncomfortable in their skins and run away from their homes in search of an identity. They join the jamat system and start obliging to the norms of the community and thus their studies are affected. Usually the transgender are ridiculed by society and hence they prefer to stay in their communities itself than come out and study.
4. **Work:** Article 23 of UDHR says: "Everyone has the right to work, to free choice of employment, to just and favorable conditions of work, to protection against unemployment."

This is the biggest violation of human rights faced by the transgender community. Only because they face a gender identity disorder they are deprived of their right to work. The transgender are forced to earn a livelihood by practicing commercial sex, prostitution, dancing and singing on streets.

Changing Status

Status of the transgender has been changing and the acceptance level has gradually started though it has to be accelerated. The formation of Tamil

Nadu Aravanigal association in 1998 has marked the empowerment of transgender, first of its kind in the country.

Social Status

The transgender are now getting acceptance from their families. Kalki, a social activist founder of Sahodari foundation, says that because she was accepted by her family she could do the good work that she is doing today. Madam Susan, social worker, who has been working with the transgender community for the past 18 years says she has seen tremendous improvements in the lifestyles of the transgender. Thus the stigma attached to a transgender is slowly getting eradicated. Social work students are striving hard to improve the status of the transgender.

Thus societal acceptance is not going to be a farfetched dream.

Economical Status

The transgender community was always shunned and looked down upon and was never given any job opportunity. But nowadays transgender are slowly making their way into the job market with some transgender working as field officers, activist, nurse, dancers, acting in films etc. Sty funds are given to transgender who are pursuing their studies.

Political Status

Tamil Nadu can take pride in declaring that it is the first State Government to form the Transgender Welfare Board (2008) under the Tamil Nadu Social Welfare Department of the Government of Tamil Nadu, which is first of its kind not just in the country but also in the world. Organizations like Transgender Rights Organization, Sahodari Foundation, Tamil Nadu Aravanigal Association, Dai Foundation are working to ensure the rights of the transgender community. The transgender have got a separate identity card called the 'Aravanigal Identity Card' apart from ration card. Voting card, Kalaingar Kapitu Thitam, Sex Reassignment Surgery (SRS) or sex change operation is provided free of cost in the government hospitals in Tamil Nadu. Above 300 houses have been provided for the transgender under the Indira Awajans Yojana.

Priya Babu, activist and President Tamil Nadu Aravanigal Association, is keen to join politics and bring policy level changes. She has a vision to get a law which recognizes the third gender in all the forms.

STRATEGIES AND MEASURES FOR INCLUSIVE GROWTH

Acceptance by Family

The problem of acceptance has to been addressed from the micro level. The transgender have to be accepted by their families first in order to be accepted by the society. Just as parents do not shun their children if they are mentally or physically challenged, parents should not drive out their children when they observe such changes in them. Parents have to be sensitized that this is the time the transgender require maximum emotional and psychological support.

Mass Level Awareness

Mass level awareness programmes should be organized in order to eradicate the stigma and discrimination attached to the transgender community. Media plays a major role in spreading this awareness. Films ridiculing the transgender should not be encouraged.

Reservation in Education

Transgender community should be given reservation in education just as other marginalized and vulnerable sections of the society are provided with reservations for their upliftment through Article 46 of the Constitution.

Inclusion about Transgender in Academic Curriculum

Awareness regarding the third gender should be inculcated at the school level itself. The students should be taught that there is a third gender when it comes to sex and it is not just male and female. All streams of education should be sensitized on transgender.

Nomination in Parliament

Transgender should be nominated as the members of Lok Sabha. Only then transgender rights would come to the forefront and the atrocities faced by transgender will be known to others and there will be an end to the human rights violations faced by them. Involving them as part of the democratic society will also show to the world about the true democratic spirit of the Indian government and commitment to serve the marginalized group and bring them on an equal platform where they can put forth their issues and get justice.

Employment Opportunities

The transgender community should be given equal opportunities and facilities to work and develop in a healthy manner and in conditions of dignity and should be protected against exploitation.

CASE STUDY 1

Name: Rambha

Age: 42 years

Family structure: Jamat system

Occupation: Begging

Born in Kerala, with two brothers and one sister, basically a Tamilian ran away to Mumbai to get a sex change operation when she could not take the humiliation, jokes and taunts by her fellow classmates for her feminine behaviour. She was in sixth standard when she decided to go to Mumbai all alone.

After undergoing the operation she wore the saree for the first time and felt very comfortable and she realized that this is what she always wanted. She again went to her home town and met her school friends and they were shocked to see her in saree. She then told her friends that if you would have not teased me for my mannerisms I would not become like this. Her friends were ashamed of their behaviour.

She then again went back to Mumbai and named herself as Helen. She worked in two dance bars in Mumbai as dancers. One day she was wearing a very short skirt when one customer complimented her that she looks like actress Rambha. Since that day she calls herself as Rambha.

She was married to a Maharashtrian in Mumbai so she learned to speak Marathi and Hindi. Because of a dispute between her and her husband she put kerosene on herself and threaded her husband that she would set herself on blaze if he didn't listen to her. Her husband didn't get scared and asked her to stop threatening and lit the matchstick and threw it on her, burning her face neck and her left hand completely. She was admitted in the hospital, her jamat spent around one and a half lakh for her surgery and hospital charges. With deep sorrow she says no one treats her like a human and we are just looked as a sex object.

When asked why do they clap their hands in a particular way she concluded by saying that it is the only way to survive and make a livelihood. Clapping hands, apart from being our identity it fetches us money as we are distinguished from beggars because of this particular mannerism of ours!

CASE STUDY 2

Name: Jayalalitha

Age: 40

Family structure: stays with her mother and also is a part of jamat system

Occupation: Social work

Born at Pallavaram, Chennai with an elder brother, Jayalalitha, now stays in a small rented house at Kannagi Nagar and pays a rent of Rs. 1000 per month along with the electricity charges. Staying in an environment of love and care she grows everyday as an individual facing different challenges in life. Before she started feeling uncomfortable in her skin she was a spokesperson on AIDMK party. After changing her sex she named herself as Jayalalitha, aspiring to be like the AIDMK leader Jayalalitha.

She is married and has a successful married life. She has been married for the fast four years. She was a member of the Planning Board for the Thiruvallur district. First time ever a member was directly appointed by the then collector. She worked as a field officer for five years at 'Tai Thitam' and then became the secretary because of her hard work, commitment and dedication towards work. She received the 'Mother Teresa Award' on Women's Day by the human rights organization for her distinguished work. She is the head of the self-help group (SHG) formed by transgender which is first of its kind in Tamil Nadu. She also formed a Women's SHG. She has featured on many televisions like Jaya TV, Sun TV, Podigai, and Vasanth TV to talk about her struggles in life.

Jayalalitha is a dynamic person with a great vision for the betterment and upliftment of their community. She is lobbying for a land with the government for setting up a township with 300 houses with electricity, sanitation, schools, and playgrounds for the transgender community. She has also asked for a MLA seat. She strongly believes that transgender should be part of the Parliament as that is the only way to be a part of the decision making and protect the rights of the transgender.

She concludes by saying before 64 years India got freedom but we, transgender, are still fighting for it!

CASE STUDY 3

Name: Amudha

Age: 50 years

Family Structure: Stays in the community care centre and also is a part of the jamat system

Occupation: Begging

Wearing a green coloured saree she was sitting in the corner of a room, waiting for her friends to get ready and leave for their daily routine of begging. I started a conversation with the lady when to my surprise I came to know that she cannot hear but can speak. With my knowledge of the sign language I told her that I want to take her interview. Readily she accepted and carefully started reading my lips. Born at Thiruvanamala, with one elder brother and one elder sister, Amudha is the youngest at home. Amudha started experiencing changes in her when she was around 12 years. She din not tell this to her parents fearing that she would be badly bashed at home.

She completed her 10th Standerd and joined a hospital to work as a compounder. She always had feminine characteristics and was always the centre of all the jokes in the hospital. Her life took a different turn when two transgender were admitted in the hospital and teased her that she did not have the courage of changing her sex even though she felt like a woman. This provoked Amudha. She went home that day and prayed the whole night and she herself castrated. She was bleeding heavily when she was admitted to the hospital and was given proper care. After she finally got her sex change operation done she went to Mumbai and got into the sex trade. She was happy with her small world revolving around her jamat and her regular customers. She was earning a decent amount till the time she got into a fight with her guru and decides to come back to Chennai.

She was again admitted in the hospital as she had some urinary problems. She claims that it at is this time that during blood transfusion she got infected with the dreaded HIV. She stopped the sex trade and goes to beg to earn a living. She said she can't hear as her hearing was affected by malaria. When asked are you aware of your rights she replied in negation.

She started becoming restless as her friends were taking too long to get ready. Threatening them to get ready fast she asked me to conclude the interview. I asked her do people still ridicule you she said educated people like you respect us for being humans but uneducated people still treat us worse than animals. She concluded by saying it is my humble request as a social work student kindly create awareness among the people that we are no different from them.

CASE STUDY 4

Name: Madina

Age: 35 years

Family structure: Jamat system

Occupation: Performer

Madina was born in Nagarcoil in an affluent family with three elder brothers, three younger sisters, one younger brother and sister. She was brought up with playing with girls. She was always fascinated by the thought of wearing a saree when she saw other transgender in her area clad in pretty sarees. She and her cousin elder sister both went to Bangalore and got a sex change operation done as they wanted to be recognized as woman. Just the way many transgender do not get acceptance from their families. Madina's case was not different from the rest. She joined the Tirunelveli transgender performing arts group which was headed by a MLAs son in Tirunelveli. Because of her beautiful looks, the leader was attracted to Madina and decided to get married. They got married in a temple and later she came to know that he was already married and had two children. She was threatened by the leader's father and father-in-law to run away else she would be killed brutally on the road. Because of this problem she decided to leave Tirunelveli and try her fate in the big bad city of Mumbai. She worked as a sex worker in Mumbai and earned around Rs. 200 to Rs. 500. One fine day she received a call from her mom saying her younger sister was going to get married and her mother invited her for the wedding. But her mother said that she has to come in pant and shirt with her hair cut like a boy. Madina told her mother she last long back left that identity and today she is anew person and if she wants her to come for the marriage she has to accept her as Madina.

That was the last time she spoke to her mother she recalls. With tears in her eyes she left for her daily routine with her friends.

Conclusion

One Earth....One Sky
Sky is the Man...Earth is the Woman
I am the "In-Between"...with No Identity to say that is mine...

Woman's soul in a man's body: transgender are the neglected, ignored and misunderstood community by the general public. But slowly the transgender are finding a place in the society and leaving a mark in the society because of their sincere efforts towards the cause.

The mainstreaming of the transgender is possible provide changes from within the transgender community comes first. The policy-makers to ensure a better life for the transgender and safeguard their rights. For long they have been traumatized because of their biological state and victimized by the society. Hence a humane, scientific and historical understanding of the problems faced by the transgender would be the right approach for inclusive growth and for fulfilling the onerous task of rehabilitating them.

24
CHAPTER

Transgender
Social and Familial Relations

Alphonsa George
M. Phil Scholar, Deptt. of Social Work, Pondicherry University

P.B. Shankar Narayan
Asstt. Professor, Deptt. of Social Work, Pondicherry University

Introduction

Gender is the fundamental aspect of human identity. It is a deeply rooted element of 'how see ourselves and how others see us'. Transgender is a term used to describe whose identity or appearance differs from stereotypical expectations of how men and women should look or act. This includes transsexual people who changes bodies to match their psychological identifications with the other gender. It also includes a much larger group of people who don't necessarily under go any medical treatment , but who don't conform to the idea men have to be stereotypically "masculine" and women have to be stereotypically "feminine".

In other words, a transgender is a person whose gender identity or gender expression differs from that associated with his or her birth sex. The family and friends do not always understand transgender issues immediately. Regardless of the child's age, most parents feel confused, angry, self-doubting, and deeply worried when they learn about their child's cross- dressing or gender identity issues. These feelings are frequently exacerbated by the parents' belief that there is no place to turn for help. So transgender people face a grave misunderstanding, prejudice and social injustice on a daily basis on their gender role. The transgender are not recognized as a distinct and equal subset of humanity and hence they face a lot of human rights issues also.

The Transgender Community

Gender identity, a characteristic that we all possess, is our internal understanding of our own gender. The term "transgender" is used to describe people whose gender identity does not correspond to their birth-assigned sex and/or the stereotypes associated with that sex. A male to female transgender individual is a transgender woman and a female-to-male transgender individual is a transgender man. There are also gender non-conforming people who do not identify as transgender and some individuals in the transgender community who do not identify as male or female.

A number of terms across the culturally and linguistically diverse Indian subcontinent represent similar sex/gender categories. In Tamil Nadu the equivalent term is *Thiru Nangai* (daughter of god), or Aravani. In Punjabi, both in Pakistan and India, the term *Khusra* is used. The word *kothi* (or *koti*) is common across India. *Hijras* are widely referred to in English with the term "eunuch" or hermaphrodite, although LGBT historians or human rights activists might label them as being transgender.

Misconceptions about Transgender

At family level and being a part of society level, the consequence of the deployment of this term is that it tends to construct sexual identity categories (like homosexual, heterosexual, and bisexual) as gender-normative, and to segregate gender non-conformity solely within the newly created minority classification of "transgender". This conceptual move allows "transgender" to be treated like a discrete identity category—setting in motion all the struggles over inclusion and exclusion—rather than perceived, like race or class, as a phenomenon that cuts across existing sexual identity categories.

At family level as well as society level the practice of discrimination has been taking place, the majority of the parents are not willing to reveal about their transgender son in the public, not only the parents but also siblings, and relatives. Many transgender youth leave their home because of the stress in the family environment or because they are thrown out by homophobic parents. Many foster homes will not accept openly transgender youth because of homophobia and fear of predation on other children in the home. The transgender people they themselves disclose their inner personality.

over the law also, recognize only heterosexual marriages, the right to marriage and family is denied to same sex couples and transgender. These misconceptions or misunderstanding, prejudice and social injustice on their gender role should not accept them to continue or maintain a normal and healthy relationship with the family as well the society. Rather than this, the transgender community is facing introvert and extrovert role and relation conflicts. Thus the transgender became the most vulnerable in the society.

Aim of the Study

The aim of the study was to analyze the social and familial relations of transgender from their perceptive.

Objectives of the Study

- To find out the familial and social communication of the transgender.
- To study about the support given by the family and the society for the transgender.
- To understand the interpersonal relationship of the transgender with their family members.

Methodology

The study was a descriptive study. Sixty samples were found through non-probability convenient sampling method. Then the data were collected through semi-structured interview schedule. The universe of the study was the transgender community, which includes *Kothis* and *Aravanis*, of SAHODARAN Community Oriented Health Development Society (SCHOD), in Puducherry.

SCHOD was started in the year 1998, under the Trust Act. The organization works with the marginalized, stigmatized sections of the society, the MSM (Men who have Sex with Men), and Transgender. It works towards their welfare; the improvement of their health conditions, to protect them from STIs and HIV, and to build their capacity for their own empowerment.

Interpretation and Findings

- The respondents of the study were in the age group of 18 to 40 years. The majority of respondents (36%) have completed their primary education. Thirty per cent of respondents completed their under graduation. Sixteen per cent of the respondents passed SSLC and 10 per cent of the respondents studied up to Plus two. Four per cent of the respondents did their diploma course and another four per cent their post-graduation. The majority of the respondents dropped their studies and came out of the school by themselves due to their gender role confusion, it made them feel ashamed in their peer group; few respondents' parents, by force stopped them from going to school due to their feminine behavior and few respondents were having economic problem.
- Majority of the of the respondents (70%) stay along with their family members. Fifty per cent of the respondents' family members do not know that they are transgender. Twenty percent of the respondents'

family members accepted them. 30 per cent of the respondents are staying away from the family; with friends, and transgender community.

- Fourteen per cent of the respondents have not been accepted by their family. Twel per cent of respondents, though discriminated at first, have been accepted later, due to reasons such as they are the only son of the family or because they are giving money at home. Four per cent of the respondents is being accepted but is treated with discrimination. The majority of the respondents were maintaining secrecy in their transgender behavior.
- The majority of the respondents (50%) said that they were controlled by their parents due to their feminine activities, 34 per cent of the respondents were ignored by their parents. Sixteen per cent of the respondents were observed by their parents, even though they ignored it because of unprediction of future consequences.
- Majority of the respondents (84%) had been subjected to societal abuse and discrimination from more than one source, of which gundas and police plays the major role. Sixteen per cent of the respondents were subjected to utter discrimination from the society. Among the respondents, 66 per cent were subjected to police torture and 34 per cent were not. This clearly indicates the violation of human rights of transgender by the law enforcing agency itself. In the everyday life of the transgender, majority of them were beaten up by the family members, police, gundas and clients.
- Majority of the respondents (58%) claim that they were treated in an abusing manner, or with lack of concern by the health care practitioners, and so they are not able to approach them again. Forty-two per cent of them were treated either good or indifferently.
- Except a very rare percent of four per cent, the majority of the respondents (96%) do not possess a ration card of their identity. Thirtey-six per cent of the respondents face discrimination from more than one source including colleagues, friends and other workers. Thirtey-two per cent of the respondents said that they don't face any discrimination but they agreed that they are working with the same community people. Thirty per cent of the respondents revealed that they face discrimination and torture from their customers. Two per cent of the respondents were unemployed.
- The societal treatment towards the transgender is very discriminative. The transgender people face a lot of abuse and torture physically, sexually and psychologically by the public servants and public. They experience isolation and discrimination at family and society in various aspects as such as functions and festivals.

Suggestions

- The homophobic parents should be aware about transgender issues, and has to take care of their children at the age group of adolescence rather than throwing them out from the home and they have to be treated equally, as the normal children. Family has to accept and construct a free environment from stress.
- More researches can be done in the areas of transgender as more issues of transgender can be brought out, so that awareness can be created among the public to a great extend.
- The rights of the transgender can be enforced through separate laws for them, especially for transgender youth to enjoy the family relations.
- A public address can be organized where transgender will come in direct to the public with the support of police and govt.

Conclusion

All over the world family is considered as a primary institution of individuals to derive love, care, and support in all kinds, especially Indian family system is recognized as a value system, comprising of all those beliefs and viewpoints that the parents pass on to their next generation and maintain strong bonds with the family members as well as relatives. But in the case of transgender children, many families are not following the ethics effectively. The traditional societal norms and believes are objecting and unscrambling the transgender group by treating them as sex icons rather than humankinds. Hence the transgender have a poor social and familial relations; they are excluded everywhere, due to a reason for which they are not responsible; that is, their gender identity.

REFERENCES

Boszormenyi-Nagy, I. and Spark, I. (1973) *Invisible Loyalties.* New York: Brunner/ Mazel.

Brown, G.R. (1998) Women in the Closet: Relationship with Transgendered Men. In D. Denny (Ed.), 353–371. *Current Concepts in Transgender Identity*, New York: Garland Press.

Sandra Laframboise RPNBeth Long Law Student, *Gender, Transgender and Transphobia.*

Stephen Erich[a]; Josephine Tittsworth[b]; Janice Dykes[b]; Cheryl Cabuses, *Family Relationships and their Correlations with Transsexual Well-Being.*

Wikipedia, the free encyclopedia, *Transgender Youth.*

25
CHAPTER

A Study on the Problems faced by Transgenders in Virudhunagar

Dr. N.M. Ganesan
Deputy Director (DDE), Madurai Kamaraj University, Madurai
S. Elangovan
Head, Department of Commerce, ANJA College, Sivakasi
S. Murugaiyan
Asstt. Professor of Commerce, ANJA College, Sivakasi

Introduction

"Social exclusion is an accumulation of confluent processes with successive ruptures arising from the heart of economy, politics and society; gradually distances and places persons, groups, communities and territories in positions of inferiority in relation to centre powers, resources and prevailing values" Beall and Piron suggest "a process and a state that prevents individuals or groups from full participation in social, economic and political life and from asserting their rights. It derives from exclusionary relationships based on power" Thus, the excluder rejects social relations denying access to resources and services, violating citizenship rights to particular individual and groups.

Social Exclusion of Transgender

Socially-excluded people or groups of people are not able to participate in societal mainstream activities. Factors contributing to social exclusion include poverty, non-dominant social identities, e.g. race, ethnicity, religion, and gender; social locations (migrants, refugees); demographic features (occupation, educational level); and health conditions, e.g. disability, stigmatized diseases, such as HIV and AIDS. Social, economic, cultural and political aspects of exclusion enforce deprivations of the basic amenities of life.

The Social Exclusion Knowledge Network (SEKN) model, developed by Popay *et al.* (2008) assumes that social exclusion is driven by unequal power dynamics and operate in four interconnected and relational dimensions (e.g. cultural, economic, political, and social) at different levels.

Economic aspects of exclusion include barriers to employment opportunities, constrained access to commodities, and livelihood opportunities, such as income, housing, land, and working conditions. Social aspects of exclusion refer to limited or no access to social, educational, legal and health services, resulting from ruptured social protection and social cohesion, such as kinship, family, neighbourhood, and the community.

Cultural aspects of exclusion refer to subordination of certain norms, behaviours, cultural practices, and lifestyles which exclude certain individuals or groups. Political aspects of exclusion refer to deprivations of citizens' rights, including restricted access to organizations, voter rights, legislations, constitutions, and decision-making in policy.

Objectives of the Study

The overall objective of the present study is to analyse the problems faced by the transgender in Virudhunagar of Tamil Nadu. However more specifically:

- To study the problems of transgender.
- To offer fruitful suggestions for solving their problems of transgender.

Methodology

The present study has covered Virudhunagar only, because the majority of the transgenders are living in this area.

The primary data were collected with the help of specially prepared interview schedule. The schedule included the questions related to the general information about the Transgender. Totally 30 respondents were selected by using convenient sampling method.

Analysis and Interpretation

- **Female psyche in male physic: nurtured for negligence:** Early childhood preference of a transgender for female clothing, make-up and attire, playing with girls rather than with boys, preferring household work culturally assigned for females, and possessing a 'soft' nature like girls, was not taken negatively by family members, particularly by mothers who enjoyed looking at 'soft' nature of their 'boys'. Other family members did make fun of these boys but only strongly opposing feminine behaviours during adolescence. 'Unusual feminine development' of early childhood tarnishes the family image. Family members felt uncomfortable with feminine behaviours of their male adolescents, particularly when the family encounters negative and unpleasant societal experiences concerning to feminine attitudes and behaviours of their children. Criticisms of neighbours and incidents of offensive teasing from neighbouring males often created unpleasant situations where parents felt offended. Feminine behaviours were initially nourished and nurtured, with time but were condemned and discouraged.

- **Humiliations in school: where to study? :** The 'unusual' growth of a feminine boy is not tolerated in schools where the informants often encountered a hostile environment for incompatible sex-gender roles and attitudes. They often experienced loneliness and abusive treatment; for example, they were not allowed to share with classmates, extending from the classroom to the playground.
- **Identity crisis: who am I? :** They wear female clothes and adopt feminine names while visiting peers. However, they wear male clothes and adopt male gestures while living with or visiting relatives. Their feminine role is denied. They cannot avoid the dilemma of their identity crisis.
- **Living for leaving: where to go? :** They preferred wearing feminine garments not permitted in the home. In front of relatives, they were discouraged to show feminine attitudes. Exhibiting 'unwanted' and 'abnormal feminine behaviours', chances of marriage of their siblings become uncertain. This decision of leaving home was finalized when they became closely associated with feminine male friends where they were fit psychologically, sexually, and socially.
- **Occupation: where to work? :** "Some got jobs but eventually were dismissed when employers learned of their feminine attitudes. In some cases, many were abused verbally, physically, and sexually at workplaces for which they never received any justice. They rather lost the job because the employers wanted to 'save the workplace from sexual pollution'.
- **Love relations: whom to love? :** A family life with a transgender perceived as neither male nor female, and unable to procreate is prohibited under socio-cultural, religious and political rules and customs. At some point, such love relationships disappear. Society does not permit any transgressive relationship beyond hetero-normativity.

- **Sexual abuse and physical harassment: where is safety? :** Most transgender described first sexual intercourse experiences at the age of 8-12 years. The first sexual relationship in most cases was developed with male relatives, neighbours, or lodging tutors. Most of these incidents occurred by force and were unprotected, putting them at risk of transmission of STI/HIV. As a result, their human dignity and self-esteem were diminished.
- **Illness of the transgender: where to seek healthcare from? :** They were not allowed to seek healthcare at the private chambers of doctors no matter whether they could pay the doctor's fee or not. "Their presence may create fear and discomfort for other patients", claimed by a private medical practitioner A transgender sex worker cannot operate sex trade at old age. Shifting occupations is not easy. Survival becomes more difficult with ageing. They stayed outside home and had no choice but to struggle against illness, poverty, and loneliness. Old age brings new and terrible threats for survival in the lives of transgender.

Though small in number transgender can do equally better like their fellow normal human being. Ignoring their manpower is a national loss. They could contribute for national development by hard work and dedication. Being a transgender is not an individual fault. It is nature on is doing. Why should opportunity be denied to them? There is wide spread misconception that transgender are untouchable, insufficient and unfit but in reality they could do any job well. Recently a transgender was a very good compaire and presented TV programmes wonderfully well. Another transgender is show talented to act in films also. Why the majority should suppress this potential minority?

REFERENCES

Popay J, Escorel S, Hernandez M, Johnston H, Mathieson J, Rispel L. Understanding and tracking social exclusion: final report to the WHO Commission on social Determinants of Health. Lancaster: Social Exclusion Knowledge Network, 2008:207.

Estivill J. *Concepts and strategies for combating social exclusion: an overview*, Geneva: International Labour Office, 2003, p. 131.

Silver H. Social Exclusion and social solidarity: three paradigms. *Int Labour Rev* 1994; 133:531-78

Index